MIND ASSOCIATION OCCASIONAL SERIES

CONNECTIONISM, CONCEPTS, AND FOLK PSYCHOLOGY

MIND ASSOCIATION OCCASIONAL SERIES

This series consists of occasional volumes of original papers on predefined themes. The Mind Association nominates an editor or editors for each collection, and may co-operate with other bodies in promoting conferences or other scholarly activities in connection with the preparation of particular volumes.

Publications Officer: M. A. Stewart
Secretary: C. Macdonald

Also published in the series

Perspectives on Thomas Hobbes
Edited by G. A. J. Rogers and A. Ryan

Reality, Representation, and Projection
Edited by J. Haldane and C. Wright

Connectionism, Concepts, and Folk Psychology
The Legacy of Alan Turing, Volume II
Edited by A. Clark and P. J. R. Millican

Connectionism, Concepts, and Folk Psychology

The Legacy of Alan Turing

VOL. 2

Edited by

A. CLARK

and

P. J. R. MILLICAN

CLARENDON PRESS · OXFORD

1996

Oxford University Press, Walton Street, Oxford OX2 6DP

Oxford New York

Athens Auckland Bangkok Bogota Bombay
Buenos Aires Calcutta Cape Town Dar es Salaam
Delhi Florence Hong Kong Istanbul Karachi
Kuala Lumpur Madras Madrid Melbourne
Mexico City Nairobi Paris Singapore
Taipei Tokyo Toronto
and associated companies in
Berlin Ibadan

Oxford is a trade mark of Oxford University Press

Published in the United States by
Oxford University Press Inc., New York

British Library Cataloguing in Publication Data
Data available

Library of Congress Cataloging in Publication Data
Data available

ISBN 0-19-823594-1

1 3 5 7 9 10 8 6 4 2

Typeset by Graphicraft Typesetters Ltd., Hong Kong
Printed in Great Britain by
Biddles Ltd., Guildford and King's Lynn

ACKNOWLEDGEMENTS

The editors are grateful for permission to reproduce the following material in this volume:

An earlier version of Frank Jackson and Philip Pettit's paper 'Causation in the Philosophy of Mind' appeared in *Philosophy and Phenomenological Research* 50 (Brown University Press, 1990), pp. 195–214, with the kind permission of Brown University Press, Providence, Rhode Island, USA.

Some of the material in L. Jonathan Cohen's paper 'Belief and Acceptance' appeared in his book *An Essay on Belief and Acceptance* (Oxford University Press, 1992), and is included here with the kind permission of Oxford University Press, Oxford, England. Readers are advised to consult that book for a more extensive development of the ideas in the paper.

Some of the material in Christopher Peacocke's paper 'The Relation between Philosophical and Psychological Theories of Concepts' appeared in his book *A Study of Concepts* (MIT Press, 1992), and is included here with the kind permission of MIT Press, Cambridge, Mass., USA, and by special request of the editors of this volume. Readers are advised to consult that book, and also the paper 'Content, Computation, and Externalism' (*Mind and Language* 9 1994, pp. 303–35), for further elaboration and development of the ideas in the paper.

CONTENTS

LIST OF CONTRIBUTORS

PAUL M. CHURCHLAND Professor in the Department of Philosophy, University of California, San Diego

ANDY CLARK Professor of Philosophy and Director of the Philosophy/Neuroscience/Psychology Program, Department of Philosophy, Washington University in St Louis

L. JONATHAN COHEN Emeritus Fellow of the Queen's College, Oxford

MARIO COMPIANI Researcher in the Department of Chemical Sciences, University of Camerino

PETER DAYAN Assistant Professor in the Department of Brain and Cognitive Sciences, Massachusetts Institute of Technology

BEATRICE DE GELDER Professor in the Department of Psychology, Tilburg University

DOUGLAS R. HOFSTADTER Professor in the Center for Research on Concepts and Cognition, Indiana University

FRANK JACKSON Professor of Philosophy in the Research School of Social Sciences, Australian National University

MICHAEL MORRIS Senior Lecturer in the School of English and American Studies, University of Sussex

JON OBERLANDER Advanced Fellow in the ESRC Human Communication Research Centre, University of Edinburgh

CHRISTOPHER PEACOCKE Wayneflete Professor of Metaphysical Philosophy in the University of Oxford and a Fellow of Magdalen College, Oxford

PHILIP PETTIT Professor of Sociology and Political Theory in the Research School of Social Sciences, Australian National University

IAN PRATT Lecturer in the Department of Computer Science, University of Manchester

AARON SLOMAN Professor of Artificial Intelligence and Cognitive Science in the School of Computer Science, University of Birmingham

IAIN A. STEWART Professor and Head of Computer Science in the Department of Mathematics and Computer Science, University of Leicester

BLAY WHITBY Tutorial Fellow in Computer Science in the School of Cognitive and Computing Sciences, University of Sussex

Introduction

ANDY CLARK

———•———

This is the second of two volumes of essays in commemoration of Alan Turing. Unlike the first volume *Machines and Thought*, the present collection does not specifically address Turing's classic contributions to the understanding of mind and computation. Instead, we here celebrate Turing's intellectual legacy: the continuing attempt to display the precise relationship between the scientific image of mind (given, we are assuming, in broadly computational terms) and our common-sense picture of ourselves as grasping concepts, acting for reasons, and possessed of a rich, subjective mental life. The space of possible relations between these two images of the mind (which Wilfrid Sellars termed the Manifest Image and the Scientific Image) is large and surprisingly complex. It is *especially* complex relative to certain philosophical projects which pursue the possible impact of new scientific images of mind upon our assessment of the folk framework as a means of properly describing and explaining intelligent behaviours. Roughly speaking, we may discern three major positions as regards the (putative) inner analogues of the class of constructs deployed in daily, common-sense mentalistic talk. These are:

(1) Gross Descriptivism: The common sense constructs (concepts, beliefs, propositionally identified contents etc.) are *nothing but* descriptions of large-scale behavioural dispositions of whole agents. According to this view, no neat inner analogues to the folk constructs are to be found.

(2) Modest Internalism: The common-sense constructs serve to pick out transient and/or large-scale features of internal (e.g. neural or computational organization). Examples might include the identification of concepts with distributed, context-dependent

patterns of neural activity (see Clark (1993)) or the identification of mental images with temporarily time-locked activity in multiple neural regions (see Damasio, 1994). In such cases the folk items (images, concepts) do not have neat, highly manipulable and/or spatially localizable inner analogues. But there remain fairly robust patterns of widespread neural/computational activity which the folk discourse at times succeeds in tracking.

(3) Gross Internalism: The common-sense constructs (or, in this case, some favoured subset such as concepts or (most) lexical items) have matching, highly manipulable, object-like inner analogues, e.g. a complex thought, folk-psychologically described might thus appear as a complex inner state with independently manipulable parts which match the independently recombinable concepts we deploy in its common-sense characterization.

These options, however, at best characterize one axis of a two-dimensional space of philosophical views. Whereas the first axis tracks views concerning the relation of the folk ontology to some scientific image, the second tracks views concerning the nature of the scientific *commitments* of the folk image. To keep things as simple as possible, consider just the following two positions:

(A) Minimal Commitment: The folk discourse is not (explicitly or tacitly) committed to any particular type of scientific inner story.

(B) Maximal Commitment: The folk discourse is (tacitly) committed to the existence of inner items which closely match (in terms of contents, manipulability and causal powers) the constructs (or some favoured subset of the constructs) of common-sense mentalistic discourse.

The combined axes yield a space of six possible positions, several of which will be familiar to many readers. Daniel Dennett (1987) is generally cast as combining Gross Descriptivism with Minimal Commitment—a combination which yields a liberal kind of realism concerning propositional attitude explanations. Paul Churchland (1989) combines the same Gross Descriptivism with a more maximal vision of the folk commitments, and thus derives an abiding scepticism concerning the folk ontology. And Jerry Fodor (1987) combines a version of Gross Internalism with, in fact, a more minimal vision of the actual conceptual *commitments* of the folk discourse (a diagnosis pursued at some length in Clark (1993)).

Turing himself was probably committed (though the issue is not as cut and dried as some would believe—see the comments by Hofstadter (this volume)) only to the position of Minimal Commitment, and hence to a broadly behaviouristic vision of the essence of mind. According to such a vision the common-sense picture of mind is applicable (if we take passing the Turing Test as at least offering a sufficient condition for the ascription of mental states) just so long as the computational innards provide for the right body of gross external behaviour. Modulo that requirement the innards might, it would seem, be of any kind whatsoever.

Acceptance of such a behaviouristic analysis of mental ascription is, however, not universal. M. Davies (1991) has argued that the discovery that an inner computational economy has a certain form could, in principle, defeat the ascription of mental states (such as believing that P) to the system. Indeed, Davies goes as far as to suggest that the discovery that the inner computational story is a *connectionist* one (see the papers by Churchland, Compiani, and Schopman and Shawky) might have such a consequence. Davies is thus exploring a new location in or around our crude 6-space; one which combines strong (though perhaps not quite maximal) commitment with a vision of (certain) connectionist models of cognition as failing to live up to those commitments. Many of the essays gathered below can likewise usefully be understood as either exploring the less well-visited locations in the 6-space (e.g. those involving some form of modest internalism) or as challenging some of the simplifying assumptions upon which it is built.

The potential interest of such explorations increases when we discover (in the papers by Churchland, Compiani, and Schopman and Shawky) that connectionist approaches are showing increasing promise as models of learning and concept-formation. If the best computational story about human cognition turned out to depict us as sophisticated connectionist devices then, if the argument of Davies (1991) were correct (for some doubts, see Clark (1993, ch. 10), the combined conclusion would be that the familiar descriptions of human beings as acting on the basis of beliefs, desires, etc. would be undermined! This is the position which has come to be known as Eliminative Materialism.

The paper by Jackson and Pettit includes a strong (negative) response to this line of argument. A proper understanding of the nature of the folk discourse, they argue, reveals its computational commitments as rather minimal: certainly not such as to yield any direct conflict with the recent connectionist proposals. Instead, Jackson and Pettit embrace a form of functionalism in which functional *role* and not inner computational format, is what fixes mental properties. A key question which then comes to the fore is in what sense a specific mental content can *itself* be a cause. For it is surely the *filler* of a functional role, and not the role itself, which does the actual causing. To identify the mental state with the functional role thus threatens to identify it with something inherently non-causal. Jackson and Pettit show in detail why this objection should not be considered persuasive.

A somewhat different way of reconciling functionalism and causal influence is pursued in the paper by Oberlander and Dayan. Oberlander and Dayan seek to resist the related temptation to construe the posits of folk psychology as (merely) instrumentally useful fictions. Their resistance involves rejecting the traditional model of computation upon which (they suggest) such an instrumentalist reading is predicated.

The discussion of the relationship between mental content and computational models of mind is continued in Peacocke's elaboration of the relationship, as he sees it, between philosophical and psychological theories of concepts. A philosophical theory of concepts, Peacocke argues, should tell us what it is for a thinker to *possess* a given concept, i.e. it should elucidate the commitments of a specific *fragment* of the folk mentalistic ontology. A psychological/computational account may then tell us how (or indeed whether—recall Davies's argument) such possession conditions are met. Peacocke's paper is followed by a critical response from Michael Morris.

The relation between philosophical and psychological theorizing about the mind also takes centre stage in the discussion by de Gelder, who relates the issues to the debate concerning logical empiricism in philosophy of science.

Shanahan introduces a new direction of influence by suggesting that the project of illuminating the nature of folk psychological discourse might *itself* be aided by the use of AI techniques—specifically, by exploiting the kind of descriptive tools used by AI workers to formalize the knowledge embodied in our grasp of 'naïve physics' (i.e. our intuitive knowledge concerning the behaviour of everyday physical objects). The parallel attempt to express our daily knowledge of the mental in a formal, machine-implementable way may lead us, Shanahan claims, to a much deeper understanding of that knowledge. To the extent that our understanding of the folk discourse is itself influenced by our theorizing about neural/computational underpinnings, the space of potential equilibria between the two images (the Manifest and the Scientific) may dramatically increase. A similar optimistic note is struck by Churchland who suggests that connectionist models of learning and conceptual change may help us understand scientific conceptual development by reconstructing it in a more revealing framework.

Further discussion of the nature of concepts and of computational models of concepts is provided by Thornton (who offers a specific information-theoretic account of one kind of concept-learning) and by Hofstadter (who discusses, in computational terms, the characteristic *fluidity* of human grasp of concepts).

Finally, some authors seek to challenge or expand the received philosophical vision of folk psychological discourse. Thus Pratt challenges the widespread characterization of the folk framework as constituting some kind of *theory* of the causes of behaviour. Instead, Pratt suggests, the cornerstone of such knowledge lies in simulation and observation. L. J. Cohen challenges the received account of the conceptual resources of folk psychology. That account, he claims, fails to distinguish between *belief* and *acceptance* —a distinction which, Cohen argues, bears on the treatment of a variety of central cases involving the folk psychological explanation of actions. Pratt and Cohen thus challenge (in different ways) a common conception of the role of the folk discourse itself. The very crude distinction drawn above between minimal and maximal models of the folk commitments is thus itself brought into question.

Taken together, these essays provide graphic proof of both the multiplicity and complexity of the issues raised by a computational perspective on mind. For such a perspective must do justice to each of its components (the mentalistic and the computational) if it is sensibly to address the relation between them. We are thus required (i) to consider the nature of computation itself (especially in natural systems), (ii) to look closely at the nature and explanatory role of ordinary mental talk, and finally (iii) to pronounce sensibly upon the relation between the two. This problematic triplet represents the contemporary legacy of Turing's persuasive commitment to a computational understanding of mind. What the current debates show us, I believe, is that over forty years since the publication of 'Computing Machinery and Intelligence', neither one of the key notions (computation and mind) is yet clearly understood. Perhaps in attempting to refine them together, we shall come better to understand the nature of each.

REFERENCES

Churchland, P. M. (1989), *A Neurocomputational Perspective*, Cambridge, Mass.: MIT Press.

Clark, A. (1993), *Associative Engines: Connectionism, Concepts, and Representational Change*, Cambridge, Mass.: MIT Press.

Damasio, A. (1994), *Descartes' Error*, New York: Grosset-Putnam.

Davies, M. (1991), 'Concepts, Connectionism, and the Language of Thought', in W. Ramsey, S. Stich, and D. Rumelhart (eds.), *Philosophy and Connectionist Theory*, Hillsdale, NJ: Erlbaum, 229–58.

Dennett, D. C. (1987), *The Intentional Stance*, Cambridge, Mass.: MIT Press.

Fodor, J. A. (1987), *Psychosemantics*, Cambridge, Mass.: MIT Press.

I

Learning and Conceptual Change: The View from the Neurons

PAUL M. CHURCHLAND

---

1. INTRODUCTION

The quest to produce an artificial but genuine intelligence presupposes or anticipates some criterion for recognizing when success has been achieved. Here the 'Turing Test' is often cited (Turing, 1950). This narrowly behavioural test gains its appeal from two sources. First, it focuses exclusively on empirically accessible data—the output of the candidate system's teletype. Inaccessible metaphysical and neuronal matters are thus deliberately pushed aside. And second, it evaluates that empirical data by comparison with the behaviour of a paradigm case of intelligence—a human being. The candidate system's teletyped behaviour must be indistinguishable from the teletyped behaviour *of a human* in the same situation.

Whatever its merits or demerits as a criterion of intelligence, it is independently clear that we are forced to fall back on 'behavioural similarity to a paradigm case' only so long as we lack an adequate *theory* of the paradigm case, an adequate theory of what intelligence is and how it is realized in physical systems. Had we such a theory, we would have no need for the austere behavioural restrictions of the Turing Test, and no need to haggle over its validity. An adequate theory of intelligence would itself make clear the relevant features, behaviours, techniques, or mechanisms that are characteristic of genuine intelligence. We could then test for those features directly, perhaps by looking inside the candidate

This essay draws and expands on the research reported in Churchland (1989*b*). Sections 2, 6, and 7 are drawn from that earlier essay. My thanks to MIT Press for permission to reprint those sections here.

system to see what is going on, or perhaps by examining the system's behaviour in contexts much richer and more demanding than that of a teletyped conversation. The Turing Test is a test precisely for people who *have no* adequate theory of what intelligence is. Alan Turing was very much in that situation, of course, and so it is not surprising that he was forced to fall back on a stopgap criterion. But we can now aspire to transcend his situation.

The 'paradigm case'—the human, or higher animal—is no longer so mysterious as it was in 1950, and its internal structures and activities are no longer so inaccessible. Magnetic resonance imaging (MRI) gives us a non-invasive and damage-revealing look at the anatomy anywhere within the alert brain to a resolution of about a millimetre. Positron emission tomography (PET) provides a non-invasive look at the local levels of metabolic activity in the alert brain to a comparable spatial resolution, and to a temporal resolution of less than a minute. Voltage-sensitive dyes focus on neural activity still more tightly in both time and space. The elaborate axonal connections between the brain's histologically and functionally distinct neuronal populations are understood in considerable detail from stain-transport studies. And at the molecular level, the electrochemistry of axonal conduction and synaptic transmission is unfolding as well.

At the systems level, the massively parallel character of the brain's processing of information is now quite evident, as is the massively distributed or vectorial character of its information coding and storage. And finally, computer models of the parallel processing of such high-dimensional vector codings yield what look like real insights into the evidently *cognitive* features of brain-like networks, such as pattern recognition, fast memory, sensorimotor co-ordination, ampliative inference, categorial frameworks, and learning.

In sum, we now possess the conceptual and experimental resources potentially adequate to the construction of a correct theory of human and animal cognition. Such a theory must aim to explain a great deal more than the capacity for teletyped conversation (not that this latter is trivial). And the empirical constraints on the theory will be commensurately greater as well. For starters, the theory must be adequate to a much wider range of input–output behaviour. More important still, it must be adequate to the internal computational realities of the system that produces that behaviour. It must cohere appropriately with the kinematical and dynamical features of the biological brain. And it must be able to account for fundamental features of cognition such as learning, perceptual recognition, and conceptual change.

These latter topics are the focus of the present paper. To a philosopher of science, a major appeal of the new PDP (Parallel Distributed Processing) or Connectionist approaches to cognitive neurobiology is their potential for throwing light not just on the nature of primitive or 'animal' cognition, but also on traditional problems concerning the nature of scientific cognition and scientific progress. That the consequences portend revolution is easily seen. Traditional approaches to scientific knowledge portray the unit of cognition as the sentence or proposition accepted by the individual or community. And cognitive activity is portrayed as the drawing of inferences from one or more such propositions to another.

The new resources, by contrast, portray the 'unit of cognition' as the high-dimensional activation vector, as a pattern of activation levels across a large population of neurons. And cognitive activity is portrayed as the transformation of such vectors into further vectors by passing them through a vast matrix of synaptic connections. What one hopes to do, *qua* philosopher, is to reconstruct in a revealing way the phenomena of *scientific conceptual development* within the framework of these novel theoretical resources. This is my aim in what follows.

2. A NEW KINEMATICS FOR COGNITION

To cognitive creatures, the world is a highly ambiguous place. Not just in the ambiguity it presents to our sensory systems, where a peripheral encoding is typically consistent with a diversity of external circumstances, but more profoundly in the ambiguity it presents to our *conceptual* systems. Behind the relatively superficial question of which of one's concepts should be deployed on a specific sensory occasion, there is the deeper question of which framework of concepts should be embraced in the first place. Here the alternatives are legion. Any conceptual framework, no matter how robust or natural its categories may seem to us, is but a single point in a practically infinite space of alternative possible frameworks, each with a comparable a priori claim on our commitment. Some of the frameworks in this vast and almost entirely unexplored volume will be closely similar to our current scheme, but countless others will be so distant and alien as to escape intelligibility to us, short of a long period of re-education.

This talk of a vast space of alternatives is not merely romantic. Each of us has a history of conceptual diversity already. For one was not born with one's adult framework. One came to it slowly, through a long period of development. There is indeed a space, through which each of us has a complex journey already completed.

An individual's conceptual history is represented by a specific trajectory through this vast space of conceptual alternatives. That trajectory is traced by a point that changes its position swiftly and dramatically in the early stages of life, more slowly in later childhood, and only very slowly throughout the adult years. Fortunately, effort and environment seem capable of prolonging the capacity for continued exploration of conceptual space, at least in some individuals, and this helps to sustain an ongoing tradition of institutionalized scientific research.

Talk of conceptual 'space' may seem metaphorical still, but as outlined in two earlier papers (Churchland, 1989*c*, 1989*d*), recent research into the training and behaviour of artificial neural networks has shown us how to make literal and very useful sense of it. If we assume that the human brain is a multilayered network of interconnected units, we can uniquely specify its current position in conceptual space by specifying the individual strengths or 'weights' of its myriad synaptic connections (see the schematic network in Figure 1*b*). That configuration of weights can be directly represented by a specific point in a multidimensional space, a space with a distinct axis for each of the brain's 10^{14} synaptic connections.

For an illustration, observe the schematic 'weight-space' in Figure 1*a*. Strictly, it should have twenty-seven distinct dimensions to represent the twenty-seven synapses of the tiny network in Figure 1*b*. (For graphical clarity only three of the relevant dimensions are portrayed.) Each point in that space represents a unique configuration of (i.e. set of values for) the network's assembled synaptic weights. If we assume that there are at least ten significantly different positions along each of its twenty-seven synaptic axes, then the tiny network admits of at least 10^{27} different possible weight configurations. Evidently, even a tiny network boasts a large weight-space.

The relation explodes exponentially. For a human brain, this

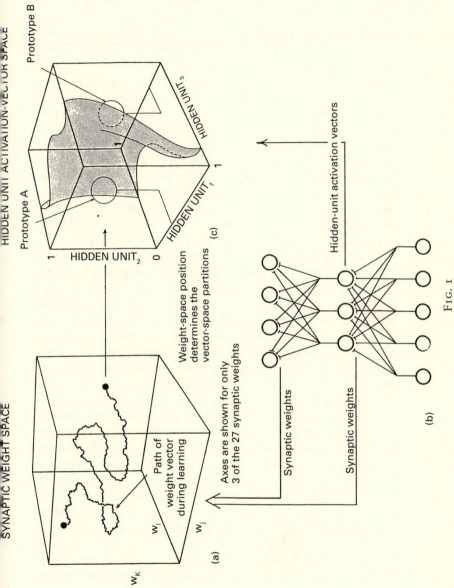

SYNAPTIC WEIGHT SPACE

HIDDEN UNIT ACTIVATION-VECTOR SPACE

Prototype B

Prototype A

HIDDEN UNIT₃

HIDDEN UNIT₁

HIDDEN UNIT₂

(c)

Weight-space position determines the vector-space partitions

w_i

w_j

w_k

Path of weight vector during learning

(a)

Axes are shown for only 3 of the 27 synaptic weights

Synaptic weights

Synaptic weights

Hidden-unit activation vectors

(b)

FIG. I

weight space will have, not twenty-seven, but fully 10^{14} dimensions. Its volume is almost unimaginably vast—at least $10^{10^{14}}$ functionally distinct positions—as our guiding metaphor suggested.

And there is a second space to consider here, comparable in extent: the space of possible *activation patterns* across the brain's 10^{11} neurons (see Figure 1*c*). This 'activation vector space', as it is called, has a distinct axis for each *neuron* in the brain, an axis that measures the level of that neuron's activity—typically, its spiking frequency. As outlined in the earlier papers, a specific configuration of synaptic weights will partition the activation space of a given neuronal layer into a taxonomy of distinct *prototypes* or *'universals'*. Such prototype patterns get activated in response to appropriate input stimuli. Figure 1*c* depicts a simple binary partition on the space of possible activation patterns, but a network's partitions will more often be elaborately hierarchical in their categorial structure.

To specify this global configuration of synaptic weights is thus to specify the global *conceptual framework* currently in use by the relevant individual. To change any of those weights is to change, however slightly, the conceptual framework they dictate. To trace a creature's actual path through the space of possible weight configurations would be to trace its conceptual history, as in Figure 1*b*. And to understand what factors induce changes in those weights would be to understand what drives conceptual change.

The present essay continues the exploration of this view. I wish to address four problems in particular. The first concerns the phenomenon of multiple conceptual competence, our capacity to apprehend or conceive a given situation in more than one way. The second concerns an important distinction between genuine conceptual change (which is slow) and mere conceptual redeployment (which can be fast). The third problem concerns the factors that drive conceptual change. And the fourth concerns the recently apprehended vastness of cognitive space, and the need to automate not just the experimental but also the theoretical aspects of the scientific enterprise if we are ever to explore that space effectively.

I open by re-raising a problem addressed in Churchland (1989*c*). Should we identify one's conceptual framework—one's global theory-of-the-world—with the configuration of synaptic *weights* in one's brain? Or with the hierarchically organized *partitions* they effect across the activation vector space of the assembled neurons to which they connect? Or perhaps with the overall in-put–output *function* that the network comes to instantiate? The weights uniquely dictate both the partitions and the input–output function, but despite the functional primacy of the weights, there are good reasons for identifying the partitions, and the function they serve, as reflecting most directly the familiar or antecedent notion of a 'conceptual framework'.

While the weights are of essential importance for understanding long-term learning and fundamental conceptual change, the parti-tions across the activation space, and the prototypical hot-spots they harbour, are much more useful in reckoning the cognitive and behavioural similarities across individuals in the short term. People react to the world in similar ways not because their under-lying weight configurations are closely similar on a synapse-by-synapse comparison, but because their *activation spaces* are similarly partitioned. Like trees similar in their gross physical profiles, brains can be similar in their gross functional profiles, while being highly idiosyncratic in the myriad details of their fine-grained arborization (cf. Quine's metaphor of the brace of apiary elephants (Quine, 1960: 8)).

Thus, a perfect identity of weight configurations will indeed produce a perfect identity of partitions on the activation space, but one can also achieve almost identical partitions with a large variety of quite different weight configurations. Synaptic contrasts in one place may compensate for further synaptic contrasts in another place, so that the categorial and functional profiles of two brains may end up practically the same. At least for now, there-fore, let us adopt the partitions across the neuronal activation space as the closest available computational analog of what the philosophical tradition conceives as our 'conceptual framework'.

3. MULTIPLE CONCEPTUAL COMPETENCE

Humans have the occasional capacity to apprehend the same thing in one of two or more quite different ways often at will. Examples range from the simple case of being able to see an ambiguous curve now as a duck and now as a rabbit (Figure 2*a*), to the more complex case of the old-woman/young-woman (Figure 2*b*), to the more unusual and global case of apprehending natural phenomena

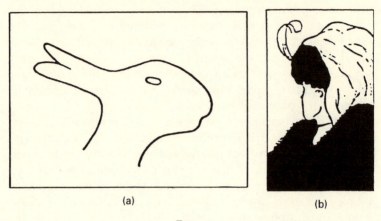

(a)   (b)

FIG. 2

at large now in an Aristotelian fashion, now in a Newtonian fashion, and now in an Einsteinian fashion. How is it possible, on the network models at issue, for a single individual to do any of this? How is it possible for one to bring distinct conceptual resources alternatively to bear on one and the same situation? How could one train a network to have this capacity?

The problem is that to train a feed-forward network to any sort of competence is to impose a function on it. A function delivers a unique output for any given input. But the situation at issue seems to require that the network sometimes deliver a different output given the same input. These demands are incompatible, and the solution is to recast the problem so that the relevant inputs are not strictly identical after all.

To do this we need to consider a vitally important addition to the feed-forward architecture of simple networks. We need to introduce *recurrent pathways* as portrayed in Figure 3. These pathways convey, back to the middle-level or 'hidden' units, the activity levels of neurons in populations somewhere higher in the processing hierarchy. Those pathways synapse onto the hidden units with various weights, just like the familiar pathways arriving from the input units.

The collective activation profile of the hidden units at any given moment is thus a function not just of the information arriving

A RECURRENT NETWORK

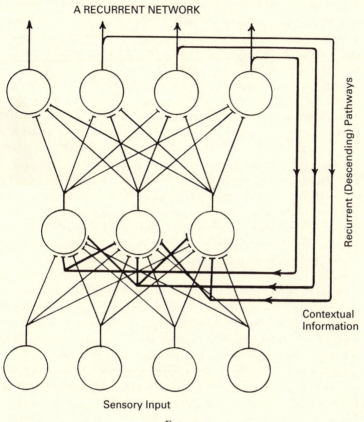

Recurrent (Descending) Pathways

Contextual
Information

Sensory Input

FIG. 3

from the peripheral input units, but also of the recurrent or 'contextual' information arriving from elsewhere in the processing hierarchy. That additional information can have a decisive modulating influence on how the hidden units respond to input from the sensory periphery. Depending on the antecedent dynamical state or 'frame of mind' of the network, a given input pattern from the periphery—the duck–rabbit curve, for example—can contribute to the production of quite different activation patterns across the hidden units: a duck-like activation pattern given one set of recurrent modulations, and a rabbit-like pattern given another set.

It is important to appreciate, of course, that a trained network will often deal quite successfully with a degraded or imperfect version of a familiar sort of input without benefit of recurrent contextual information. For trained networks are typically capable of *vector completion*. Their antecedent training produces a set of lasting partitions and similarity gradients across the hidden-unit activation space, and slightly atypical input stimuli tend to get classified along with (i.e. to get represented within the hidden-unit partitions appropriate to) the prototypical inputs that the atypical inputs most closely *resemble*. In this way, a network's categorial response to an input is almost always *ampliative*. Its response at the hidden units presumptively represents substantially more than is strictly present in its input. The network tends to 'see' the world in terms of the antecedent categories to which it has already been trained. Steered by what it has learned to regard as relevant vectorial similarities, its conceptual response at the hidden units might naturally be called an 'inference to its best understanding' of the input.

What recurrent neural pathways can add to this already prodigious feed-forward activity is a variety of temporary and context-dependent 'tilts' to the classificatory playing-field at the hidden units. A recurrent vector arriving at the hidden units can contribute a pattern of (partial) activation that is already tending in the direction of a duck-like pattern independently of the input arriving from the sensory periphery. That is why the same input can at different times be processed in different ways. The peripheral inputs arrive to a population of neurons that may already be biased in one cognitive direction or another by contextual information arriving via recurrent pathways. This is clearly a good thing when the network as a whole has some vital background information not currently available from the sensory periphery.

In this way, recurrent pathways produce a network where the manner in which the sensory input is processed is both variable and under the control of the network itself. Such a network can process a given perceptual input in any one of several different ways, depending on which of its activational subspaces (conceptual resources) has been temporarily favoured by the relevant context-fixing recurrent inputs. This is true not only at the level of perceptual processing, but at higher levels as well. A situation drawn from memory, or contemplated in imagination, or apprehended from a printed description can also be processed in a variety of different ways, depending on what contextual information accompanies its apprehension at the relevant population of neurons.

It is entirely to be expected then, on the model of cognition here being explored, that one can see ambiguous figures in diverse ways. Nor is it mysterious that one can learn to perceive/understand the world in an Aristotelian fashion, and in a Newtonian fashion, and in an Einsteinian fashion, and then use each framework (= subvolume of the relevant activation space) by turns, to suit aesthetic whim, theoretical occasion, or practical demand. What is required is independent training-to-competence in all three frameworks, and then some recurrent manipulation of whatever neural population embodies that competence. This capacity for multiple conceptual competence is a central feature of recurrent nets in general. It is an automatic benefit of their recurrent architecture.

[Though it will loom large in what follows, this feature of recurrent nets is not the only nor even perhaps the most important feature they introduce. Recurrent nets can be trained not just to a prototypical vectorial response to a favoured class of inputs, but to a prototypical *sequence* of vectors. They can, in other words, be trained to represent important temporal sequences in the world, such as causal sequences or the behaviour of an individual over time. Moreover, they can be trained to trace highly specific closed loops in activation space, loops that represent periodic phenomena. They are thus fit both to recognize locomotor behaviour (such as walking or swimming) in other creatures, and to generate such behaviour themselves. These virtues will not be explored here.]

A recurrent net's capacity for self-modulation in the face of bivalent ambiguity is further displayed in cases where one of the available conceptual alternatives represents the input as little more than scattered trivia or unstructured noise. Consider Figure 4*a*, which typically looks like a mottled chaos unless one has chanced to encounter it before. In fact, it portrays a perfectly ordinary scene, but the image has been degraded, by repeated high-contrast copyings, to the point where its context-free presentation produces only confusion in most observers.

Let me now provide you with some contextual information, in the hope that the relevant recurrent pathways within your visual system will modulate your vectorial response to Figure 4*a* in such a fashion as to permit visual recognition. In the very centre of the

(a)

(b)

FIG. 4

picture is a spotted Dalmatian dog as seen from a standing position perhaps ten feet away. The dog is walking left and slightly away from you, with its nose to the ground and the outline of its head and left ear just visible. Beyond and to the left is the bottom of an ornamental tree with a dark shadow underneath, as if the entire scene were lit with brilliant sunshine. Very likely you now see the scene quite differently: it shows a structure and coherence that was not evident at first viewing.

Figure 4*b* provides a second and more difficult example. But the scattered marks one initially apprehends (perhaps you see an absurdly smiling face at the top of the picture) suddenly resolve themselves into a highly specific and coherent pattern when you are given the following collateral information, recurrently delivered to the relevant population of neurons in your visual system. You are looking at a man on a horse. The horse's head is at the upper left, with two small ears just showing. From the head you may trace the horse's neck down to its chest and two front legs towards the bottom of the picture, passing the rider's two splayed riding-boots on the way. The animal's hind legs and tail are to the right, and the rider is carrying a lance, pointing leftward. In the end, Don Quixote emerges from the scatter.

Such perceptual shifts, I suggest, are not different in principle from shifts encountered in the classically ambiguous figures portrayed in Figures 2*a* and 2*b*. The classical examples are famous, of course, precisely for their bivalence and rough 'symmetry': each of the interpretive alternatives is equally likely to be adopted, and each alternative is a stable, specific, and familiar category. Figures 4*a* and 4*b*, however, are multivalent; and the alternative spontaneous interpretations are all unstable and unspecific, save for the initially improbable interpretation that collateral information eventually helps to activate—a spotted dog in the first case, and a mounted rider in the second.

Taken jointly, a trained network's talent for vector completion and recurrent modulation provides us with a possible account of how living creatures are able to recognize, often in milliseconds, an instance of a familiar category despite partial or severely degraded sensory inputs, and also of how they are able to modulate their cognitive response so as to discover alternative interpretations of those same sensory inputs. The possible applications of this account to scientific cognition are moderately obvious, but before exploring its virtues, let us examine some severe problems that currently confront a neural-network account of human cognition.

4. THREE PROBLEMS ABOUT LEARNING

The currently dominant technique for training artificial networks is the familiar Generalized Delta Rule or 'Back-Propagation' procedure as it is commonly called. This procedure calculates, for each synaptic weight in the student network, its local contribution to the net's global error in performance on a particular input–output trial. It then makes a small adjustment in each weight accordingly—to a new configuration that produces a very slightly improved performance on the specific trial task in question. Repeated applications of this procedure, over many different input–output examples drawn from the function-to-be-learned, leads the network down a meandering but ever-descending path in weight/ error space until it reaches at least a local error minimum in that space.

There is no guarantee that said local minimum will be the global or lowest possible minimum in the network's weight-error space, but there are a variety of auxiliary procedures designed to bounce the weight-space point out of merely local minima so as to increase its chances of finding the truly global error minimum. In all, the augmented procedure is robustly effective at finding weight configurations that yield excellent performance (i.e. close approximations to the target function), at least in relatively small networks.

There is no pretence, however, that back propagation might be the specific procedure by which biological brains adjust their synaptic weights. It is a flawed candidate for several reasons. First, a real brain rarely possesses an exact error measure for each new performance, as the back-propagation procedure requires. Second, a real brain displays no central administrator to transform such a measure into a proprietary adjustment for each of its many billions of synapses. And third, it has no distribution system to effect such adjustments even if it could compute them. Back-propagation is just a very useful instance of a much more general class of 'gradient descent' procedures for exploring a network's weight-configuration space. It has been of decisive importance in furthering research into the capacities of neural networks. But the brain itself exploits some other technique within the enveloping class of gradient descent procedures.

Just what that technique might be is still an open question, although Hebbian procedures provide our current best guess. The problem I have been leading up to, however, is highly general, and it will arise on any gradient descent procedure whatever. Indeed, it will arise on every weight-adjusting procedure of which I am aware. For such procedures are all instances of *curve-fitting* in a hyperspace: the various training examples are all points lying on the function-to-be-learned, and any gradient descent procedure attempts to approximate a (hyper-) curve that minimizes the deviation from those training points. With multiple input units and multiple output units, the problem becomes a high-dimensional one, but it differs none in principle from the two-dimensional case illustrated in Figures *6a* and *6b*.

Although some functions are more difficult than others, and deliberately 'pathological' functions are always possible, there is no essential problem encountered by the familiar weight-adjusting procedures, so long as the elements related by the target function are all *observationally available* to the student net, so long as the functionally related elements are all explicitly or implicitly *present* in the training examples.

But sometimes they are not. To take a deliberately trivial example, consider the problem of training a net on the functional relation between the pressure P and the volume V of a confined gas (Figure 5), in an environment where the ever-changing temperature T of the gas is hidden or ignored. The problem is that there is no functional relation between P and V when T is left to wander. The result of plotting P against V in that environment will show a disordered scatter as portrayed in Figure *6a*. A net trained on such a scatter will learn nothing.

That scatter does reflect a hidden order, of course, an order that emerges when the hidden variable T is taken into account: all of the original points lie on curves of constant temperature, as portrayed in Figure *6b*. The true functional relationship is $P = cT/V$. This function is easily learnable, but it cannot be learned if the network is denied access to the variable T.

You can see the problem emerging. If nets are instructed by what is essentially a curve-fitting procedure, then they are limited

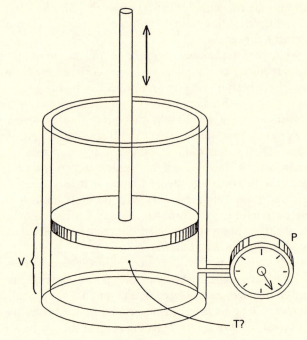

FIG. 5

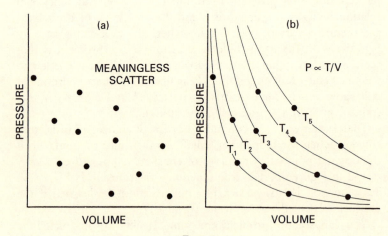

FIG. 6

to the discovery of 'phenomenological' or 'observation-level' laws, to the discovery of functional relations between observables.

This limitation must not be conceived too naïvely. One of the impressive and endearing features of neural networks learning under gradient descent procedures is that they are plastic about what counts as a functionally relevant 'observable'. A net's search for functional order is at the same time a search for observational categories that take part in such an order, and those categories will often be strange or unfamiliar to us. By adjusting the weights from the input units to the hidden units, a net can come to focus on a large variety of different aspects of or configurations within its complex input vectors, in hopes of finding those aspects or configurations that are functionally relevant. In this sense it is 'theorizing' about what *observational* categories it should embrace. And it will generally succeed in finding both the categories bound and the function that binds them, so long as the functionally important categories are at least implicit in the network's input vectors.

But sometimes a functionally essential category is simply not present in the input vectors at all, not even implicitly. Here the network must fail to learn, if there is no functional relation that binds the observationally available categories in the absence of the hidden category. A net cannot learn a function that does not exist.

The first problem, then, is this. How can a network theorize successfully about the possible existence and relevance of factors that lie hidden from its observation? How can a network theorize about *un*observable categories, entities, or processes and their functional relationship to observables? How can a network reach *behind the appearances*?

The history of science illustrates that we humans do this all the time, occasionally with great success. In postulating molecules, atoms, nuclei, electrons, electromagnetic waves, and so forth, we have presumed to portray a rich reality behind the appearances, a reality bound in specific functional relations to the appearances, much to our explanatory and manipulative advantage. How could we do this if our capacity for learning were limited, as in the artificial network models, to curve-fitting over observables? Those models, therefore, appear inadequate to the facts of human cognitive behaviour.

There is a second and equally serious problem with the standard account of learning and conceptual change as a process of synaptic-weight modification. It concerns the time course of conceptual change. On the face of it, the unique determinant of a network's conceptual framework (= its activation-space partitions) is the network's configuration of synaptic weights, and the only way to change the former is to change the latter. But in living creatures as well as in artificial nets, changes in the weight of any given synaptic connection happen only in small increments. Accordingly, the learning network's global trajectory through weight space (see again Figure 1a) must always approximate a continuous path. Moreover, synaptic change takes time, and so the velocity of the weight-space point must always be fairly low: it must move through the relevant space as if embedded in molasses.

But in humans conceptual change is a process that at least occasionally displays dramatic *dis*continuities. Sometimes it is very sudden, occurring on a time scale of minutes, or seconds, or even milliseconds: as when the light dawns, the scales fall from one's eyes, the structure is suddenly apparent, and so forth. Unlike weight-change in nets, which is always smooth and gradual, conceptual change in humans is sometimes sudden and cathartic. How to reconcile the apparent conflict?

Lethargic change is not the only problem here. A third problem is as follows. However the weight-space point might be made to move to new positions in configuration space, *as* it moves it *dissolves* the old conceptual framework in the same act that gives form to the new one. Accordingly, even if one could hasten the weight-space point on its journey towards a deeper understanding, or make it move in discontinuous jumps, in every case one would be leaving behind, irretrievably, the framework of one's past. To each point in weight space there corresponds exactly one partitioning of the network's activation space, exactly one hierarchy of prototypes. As the weight-space point moves and a new family of prototypes is created, the old family inevitably disappears.

But this is unfaithful to the facts of human cognition. When one learns the Newtonian framework, one does not thereby lose one's Aristotelian capacities. When one learns the Einsteinian framework, one does not thereby lose one's Newtonian capacities. Past modes of thinking may become faint, through disuse or disinterest, but they do not disappear, utterly and automatically, by the mere discovery of conceptual alternatives.

In summary, a network model of cognition confronts three major problems. First, how can a mere observational 'curve fitter' reach behind the appearances to the hidden reality that produces them? Second, how can a system that learns by slow and continuous gradient descent ever display the sudden flashes of conceptual insight that humans occasionally display? And third, how can such a system find new ways of conceiving the world without thereby losing competence in its old conceptual habits?

5. CONCEPTUAL CHANGE VS. CONCEPTUAL REDEPLOYMENT

The problems of section 4 are serious, but the ideas set free in section 3 provide the materials for their solution. There is a way to account even for large-scale conceptual shifts, on a time scale as short as milliseconds, that requires no motion from the weight-space point whatsoever. We have already seen the trick at work in the earlier account of how a network with recurrent pathways can manipulate the manner in which its hidden units respond to stimuli from the input layer. The crucial idea is the idea of *conceptual redeployment*, a process in which a conceptual framework that is already fully developed, and in regular use in some other domain of experience or comprehension, comes to be used for the first time in a new domain.

Examples are many and familiar. Consider Huygen's seventeenth-century realization that optical phenomena, previously grasped via the ray traces of geometrical optics, could be more comprehensively understood as instances of wave phenomena. Here the theory of waves in mechanical media—a theory already well-formed in Huygen's mind in connection with water waves and sound waves—was applied in a domain hitherto unaddressed by that framework, and with systematic success. There was no need for Huygens to effect a global reconfiguration of his synaptic weights to achieve this conceptual shift. He had only to apprehend a familiar class of phenomena in a new cognitive context, one supplied largely by himself, in order to have old and familiar input-unit vectors (those concerning light) activate hidden-unit vectors in an area of his conceptual space quite different from the areas they had previously activated. The difference lay in the context-fixers brought to the problem. And the result was a radically new understanding of optical phenomena: they arise from the propagation and interaction of waves. The cognitive novelty, however, consisted in the unusual redeployment of old resources, not the creation from scratch of new ones. No new conceptual resources were created; nor were any old resources destroyed.

Conceptual redeployment therefore solves immediately the second and third problems listed in the previous section. Since recurrent manipulation of the hidden units takes place on a time scale of only tens of milliseconds, a change in one's conceptual apprehension of any phenomenon can take place with comparable swiftness. This is not to say that the search for recurrent manipulations that yield genuinely *successful* conceptual redeployments will be completed so swiftly—the search might take days, or years, or decades—but if and when the lucky context-fixers finally arrive, activation of the relevantly virtuous hidden-unit vector can happen as swiftly as does the shift from the old woman to the young woman in the ambiguous Figure 2*b*. And as with ambiguous figures generally, the redeployment of one's conceptual resources is not a process that automatically destroys the resources typically applied before the shift. Those old resources remain in place, perhaps to be redeployed themselves as future occasion demands.

More importantly, the phenomenon of conceptual redeployment offers us a solution to the first problem of the preceding section: how can an observational 'curve-fitter' reach behind the appearances to the hidden reality that produces them? As follows. We illustrate with a real example. Christian Huygens originally developed his systematic conception of wave phenomena in the context of the behaviour of *water* waves, a context in which all of the relevant variables—wavelength, velocity, frequency, amplitude, etc.—are observationally available. Here there is no especial problem for a 'curve-fitting' cognitive system: the functionally related factors are all out in the open. One can discover inductively that $f = v/l$; one can see diffraction and interference effects directly; and so on. But once those conceptual resources are fully developed in this fortuitously transparent domain, they are then candidates for redeployment in domains whose behavioural profile is in fact similar to that of water, but where some or even most of the relevant variables are typically hidden from view.

Historically, the first major redeployment discovered 'waves' of a sort in the air: sound was fruitfully reconceived as a variant form of wave motion. The second major redeployment discovered waves of a similar sort in a possible universal 'aether': Huygens began to reconceive light itself as a wave phenomenon. A third major redeployment was effected by James Clerk Maxwell, of which more in a moment. While the conceptual prototypes of wave phenomena could not have been *learned* in either of these comparatively opaque domains, they were certainly capable of being *redeployed* there on the strength of a network's recurrent manipulations of its own cognitive activity and its ever-present capacity for vector completion of partial or degraded inputs.

In illustration of where and how this can happen, Figure 7 portrays two situations that might be seen—by someone already adept in wave phenomena—as instances of the same basic structure. Figure 7*a* portrays the observable behaviour of water waves arriving at a sea-wall after passing through two slits in an earlier barrier. Figure 7*b* portrays the observable behaviour of light arriving at a wall after passing through two slits in an earlier barrier. The parallel between the resulting patterns on the two walls is striking on the face of it, and it becomes more striking still as one varies the distance between the wall and barrier, or the distance between the two slits, or as one varies the presumed wavelength of the arriving periodic disturbance: the pattern of amplitudes on the wall is always modified identically in both cases. If recurrent manipulation of the hidden units is doing anything at all to suppress the prior (i.e. the rectilinear-ray) interpretation of optical phenomena, then vector completion will have a good chance of activating wave prototypes in any observer who has already developed the relevant conceptual prototypes in some other context, despite the comparatively degraded or partial character of the observational inputs, *qua* instances of waves. Most of the relevant structure is hidden, but there is enough structure evident in the two-slit optical experiment, and in many other observable optical phenomena, to suggest wave-like activity to a suitably trained and suitably imaginative observer.

It is evident then, that an observational curve-fitter *can* aspire to reach behind the appearances, by first learning a rich repertoire of prototypes in the clear, and then by exploiting its capacity for recurrent manipulation and vector completion of patterns that are only incompletely evident at the level of current observation. And

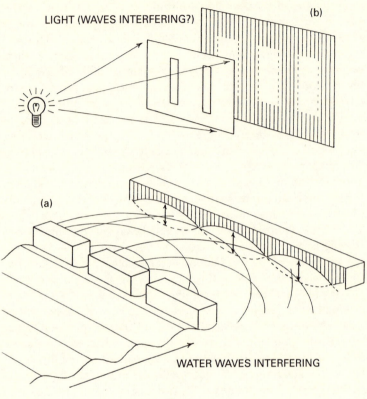

LIGHT (WAVES INTERFERING?)

(b)

(a)

WATER WAVES INTERFERING

FIG. 7

once a possible reinterpretation of a familiar phenomenon has been found, recurrent manipulation can enhance the chance of finding further opportunities for redeployment of the relevant conceptual resources, as the empirical domain containing the original phenomenon is systematically re-explored with a 'new eye'.

Of course, the story so far accounts only for the 'context of discovery' in science. We need to look further if we are to account for the 'context of evaluation or justification' as well. But we can see how to begin. Since vector completion is a dramatically ampliative process—a prototype is a digest of a great many training examples and thus embodies far more structure and detail than is evident in most inputs—the activation of any prototype constitutes a set of expectations about things perceivable (perhaps), but so far unperceived. Those expectations may or may not be systematically satisfied, and the usefulness of redeploying the relevant prototype is thus open to evaluation.

The reader familiar with the philosophy of science will recognize that this neurocomputational account of theoretical activity is a new incarnation of an old and venerable idea: the idea of exploiting *models* and *analogies*. Russell Hanson (1958), Mary Hesse (1966), Wilfrid Sellars (1961), and Thomas Kuhn (1962) have each put these notions near the centre of their accounts of science, as more recently have Bas van Fraassen (1980), Ron Giere (1985), and Nancy Nersessian (1992) in their somewhat different ways. What the new setting adds to this older approach is a novel and unexpectedly powerful account of both representation and computation, an account that is faithful, moreover, to the empirical microstructure and the physiological activity of the human brain. It also provides a physical mechanism for the 'creative process' in science and elsewhere, as it has recently been characterized by Margaret Boden (1991).

The genesis of the wave theory of light is but one historical example of conceptual redeployment. A second example is provided in the various seventeenth-century attempts to apply the conceptual resources of *terrestrial* mechanics to the case of motions in the superlunary heavens, a domain long thought to be governed by distinct and divine principles. From the rectilinear perspective of the recently developed terrestrial mechanics, the circular motion of the planets around the sun—which constitutes a centripetal acceleration *toward* the sun—clearly asked for a *force* on the planets directed toward the sun. It could be a push from the outside or a pull from the inside, but from the new perspective it needed somehow to be there. Descartes' vortex theory tried to fill out the story in the first way; Newton's gravitational theory tried, with more striking success, to fill it out in the second. But in both cases, existing conceptual resources were being reapplied in a new domain. Contemplation of the heavens was now activating, on a regular basis, prototype vectors that were initially learned in, and used only in response to, terrestrial situations.

A third and very striking example is the systematic reconception of optical phenomena as *electromagnetic* phenomena, a shift that spread quickly throughout the scientific community of the late 1800s. Maxwell's beautiful summary of the relations between electric and magnetic fields entailed the existence of a wave-like electromagnetic disturbance, spreading out from any oscillating charge, with a velocity of $(\mu * \varepsilon)^{-1/2}$, where μ and ε represent the magnetic permeability and the electric permittivity of the surrounding medium. For the atmosphere, these two values were well known. A quick calculation yielded a velocity of roughly 3.0×10^8 metres/sec. for such spreading electromagnetic disturbances, a velocity indistinguishable from the measured velocity of light in air. This extraordinary coincidence invited an attempt to see further optical phenomena as facets of oscillatory electromagnetic phenomena.

As it developed, this electromagnetic reincarnation of Huygen's much simpler vision immediately displayed all of the virtues of its antecedent, plus an unexpected cornucopia of further virtues. EM waves were transverse, and thus were polarizable, just as light had proved to be. Unfamiliar features of transparent substances—such as their permittivity (ε) and permeability (μ)—suddenly became salient, since it is they that dictate the differing velocities of EM waves in the relevant substances, and it is those relative velocities that dictate the refractive index of any substance. The refractive indexes for transparent substances were already well known, and the agreement with the predictions of the new theory was striking if occasionally imperfect. These various optical indexes suddenly emerged as systematic reflections of the electric and magnetic properties of matter.

Here again a familiar domain was ambiguous, and proved to be understandable in more than one way. When addressed with the appropriate context-fixing inputs (perhaps no more than the admonition, 'Any ray of light *is* a train of EM waves!'), optical phenomena began systematically to activate vectors in an unexpected subvolume of conceptual space, a subvolume that was initially partitioned by its extensive training on entirely non-optical phenomena. Moreover, after extended practice at approaching the old phenomena with the new electromagnetic subvolume in gear, one clearly did better at understanding things than one did with the old framework. And finally, a major virtue of this shift—a virtue displayed in both of the preceding examples as well—is that one now had a *unified* understanding of what initially appeared as disjoint empirical domains.

It is clear from these three examples that conceptual change is regularly a matter of conceptual redeployment, as opposed to fundamental conceptual novelty. It is also clear that such shifts can initially take place, in a given individual, on a time-scale of seconds or less, although the full exploration of the novel use of old resources may well take years. Indeed, so many of the historical examples fit this redeployment mould that one may begin to wonder if history contains *any* examples of real conceptual novelty. I believe that it does—Faraday's conception of a 'field of force' comes quickly to mind—but I also suspect that such cases are relatively rare. The bulk of the conceptual discontinuities displayed in the history of science are clearly cases of conceptual redeployment.

These can often be cases of learning, however, in the deeper sense and beyond the making of the shift itself. The redeployed resources seldom survive extended contact with the new domain entirely unchanged. The redeployed resources are now subject to a new regime of training examples. This will often lead to a yet more subtle articulation of the antecedent partitions, a process of learning that is comparatively slow and thus easily explained in terms of the gradual motion of one's weight-space position.

Figure 8 illustrates the manner in which sudden conceptual redeployments can produce sudden improvements in a network's performance without any change at all in the network's synaptic-weight configuration. The several short vertical lines represent sudden reductions in performance error, but since they are purely vertical, they represent no change in any of the weight dimensions. The change in the network's behaviour is due not to a change of its weights, but to a fortuitous recurrent modulation of the activation patterns at its own hidden units. Once we add recurrent pathways as in Figure 3, we have changed a stimulus-response machine into a partially autonomous dynamical system. And since the behaviour of its many interacting units is non-linear, the behaviour of such a network can prove highly idiosyncratic and unpredictable.

What we have to acknowledge is that the notion of 'learning' is starting to fragment in interesting ways. Beyond the basic but comparatively slow process of synaptic adjustment, there is the more short-term process whereby one learns how to deal with a puzzling new situation by repeatedly reapprehending it in conjunction with various context-fixing auxiliary inputs, in hopes of eventually activating some robust prototype vector within a subvolume that is already well trained. The ten-year-old takes apart the old

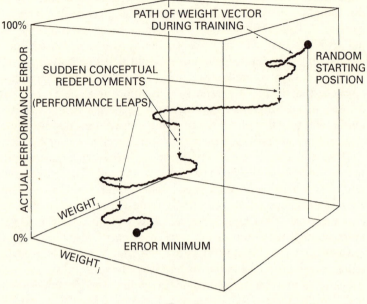

FIG. 8

alarm clock and after a half-hour's pondering sees how it all works. The maths student puzzles over a homework problem and after several false starts suddenly sees the path through it. The physician confronts a confusing set of symptoms and, several failed tests and incoherent diagnoses later, finally lights on a successful one. These are all genuine cases of learning, in the sense of 'coming to understand', but the underlying process here is quite different from the slow process that partitions one's activation spaces in the first place.

The frequency and importance of conceptual redeployment requires us to acknowledge a further divergence, which I have been suppressing to this point, between the partitions across one's activation space(s) and the input–output function one instantiates. Plainly it is possible for two people to have closely similar partitions, but widely divergent deployments: they may command essentially the same conceptual resources, but apply them to quite different domains. Two physicists (Newton and Huygens, say) may have a comparable command of both projectile mechanics and wave mechanics, and yet one chronically understands light as the high-speed ballistic motion of tiny corpuscles, while the other chronically understands light as a train of compression waves in the aether. The same sensory inputs produce different conceptual responses in each, and thus different behaviour from each, since particles and waves often call for different techniques of manipulation and they behave differently in many circumstances. Because of their divergent deployments, the two physicists will have very different input–output functions, despite commanding essentially the same conceptual resources.

Such cases give us reason to regard a person's trajectory through weight-space as capturing only a part of what we would normally regard as one's conceptual evolution. The repeated redeployment of existing conceptual resources can produce some profound changes in one's cognitive and practical life, with only minimal changes in the configuration of one's synaptic weights and in the activation-space partitions that they produce. If we want to know what drives conceptual change, then, we must address both the dynamics of the moving point in weight-space, and the more superficial but still vitally important dynamics of conceptual redeployment.

6. WHAT DRIVES CONCEPTUAL CHANGE?

Weight-change procedures are currently a topic of intense research, both in connectionist AI and in neurophysiology. Hinton (1989) provides a useful summary of research in the former, and Churchland and Sejnowski (1992) provide a recent summary of research in the latter. In this section I shall confine attention to the narrower question of what drives conceptual redeployment, a process that involves little or no change in one's synaptic weights.

Clearly, frustration with the poor performance of older frameworks figures prominently. Recall Kuhn's analysis of gathering anomalies, crisis science, and the resulting radiation in conceptual approaches to old problems. Individuals show an increasing willingness to explore, and the scientific community shows an increasing willingness to tolerate, unorthodox conceptions of recalcitrant phenomena. Old inputs are repeatedly re-entered into one's already trained network, with a variety of increasingly unusual context fixers, in hopes of activating some antecedently developed prototype vector in a subvolume of activation space hitherto devoted to other phenomena entirely. Should success be achieved, the (hyper)distance between the old and new prototype vectors is a measure of how great the conceptual change effected.

Though gathering anomalies are perhaps the most common force behind such explorations, they are clearly not *necessary* for conceptual exploration of this kind. The simple desire for *theoretical unity* can drive a systematic search for new ways of comprehending old phenomena, even when the old ways are still functioning quite nicely. Here the only defect that need be felt in one's current conceptual resources is the fact that they are still diverse rather than unitary.

Examples are common enough. Classical or 'phenomenological' thermodynamics was enormously successful (it helped to produce the Industrial Revolution), but this did not dissuade the tradition of Bernoulli, Joule, Kelvin, and Boltzmann from repeatedly trying to reconceive thermal phenomena within the broader framework of kinetic and corpuscular theories. Newtonian mechanics had conquered motion at both the astronomical and the human scales. One had to wonder if it also held true at the submicroscopic scale. The possibility of apprehending heat as mechanical energy at some micro-level was therefore very inviting.

An unusual sensitivity to failures of unity seems to have driven the greater part of Einstein's theoretical work. Special relativity was an attempt to bring mechanics and electrodynamics together under a common and internally coherent roof. General relativity was an attempt to unify the physics of both accelerated and unaccelerated reference frames. In both cases the new conceptual perspective was provided by four-dimensional geometry with non-standard metrics. But in neither case was the search for this more unitary perspective driven by any prominent experimental failing in any of the older views. His later search for a Unified Field Theory is a further instance of the same general yearning.

This impulse toward unity is vitally important in any cognitive creature, an impulse coequal with sensitivity to the data, for reasons we can now understand (see Churchland, 1989*a*, ch. 9, sect. 5). It is curious that the relative strengths of these two impulses seem so variable across individuals. A major imbalance in either direction yields a familiar pathology. Valuing unity at the radical expense of local empirical success yields a castle-in-the-air fantasy world for its victim to live in. And valuing local empirical success at the radical expense of synoptic unity traps its victim in a disconnected set of small and windowless rooms: it yields a hidebound and narrow vision that will not generalize successfully to unfamiliar cases.

Finally, conceptual redeployment is occasionally prompted by some fortunate novelty in one's experience. Ampère's observation that a cylindrical coil of current-carrying wire produced a bipolar magnetic field moved him to reconceive the long-familiar case of magnetized iron bars as having circular currents somehow flowing inside of them as well, just as in the coil. Fresnel's striking demonstration of concentric circles of light at the centre of a tiny circular shadow moved many thinkers to forsake Newtonian corpuscles and to set about reconceiving light on a wave model. And Einstein's much later observation of the curious photoelectric effect moved him to reconceive light waves as quantized after all. In such cases, the striking new phenomenon discovered in a familiar domain is capable, all by itself and without arduous context-fixing, of activating specific vectors in some heterodox portion of one's activation space. Here the phenomena themselves have the salient character necessary to activate an unusual interpretation directly.

Conceptual shifts of the kind under discussion constitute perhaps the greater portion of our scientific development, but they seem superficial relative to the prior and deeper learning process by which our activation spaces are partitioned in the first place, and by which they must be readjusted. What factors drive change at this most fundamental level? By what procedure(s) is the weight-space point made to move? Until this question is answered, our account of learning and conceptual change in science must be radically incomplete. However, even in the absence of a clear answer to this question, one or two very general lessons can safely be drawn from the account as it stands. They are worth noting.

7. TWO LESSONS ABOUT LEARNING

The first lesson concerns the character of the factors that drive synaptic adjustment and conceptual change. Are they exhausted by considerations of mere 'professional interest', as some theorists have argued (cf. Pickering, 1981, 1984), or does the world itself exert a robust influence on the process? In the many network models that have appeared in the research program under discussion, it is clear that it is the world itself that is driving the learning process, whether by means of back propagation of measured error, by means of the progressive reduction of cognitive dissonance with imposed output vectors, or by means of a progressive accommodation to the objective statistical distribution among inputs.

It must immediately be admitted, of course, that these networks are not functioning in a complex *social* world, as is a real scientist. And it must also be admitted that for a network as complex and sensitive as a human brain, the pressure to instantiate socially acceptable functions can often be overwhelming. But while the character of social pressures will have a vital role to play in any adequate account of learning in scientific communities, there is no reason whatever to regard them as *exhausting* the dynamical pressures. We know that in non-social cases of learning (artificial networks, simple animals), it is the non-social world itself that is the instructor, a relentless and often highly successful instructor. And unless institutionalized science somehow represents a total *corruption* of a process that shows systematic integrity elsewhere, there is no reason to embrace the extremely sceptical, anti-realist social determinism suggested above. On the contrary, science has outperformed those purer but simpler creatures.

On the other hand, from the perspective of the present paper, the naturalism of the 'strong program' in the sociology of knowledge (Bloor, 1976, 1981) appears entirely justified. (Bloor in particular has been entirely clear in asserting that sociological factors are only some among a great many factors that steer our cognition, the non-social world itself being prominent among them.) Throughout this essay we have been exploring causal accounts of the learning process—accounts, moreover, that are uniform for successful and unsuccessful cognitive configurations alike. And we have found it neither necessary nor useful to fall back on the language of observation sentences, logical inferences, rational beliefs, or truth. To reassure the reader, however, let me hasten to add that the alternative to these antiquarian semantic and syntactic notions need not be a sceptical or a deflationary account of knowledge, as some urge and as so many fear. Rather, one hopes, it will simply be a better account of knowledge.

The second major lesson I wish to draw, from the picture of cognition explored in this paper, concerns the appalling vastness of the conceptual space in which we find ourselves. I am reminded here of the shock that must have confronted Greek thinkers when Aristarchos of Samos first put a realistic metric on the dimensions of the physical universe. While scholars of the period were quite prepared to believe that the heavens were very large, Aristarchos' crude but well-conceived calculations caught them quite unprepared for just *how* large. To a community used to thinking of the scale of the heavens in terms of thousands of miles at most, Aristarchos brought compelling geometrical reasons for extending the yardstick to hundreds of thousands of miles in the case of the moon, millions of miles in the case of the sun, and many thousands of millions of miles in the case of the stars. An expansion of this magnitude changes one's perspective on things.

I believe we are now confronting a similar lesson. Contemporary scholars, with a few notable exceptions (e.g. Davidson, 1973), are prepared to concede the possibility of alternative conceptual schemes, perhaps a great many of them. But the reckoning of the true extent of the space of alternatives that arises from the point-in-weight-space model of human knowledge is one that catches us unprepared, however liberal our prior sentiments. $10^{100,000,000,000,000}$ (just barely discriminable) alternatives is not a number one would have picked, and yet that is a minimum reckoning. (Given that each synaptic connection admits of at least ten possible values, and given that the brain has at least 10^{11} neurons, each of which has at least 10^{3} synaptic connections, then the total number of synapses is at least 10^{14} and the total number of possible synaptic configurations is at least 10 to the 10^{14} or $10^{100,000,000,000,000}$.)

The significance of this number will be clearer if we note the following points. Simple networks have already been trained up on a wide range of dramatically different problems: phoneme recognition, shape discrimination, multiplication tables, music composition, loan-application evaluation, hand-eye co-ordination, text reading, and so on. Each of these trained skills represents what we would call a 'dramatically different conceptual configuration' of the network. The number of such dramatically distinct skills already produced by various researchers, many of which are now available for sale, is into the thousands and is still climbing. But effectively all of them are achieved in networks of less than 10^{3} units. This means that any one of them is a skill that a standard 10^3-unit network could have: it needs only to be weighted properly.

As we noted, such a network commands, at a bare minimum, a thousand dramatically different possible conceptual configurations, and it has this capacity with only 10^3 units and something like $(10^3)^2 = 10^6$ synaptic connections. Assuming, as before, ten distinct possible values for each synaptic weight, such a system has $10^{10^{\wedge}6}$ distinct possible weight configurations. This is a very large number indeed, but it is a paltry fraction of the figure for a human brain. In principle, our combinatorial options are greater than the small artificial network's by a factor of $10^{10^{\wedge}14}/10^{10^{\wedge}6} = 10^{(10^{\wedge}14-10^{\wedge}6)} = 10^{99,999,999,000,000}$! The number of 'dramatically different conceptual configurations' open to us should therefore be greater than the small network's by the same factor.

One's excitement at the extent of the opportunities available here is quickly joined by a dismay at the problem of how to explore that space effectively. Supposing one could make an arbitrary change in each one of one's synaptic weights ten times every second, and did so for every second of one's life (= 10^{10} changes), one would still have visited a total of only $1/10^{(100,000,000,000,000-10)}$th portion of the functional positions available. Figures like this, and those in the preceding paragraphs, change one's perspective on things, for they begin to put a recognizable metric on the space. A maximal reckoning of any possible human cognitive excursions comprehends but an infinitesimal part of a minimally reckoned cognitive space.

As with astronomical space, it is clear that the effective exploration of cognitive space will require major instrumental help. We cannot run fast enough, jump high enough, or see far enough to explore the heavens without technological augmentation of our native resources. We need manned spacecraft, unmanned probes, and optical and radio telescopes. The same is true for the exploration of cognitive space. Our native resources are inadequate to the task, by many orders of magnitude. But we need not be limited by our native resources. Let me close by discussing the possibilities.

8. AUTOMATED SCIENCE

The advent of artificial neural nets, and of automated procedures for teaching them, opens the possibility of automating aspects of the scientific enterprise itself. Computers, of course, have been helping us to assemble, organize, and filter *data* for decades. But teachable networks promise returns far in excess of these humble duties. For they promise to do something *conceptual* with the data, something similar to what intelligent creatures do with it. They promise the possibility of effectively automating, for the first time, the *theoretical* part of the scientific enterprise.

The prospects here cover a wide range of possible achievements. Let us begin with some of the simplest. 'Expert systems' are now a part of the market-place. These are carefully written programs, typically diagnostic in their practical applications, that attempt to encapsulate and to exploit the expert knowledge available in some domain. They are regularly good enough to be useful, but chronically they are poor enough to be frustrating. Part of the problem is that such programs inevitably represent someone's attempt to *articulate* the available wisdom in the relevant domain. Such reconstructions typically fall well short of the detailed expertise of a skilled professional, though in programmed form they do display the virtues of tirelessness, speed, and uniformity of treatment. They fall short because much of an expert's wisdom is *in*articulate: it consists of knowledge that is not stored in linguistic form and is difficult both to recover from the expert and to recast in the idiom of a programming language (cf. Dreyfus, 1979).

From the perspective of knowledge representation in neural nets, these difficulties are not surprising. One's capacities for discriminating subtle and complex patterns typically resides in a very high-dimensional representation space, a space whose individual dimensions each codify some intricate feature of the input space (remember that each hidden unit receives weighted inputs from thousands of sensory units). Recovering all of this information from a living expert is effectively impossible, and exploiting all of it effectively in a serial machine might take too much time even if it could be recovered.

The solution is to forget the task of trying to articulate the desired knowledge within a set of explicit rules. Instead, just train up an artificial neural network on the same dataset that trained the human expert. For example, if medical diagnosis is the expertise being modelled, then what is needed is a large number of pairs where the input is the profile of metabolic parameters and pathological symptoms of a real patient, and the output is the correct diagnosis as to his disease. Here no attempt is made to articulate rules that will connect complex symptoms to specific diseases. The network is left to generate its own 'rules' in response to the patterns implicit in the large dataset. We do exploit the human expert's knowledge, of course (to provide the diagnoses on which the network is trained), but it is the many examples that do the work: no attempt is made to articulate that knowledge. We wish only to recreate it—and perhaps to exceed it in speed, range, and reliability—in the trained artificial network.

Once that expertise has been achieved we can read out the configuration of weights that sustains it and then fix those values immediately into any number of new networks. The expertise can thus be mass produced without further training. More importantly, we can also read out the partitions effected across the various activation spaces of the various layers of hidden units, in order to discover what taxonomic strategies were found by the network as its solution to the general problem set it. Perhaps its taxonomies will parallel our own and perhaps they will not. The network may find new groupings of old cases, and it may identify as diagnostically important features that went unnoticed by human experts. In this way might artificial networks provide us with new insights into the taxonomy and causal structure of the world, even in domains we already command.

This approach is repeatable in a wide variety of contexts, psychological, chemical, geological, economic, meteorological, and industrial. And no doubt it will be, since PDP expert systems will offer real advantages over the conventional programmed expert systems available today. Instead of struggling to equal human expertise in a specific domain, they promise to exceed it in almost every respect.

These minor prognostications are not what motivate this closing section, however. They serve only to introduce the shape of the larger project. What we need to address is the problem of training networks to a useful understanding of domains where human experts have no understanding, or none that is satisfactory. This will require that our artificial networks use learning strategies that place negligible reliance on antecedent knowledge and expert teachers, beyond what instruction the world itself can provide. If we can construct genuinely parallel *hardware* realizations of the large networks that will be needed, and if we can automate such learning procedures so that they will take place many orders of magnitude faster than they do now, either in serial machines or in human brains, then we can turn such systems loose on existing datasets like stellar and galactic surveys, the behaviour of national economies, the properties of millions of chemical compounds, and the varieties of psychological dysfunction. Presentation of the data must be automated as well, to exploit the network's great speed. We can then examine with interest what order our artificial networks manage to find in such complex and teeming domains. For they will be able to explore the space of cognitive possibilities—large subspaces of it, anyway—far more swiftly and extensively than we can ever hope to explore it without their help.

What sort of symbiotic relationships may emerge here, between existing human brains on the one hand, and very large and fast neural nets on the other, is an engaging question that invites the imagination for a ride. Making a network equal in all respects to the human brain, but just faster, seems still much too hard a job to be completed in the near future. So we must not expect to have something to which we can simply *talk*. If we are willing to settle for less familiar kinds of interactions, however, then networks large and fast enough to be useful seem designable and buildable right here and now. The difficulty will lie in making *accessible* to us the cognitive achievements we may expect them to make. The goods will always lie in the structured partitions that emerge, in the course of learning, within the hidden-unit activation spaces. But as the networks get larger and the dimensionality of those spaces goes up, it will be progressively harder to display in accessible ways, and to make sense of, the structures that develop within them. For we can expect them, after all, to develop conceptual resources that are alien to us. Internalizing a penetrating new framework may thus take some time, even if it is handed to us on a platter.

Supposing that we do develop such turbocharged versions of or adjuncts to our native cognitive capacities, the space confronting us remains abyssal. An electronic or optical realization of the neural organization of the human brain will have transmission velocities 10^7 times faster than axonal velocities, and this may allow the artificial system to learn 10^7 times faster than a human brain. This would be an impressive gain. But the conceptual space it could explore in a lifetime would still comprise but a minuscule portion of the space available: it would discharge less than a single zero in the superscript of the denominator of the tiny fraction discussed earlier. There is little prospect, therefore, that a 'final, true theory of the cosmos' is something we can ever expect to discover. Nothing guarantees that *any* point in human cognitive space is such as to yield a network with zero error on every performance. And should such a point exist, which I very much doubt, it would still be a needle in a monumental haystack.

And yet, if there is no real prospect of an end to our cognitive journey, there is every prospect that our conceptual frameworks can continue to get better and better, *ad infinitum*, especially since we can always artificially expand the number of neuronal units and synaptic connections available to a given thinker, and thus expand the conceptual space to be searched. In the long run, this may be a more effective incentive to intellectual progress than the prospect of a final resting-place could ever be.

REFERENCES

Bloor, D. (1976), *Knowledge and Social Imagery*, London: Routledge & Kegan Paul.

—— (1981), 'The Strengths of the Strong Programme', *Philosophy of the Social Sciences*, 11: 199–213.

Boden, M. A. (1991), *The Creative Mind: Myths & Mechanisms*, New York: Basic Books.

Churchland, P. M. (1989a), *A Neurocomputational Perspective: The Nature of Mind and the Structure of Science*, Cambridge, Mass.: MIT Press.

—— (1989b), 'Learning and Conceptual Change', ch. 11 of Churchland (1989a), 231–53.

—— (1989c), 'On the Nature of Theories: A Neurocomputational Perspective', in W. Savage (ed.), *Scientific Theories: Minnesota Studies in the Philosophy of science*, XIV, Minneapolis: University of Minnesota Press, 59–101; repr. as ch. 9 of Churchland (1989a), 153–96.

—— (1989d), 'On the Nature of Explanation: A PDP Approach', ch. 10 of Churchland (1989a), 197–230.

—— and Sejnowski, T. J. (1992), *The Computational Brain*, Cambridge, Mass.: MIT Press.

Davidson, D. (1973), 'The Very Idea of a Conceptual Scheme',

Proceedings and Addresses of the American Philosophical Association 47; repr. in D. Davidson (1984), *Inquiries into Truth and Interpretation*, Oxford: Oxford University Press.

Dreyfus, H. (1979), *What Computers Can't Do*, New York: Harper & Row.

Giere, R. N. (1985), 'Constructive Realism', in P. M. Churchland and C. A. Hooker (eds.), *Images of Science*, Chicago: University of Chicago Press, 75–98.

Hanson, N. R. (1958), *Patterns of Discovery*, Cambridge: Cambridge University Press.

Hesse, M. B. (1966), *Models and Analogies in Science*, Notre Dame Ind.: Notre Dame University Press.

Hinton, G. E. (1989), 'Connectionist Learning Procedures', *Artificial Intelligence*, 40/1–3: 185–234.

Kuhn, T. S. (1962), *The Structure of Scientific Revolutions*, Chicago: University of Chicago Press.

Nersessian, N. (1992), 'How do Scientists Think? Capturing the Dynamics of Conceptual Change in Science', in R. N. Giere (ed.), *Cognitive Models of Science: Minnesota Studies in the Philosophy of Science*, XV, Minneapolis: University of Minnesota Press.

Pickering, A. (1981), 'The Hunting of the Quark', *Isis*, 72: 216–36.

—— (1984), *Constructing Quarks: A Sociological History of Particle Physics*, Chicago: University of Chicago Press.

Quine, W. V. O. (1960), *Word and Object*, Cambridge, Mass.: MIT Press.

Sellars, W. (1961), 'The Language of Theories', in H. Feigl and G. Maxwell (eds.), *Current Issues in the Philosophy of Science*, New York: Holt, Rinehart & Winston, 57–77; repr. in W. Sellars, *Science, Perception and Reality*, London: Routledge & Kegan Paul (1963), 106–26.

Turing, A. M. (1950), 'Computing Machinery and Intelligence', *Mind*, 59: 433–60.

Van Fraassen, B. C. (1980), *The Scientific Image*, Oxford: Oxford University Press.

2

Remarks on the Paradigms of Connectionism

MARIO COMPIANI

---

1. INTRODUCTION

Connectionism is the most interdisciplinary branch of Artificial Intelligence [1]. The current state of this very recent line of research is characterized by a certain openness towards the current cultural context and to historical contingencies, typical of the high-level sciences [2], and implies a substantial osmosis of methodology and paradigms originating in other disciplines. Naturally there is a counteracting effect through which the acquisitions of computer science and AI influence the directions taken by other disciplines (e.g. the theory of cognitive processes [3, 4]). In this paper, however, we will not consider the historical details of these reciprocal influences (more generally outlined in [5]) but will compare the paradigms of connectionism with the paradigms of other disciplines, confident that this will contribute towards a critical evaluation of the connectionist approach especially as compared with classical AI.

2. THE ORIGINS OF THE PARADIGMS OF CONNECTIONISM

Given that connectionism aspires towards obtaining objects with cognitive abilities qualitatively akin to those of living organisms, one can easily understand why psychology and neurophysiology

This work was initiated at ENIDATA (ENI Group) in the framework of a project on connectionist systems and their applications and completed with the support of the Ministero per la Ricerca Scientifica e Tecnologica.

have strongly conditioned its development. In the field of psychology, the change from behaviourism to cognitivism is certainly relevant to the present evolution of connectionism [6]. Another just as momentous change for the development of connectionism and which *mutatis mutandis* echoes certain basic themes of the cognitivist revolution, is precisely that which in physics has focused, over the last few years, much interest on the so-called complex systems [8, 17].

Finally, we can cite the increasing attention which in the framework of connectionism is directed towards mechanisms of evolution, natural selection, and adaptation to be found at many levels in the biological world (from macromolecules to cells and up to the level of populations). The most explicit antecedent of this orientation lies in the theses of Piaget [9] which are proving to be extraordinarily up-to-date in the light of the most recent developments in connectionism. Piaget sees, in the science of cognitive processes, a chapter of biology and in cognitive processes an extension of biological adaptative and regulatory processes.[1] Thus, connectionism is currently facing the following dichotomies, which have distinguished a relevant part of the recent history of psychology, physics, and biology:

- behaviourism/cognitivism
- hetero-organization/self-organization
- creationism/evolutionism
- nativism/epigenesis

These dichotomies will be used to discuss both classical AI and the new directions related to the advent of connectionism.

2.1. *The cognitivist revolution*

The phase through which the field of connectionism is passing has various points in common with the transition from behaviourism to cognitivism which has interested psychology since the 1950s. We recall that behaviourism [11, 12] recognizes the environment as playing a determining role in directing and conditioning the actions of the subject, whose internal state can be completely characterized using externally controllable parameters. Consistently, the conditioning of the system can also be obtained through an

---

[1] This point of view is also espoused by Popper in [10].

extrinsic supervision mechanism based upon gratification or frustration as a function of the response to stimuli. In this way intelligence acquires a strictly associationist character and is identified with the learning of behavioural schemes which guarantee the individual a certain ability to adapt. This conception of intelligence underlies Pavlovian practice which takes conditioned reflexes as elementary modules, perfect archetypes of behavioural analysis in terms of stimulus and response [13]. This reasoning exclusively in terms of external parameters (stimulus and response) assumes that the processing by the system does not add anything at all to the information content of the input; that is, the performance of the system can be completely characterized externally without recourse to the internal properties of the system [12].

Cognitivism, on the other hand, recovers the richness and the extension of the internal representation and of the system's internal processes. In other words, this veering from behaviourism to cognitivism entails a greater emphasis on the processes of self-organization of the cognitive system. In this context the contribution of the system increases and, indeed, the hierarchy advocated by behaviourism is inverted in the sense that now the system's processing ability may dominate and completely upset the information content of the stimulus. Actually, the rediscovery of internal dynamics is one of the main results of recent developments in connectionism [14, 15, 16, 17]. A rediscovery which concludes the parable moving from the hetero-organizational paradigm which has its most radical version in the dream of *l'homme machine* [18] to the specular paradigm of *la machine humaine*. This overturning of the perspective of connectionism is concretized in the production of systems (computers or algorithms) with a strong biological inspiration (we will come back to this point in Section 4).

On this point we cite here the attempt by Braitenberg [19] who, with a 'bottom-up' approach which the author qualifies as a synthetic psychology, attempts to fill the gap between man and machine showing how the machine can, from certain points of view, be assimilated with an intentional system. More precisely, Braitenberg's analysis suggests how even simple automata from a structural point of view may show a kind of behaviour which an external observer could succinctly describe in terms of affections, fancies, and inclinations using the 'mentalist' terminology so unpopular with behaviourists.

Braitenberg's arguments show a less paradoxical character when accompanied by a more detailed analysis of the levels upon which the discourse is articulated [20]. The anthropomorphic or intentional description of many cognitive systems is justified if related to a purely exterior characterization of the performance formulated at a very high level so that one can leave aside the microscopic design of the system.

It can be understood how, in relatively simple automata (such as those of Braitenberg), the intentional description offers only a paraphrasal of the performance which, moreover, would be perfectly predictable on the basis of a structural analysis of the system. On the contrary, in much more complex systems where the overall function is no longer deducible from the description of the partial functions, it may happen that the intentional description remains the only practicable alternative.

Breitenberg's argument applies not only when we are unaware of the internal architecture of the system but can be extended to those cases where the internal structure or design is known but it is hard to deduce all of the 'system's moves' from a mere list of its components and the way they are arranged [59]. In these circumstances, a discontinuity sets in that separates the low-level (microscopic) description of the system and any higher-level representation (e.g. an intentional picture) and the latter cannot be deduced from the former. The only way to bridge the gap is to create a phenomenological mapping that connects the two levels of interest. This is exactly what a connectionist system, like a neural network, is expected to do when it is used to study a complex system. A case in point is the prediction of protein structures starting from the set of the elementary building blocks [60, 61]. In this context the protein structure stands for the higher-level description whereas the sequence of amino acids provides the lower-level picture of the system. In this case the neural network reconstructs a mapping from the amino acid sequence to the set of possible structures, which stands as a deputy of the real (up to now unpredictable) chemico-physical process (folding) during which the unstructured chain acquires its stable structure.

2.2. *The paradigm of complexity*

The observations of Braitenberg and Dennett suggest that changing the level of representation may obscure apparently incontrovertible distinctions so that one may associate, for example, from a macroscopic point of view, a kind of psychological dynamics with a system which at the microscopic level is extremely hetero-organized. Many dichotomies may then vacillate and fade once the description covers different levels of representation. Analogously, another extremely problematic antonym, that which counterposes order with disorder, is recomposed as soon as the two terms are scaled to their respective descriptive levels (macroscopic and microscopic) [21]. Thermodynamics and statistical mechanics heralded the relativization of these two antithetic notions. The concept of disorder, of molecular chaos, becomes valid at the microscopic level for equilibrium states which from a macroscopic point of view possess characteristics of maximum order and homogeneity. The contradictory assignment of incompatible attributes to the same entity becomes acceptable only by paying the price of introducing a distinction between levels of description.

Synergetics presents itself in the same stream as thermodynamics, accepting as its own the study of complex systems (with particular emphasis on self-organization phenomena) and the formalization of the notion of disorder [17, 8]. The physics of complex systems has opened a breach in the physico-mathematical construction consolidated in the tradition of classical rational mechanics. Disorder, relegated by thermodynamics to an asymptotic condition of any isolated system, with the physics of complex systems breaks into the ordinary evolution of systems. Exception becomes recurrent behaviour which even emerges enigmatically from those same equations into which classical mechanics had only read ordinary, reproducible, and predictable motion. On the other hand Bachelard [22], long before the birth of synergetics, had stressed that 'determinism implies the abandonment of perturbing phenomena (and forms the basis) of a spirit of simplification . . . the real order of nature being that which, while arguing for the simplicity of nature, we ourselves introduce'. Recalling the metaphor of Monod [23], this is an approach which has privileged necessity and neglected and even removed the intervention of chance.

Besides the genesis of disorder, synergetics examines the encounter between chance and necessity utilizing the instruments of the theory of stochastic processes. Chance intervenes in the form of noise which interferes with the deterministic behaviour dictated by the intrinsic structure of the system; it is a generator of variability which has a much more fundamental status than that of an undesired diversion from a predefined law: 'chance is, since the beginning of time, the unavoidable counterpart of the regulating forces' [24].

Regarding the paradigmatic role of physics in the formulations of the behaviourists, it is clear that for behaviourism the reference framework was that of the physics of 'simple' systems. Complex systems are scandal for behaviourists as there is no longer a univocal correspondence between stimulus and response. Complex systems are capable of developing conditions of homeostasis which ensures, in fact, an unchanging response even in the presence of variable stimuli, but may even respond, for example, to stimuli which do not change with time, by entering an oscillating regime [17]. In this case internal complexity becomes necessary to counterbalance the weight of the external influences and allows the system to break out of the bottlenecks of hetero-organization. This becomes even more evident in the response of complex systems to chaotic stimuli. While simple systems when subjected to random forces show a stochastic behaviour, complex systems can use external noise to effect a transition from a chaotic regime to an ordered one [17].

2.3. The evolutionary paradigm

The currently available methods for the analysis of complex systems show their limits when systems subject to evolutionary mechanisms are considered. The evolutionist paradigm encounters the approach which is typical of the physico-mathematical sciences, which pay more attention to finding invariants and laws of conservation rather than the study of mechanisms of variability and renewal. Rational knowledge, as Musil [25] observes, goes 'under the banner of repetition of the fixed concept which does not take into consideration any deviation'. The evolutionist paradigm places us before a more radical variability. While in stochastic systems the only mechanism of variation was represented by noise, deviation from a norm dictated by the structural identity of the system, we now have a prospective of a more profound variability which we could define as qualitative or structural. The paradigm of evolution introduces an additional mechanism of variability with respect to the usual progression of states, which magnifies the plasticity of the system, and by involving the architecture itself of the system. A related distinction was made in genetics by Waddington [9], who distinguished between homeorhesis and homeostasis. Homeorhesis is diachronic, structural, and involves regulatory mechanisms which affect the system's structure. In the meantime, in the structure established by the homeorhetic process a synchronic mechanism of functional regulation (homeostasis) comes into play; it no longer alters the structural physiognomy of the system and only governs the dynamics of the states compatible with that structure. We will see how certain classes of connectionist systems have adopted a double regulatory mechanism (structural and functional) which reproposes the homeorhesis–homeostasis dualism, and it is the pillar of the phenomena of self-organization which arise in the system [26].

The Piaget thesis (mentioned in Section 1) is profoundly evolutionist, and excludes the possibility of conducting a discourse on intelligence in purely nativist terms. The central point of Piaget's position is the assertion that learning and intelligent behaviour in general cannot derive from a structure which is incapable of changing but is linked to the possibility of submitting the structure of a cognitive system for revision.[2]

3. REGULATION, ADAPTIVITY, AND COGNITIVE PROCESSES

In this section we would like to compare several classes of connectionist systems with systems of natural intelligence (biological systems) to highlight the remarkable functional analogies and, in the light of this, underline how there is basic agreement between the thesis of Piaget and the philosophy of cognitive processes which is gaining increasing support in the framework of connectionism. In the second place, we would like to examine the tendencies of development in the field of connectionist models in the light of the paradigms examined so far and show how connectionism, from certain points of view, still has a certain behaviourist nature, and is

---

[2] This view is clearly stated in [27] with reference to as different systems as the nervous system and the immune system.

TABLE 1

Biological Systems	Connectionist Systems
Immune System	Classifier Systems
Nervous System	Neural Networks
Genetic Regulation	Cellular Automata

undergoing a revision of its own original paradigms and becoming inspired above all by the paradigms of complexity and evolutionism.

3.1. Connectionist models as metaphors of adaptive biological systems

The interesting point is that various types of connectionist models turn out to be practically isomorphous with adaptive biological systems of fundamental importance in a vast range of organisms. Table 1 presents three classes of connectionist systems together with biological systems with which they have a strong functional analogy.

Neural networks were born precisely as a schematization of the nervous system, whereas cellular automata, were proposed as models for the study of regulatory phenomena in DNA [28, 29, 30, 31]. Holland's classifier systems [32, 33], on the other hand, have a different appearance even though substantially their effective functioning has various parts in common with neural networks and cellular automata. A general discussion of the mathematical similarities of the above-mentioned connectionist systems is given in [34]; a detailed comparison between classifier systems and neural networks can be found in [35], whereas isomorphism between classifier systems and the immune system is discussed in [36].

Moreover, all of these systems not only have in common the structure of interconnected entities, but also, and above all, a mechanism of adaptation of the connections (that is, of the interactions). Such regulatory mechanisms are known as learning algorithms (e.g. technique of back-propagation in neural networks or bucket brigade in classifier systems) as they are responsible for the ability, shown by the system, of learning by examples. If one now, in a perspective which essentially takes the point of view of Piaget, assimilates the cognitive performance of a system with the phenotype, and the topology and intensity of the connections with the genotype, we once again find in the dynamics, which arise from the learning algorithms, the same interplay between genotype, phenotype, and environment which forms an integral part of the regulatory mechanisms ruling the expression of the genetic heritage. In line with this genetic paraphrasal of the functioning and of the structure of these connectionist systems one collocates the implementation of mechanisms of structural variability (genetic algorithms), which mimic processes of recombination and of genetic mutation, in neural networks [37, 38, 39, 40] and in classifier systems. The same evolutionary strategy is at work in the genetic programming approach [41] that in a sense is intermediate between expert systems and connectionist systems. In the former class of systems semantically acceptable pieces of information are combined via semantic tags while in the latter class the semantic value of the internal representation is often hardly amenable to interpretation due to the prominent weight of the internal dynamics (see Sections 2.1, 3.3, and 4).

3.2. *Self-organization and learning*

The implementation of genetic algorithms and of learning algorithms has a double effect upon the properties of connectionist systems: it renders the systems extremely plastic and automates the learning phase, characteristics which qualitatively differentiate connectionist systems from systems of classical AI. And it is precisely in this question of learning that one sees a change in paradigm. In fact, hetero-organization and self-organization are methodological alternatives which have produced, in classical AI and in connectionism, profoundly different systems precisely because of the way in which the transfer of knowledge from the environment or from the human expert to the system is carried out. Traditional systems are inspired by the former alternative and they reflect an authoritarian pedagogical outlook. Following a model which recalls the combinatorial psychology of Locke, knowledge is explicitly and punctually coded in the form of rules or prescriptions which the system combines in order to discover the resolutive strategy (regarding the combinatorial character of internal representations of classical systems see the remarks made by [42]).

In various connectionist systems, on the other hand, the paradigm of self-organization offers an alternative to explicit programming and suggests the possibility of utilizing the combined interplay of internal mechanisms and external forcing so that the system can select, autonomously, the most suitable cognitive strategy.

The counterposition between hetero-organizational and self-organizational learning recalls the debate which in the eighteenth century saw the confrontation between nativists and epigenists regarding the dilemma of spontaneous generation [43]. The genesis of the systems in traditional AI (e.g. expert systems) conforms to the nativist point of view according to which every structure and functionality, in our case every cognitive capacity, must pre-exist in an anterior clichè, it must be preformed and pre-coded, and it must be excluded from any kind of evolutionary process. The learning phase is completely indistinguishable from the creation phase of the system.

Connectionist models conform to an epigenist philosophy. In these models learning (as embryogenesis) is a completely separate phase and is founded upon the above mentioned algorithms. The mechanisms of variability and adaptivity, established in this manner, simulate evolutionary and adaptation processes which, as in natural organisms, allow the individual species to survive the selection operated by the environment (selection which is carried out by the supervisor in systems with supervised learning). From a functional point of view, therefore, there is a basic homogeneity between the mechanisms of adaptation and of self-regulation which operate in biological systems and mechanisms of self-regulation and of the processing of cognitive strategies in connectionist systems. The homeorhetic process which such mechanisms implement, leads one to conclude that connectionism is aligned towards the position of Piaget and is openly inspired by the evolutionist paradigm.

3.3. Self-organization and reasoning; the role of complex dynamics

Connectionist systems are distinct from classical systems not only because of the presence and the modality of the learning phase but also because of the peculiarities which distinguish the reasoning phase. In this connection we will discuss the role played by internal dynamics with different degrees of complexity (dynamical regimes of the same kind play a central role also in systems of natural intelligence [44]). More specifically, we will show that the increasing importance assigned to internal dynamics firstly is conducive to internal representations with systematic (non-combinatorial) character and, secondly, shows an increasing acceptance of the paradigm of complexity.

To begin with, let us remark that connectionist systems essentially are classified as sophisticated associationist systems [1, 42] in which computation takes advantage of the existence of simple attractors (fixed points). Accordingly, learning amounts to sculpting basins of attraction and reasoning has been restricted to a mere relaxation process towards the appropriate attractor. In the reasoning phase, the response is coded into the asymptotic state of the system and the dynamics which produce it are actually seen as an irrelevant transient. As far as the cognitive performance of the system is concerned, meaning is ascribed only to the final state in which the system eventually settles.

In general, the possibility of assigning semantic value to internal representations in AI systems is a matter of debate in the current literature [42, 45, 46]. In this paper we take it that in connectionist systems the systematic character of the internal representations [47] introduces a novel element with respect to the combinatorial character of the representations typical of traditional cognitive systems [42]. Put in another way, in a cognitive system of a traditional type the functioning of the system is legible in the logical structure and in the semantics which code the knowledge relating to the specific field of application. On the contrary, in a connectionist system, the intermediate steps (in time) of the computation or the states of the internal components of the system cannot generally be translated into defined logical steps and it is not always possible to specify their semantics.

To substantiate this claim we discuss how the character of the internal representation may be affected by the presence of more complex internal dynamics than those involved in reaching fixed points. In particular we discuss the existence of a trade-off between the legibility of the semantics of the internal representation and the emergence of internal dynamics, in the sense that the more elaborate the dynamic regime supporting the reasoning phase, the less transparent are the semantics of the representation. This point is particularly clear in hybrid systems like classifier systems[3] in which the computation possesses a symbolic component beside a subsymbolic one.[4]

Let us assume that a classifier system is faced with the problem of predicting the displacements of a frictionless pendulum; more precisely, the system is expected to predict the next position from a knowledge of the present position (for the sake of simplicity we make reference to a discretized trajectory such that A, B, and C represent respectively, the position of rest and the two positions of maximum deviation from equilibrium). The original problem is then equivalent to learning the symbolic sequence $ABACABAC\ldots$ so as to be able to forecast the next coming letter on reading one letter at a time.

It is apparent that the task can be divided in a non-ambiguous subtask (predicting $B \to A$ and $C \to A$, where the arrow indicates temporal consecutivity) and an ambiguous subtask (predicting $A \to B$ and $A \to C$).[5] In the following we focus on the latter, since it represents a major challenge for the self-organizational capabilities of the system.

An examination of the internal representations synthesized by the system has led to the identification of two possible types of representation in which the symbolic and the dynamic components have different relative weights [17, 48, 49] (in the following they will be referred to as symbolic solution and dynamical solution). Although in both of them the system succeeds in performing associations which are semantically equivalent to $A \to B$, $B \to A$ etc., the internal representations differ in some fundamental aspect as it will be clear from the following comparative analysis.

The symbolic solution has a logical structure which is decipherable merely by examining the concatenations of the classifiers (i.e. the semantic and syntactic features of the representation). In this

---

[3] On classifier systems viewed as connectionist systems see [16, 35].

[4] In classifier systems there is the coexistence of mechanisms of pattern-matching amongst rules (called classifiers) and messages and a process of dynamical reallocation of the strengths assigned to each rule (see [32, 33]). This is also reflected in the double nature of the adaptive algorithms (bucket brigade and genetic algorithms) that operate respectively on the dynamical (subsymbolic) and the symbolic component.

[5] Clearly, ambiguity would disappear on allowing the system to include two symbols in the current input.

respect the steady-state functioning closely resembles that of a classical system, in which the bucket brigade (viz. the subsymbolic mechanism) is irrelevant to the reasoning stage although it remains active during this phase. None the less, the strengths play a significant role during learning as they are responsible for the emergence of the correct rules. In the end the system learns alternately to activate one or the other of the associations $A \rightarrow B$ and $A \rightarrow C$ in response to the same input A. The requisite selection of the appropriate rule is made autonomously by the system which, to this aim, identifies the context sufficient for carrying out the discrimination; the context is the position of the pendulum on the previous time step $t - 1$. This position is memorized and used at the next time step t for integrating the information A (t) (which alone is ambiguous) and to transform it into the non-ambiguous antecedents $A(t)\&B(t - 1)$ or $A(t)\&C(t - 1)$. It should be noted that the system exhibits a feature which is typical of intentional systems; namely it is not exclusively moved by the current input but also by information contained within the system ('beliefs' [20] or 'anticipatory theories' [10]). This entails that the internal state of the system contributes to interpret and integrate the knowledge carried by the input before the system elicits any action on the external environment.

It is to be emphasized that the selection of the appropriate rules (and only of them) on each time step is achieved by means of a mechanism which is independent of the strengths; in fact the wave of activation propagates through semantic tags which, in the course of the learning phase, are attached to the strings which code for each classifier. In this respect the system exhibits an all-or-none mechanism of activation, typical of classical systems, which is mediated by the pattern-matching mechanism. The internal representation which eventually gets stabilized is essentially symbolic in nature; furthermore, it possesses the property of structure sensitivity since 'the operations apply to representations by reference to their form' [42].

In the dynamical solution towards which the system is able to converge, the solving strategy has to be founded upon the concomitant dynamics of the pattern-matching (symbolic) mechanism and the dynamics of strengths. This is due to the fact that the system does not develop a complete set of auxiliary semantic markers which forestall the concomitant activation of rules leading to contrasting conclusions. Consequently, the rules responsible for the associations $A \rightarrow B$ and $A \rightarrow C$ can be simultaneously activated. The ensuing situation of competition is ruled by a conflict-resolution mechanism; this is entrusted to the dynamics of the strengths which settle into a regime of synchronized oscillation with just the same periodicity as the ambiguous input A. The oscillatory regime has an appropriate phase such that each of the competing rules wins the competition exactly on each two presentations of the input A. Those symbolic features which are lacking in the dynamical solution are superseded by dynamical (i.e. subsymbolic) features.

Concerning the symbolic components, the dynamical solution capitalizes on the same building-blocks which are to be found in the symbolic solution; more precisely, it is a juxtaposition of structures of classifiers which are drawn from the symbolic solution and one-shot rules which occur in the solution to the non-ambiguous subtask.[6] The occurrence of the same structure of classifiers preserving their meaning and function in both the dynamical and the symbolic solutions attests to another characteristic which has been ascribed to the representations of classical systems, namely their having combinatorial semantics and syntactics [42]. This implies that the same building-blocks can participate in different representations preserving their own semantic value which, accordingly, is context-independent. However, though the semantics inherent to the individual components does not vary, the overall meaning of the representations undergoes quite a substantial change in passing from the symbolic to the dynamical solution. Actually, interpreting the action of the system is no longer feasible in terms of patterns of activation in the case of the dynamical solution, since coactivated rules may generate contradictory guesses. On dealing with the ambiguous input, the system activates the rules coding for all possible responses so that the decisive choice is left to the strength dynamics. In this context, the building-blocks which represent $A \rightarrow B$ and $A \rightarrow C$ can be thought of as creating two attractors within which the system oscillates. In other words the internal dynamics serve the scope of making accessible at the proper time the individual contents previously stored as attractors. This can be interpreted as the deterministic equivalent of the mechanism

---

[6] The non-ambiguous subtask is coped with in the same way in both the symbolic and the dynamical solutions.

proposed in [50] on the basis of experimental evidence of the dynamical regimes detected in a biological neural network.

4. CONCLUSIONS

The artificial systems of Table 1 can be distinguished according to the effectivness of their own internal dynamics. Classifier systems, unlike most neural networks, for example, are endowed with dynamical processes (see the dynamical solution illustrated in Section 3) that remain active even in the testing stage, when the learning process and the attendant dynamics are inactive. This enhances the plasticity of the system since the extant dynamical processes can counterbalance the architecture that sometimes turns out to be insufficient to ensure the expected performance. In the above-mentioned example the dynamical solution leads to the emergence of internal memory that compensates the deficient input window of the system. When the dynamical potentialities of the connectionist system are not commensurate to the dynamics to be studied, the only thing the system can do is to reproduce an impoverished representation of the target dynamics, which stands to the original one like a map is to the full dynamics of the dynamical system from which it is taken [7]. The word 'map' is used here in the sense of dynamical system theory, as a discretized version of a continuous dynamics. The mapping reconstructed by the neural network in the real-world problem of the prediction of protein structures (mentioned in Section 3) can be viewed as a reduced and discretized picture of the continuous process of folding.

In neural networks the creation of a mapping is supported by internal dynamical processes only in the learning stage. It follows that the resulting mapping is essentially static; this implies that the neural network is typically not in a position to process, in an appropriate manner, ambiguous inputs similar to those described in Section 3 for the prediction task solved by the classifier system. When such ambiguities occur (see [62] for a classification) the neural network is forced to record the probabilities of the alternative events, the final response of the network being guided by a maximum probability principle [62, 63].

Internal dynamics allow classifier systems to be more flexible and thus be able to devise more efficient strategies than those relying on probabilistic information in order to deal with ambiguous tasks.

The discussion of Section 3 on classifier systems shows that dynamical self-organization has some bearings on the reasoning phase and on the nature of the ensuing internal representations. The symbolic and dynamical solutions are the archetypes of two classes of solutions which have, respectively, a purely logical and a mixed logical/dynamical character.

This suggests some comments on the associationist approach to learning and reasoning. Mapping the frequency of occurrence of external events in the strengths (this is the very essence of associationism [42]) presupposes the possibility of effectively discriminating on the basis of frequency only. In our example, recording the frequencies of occurrence of the mutually excluding events $A \to B$ and $A \to C$ (on which the system is trained) does not allow a solving of the inherent ambiguity since the two associations are equiprobable in the training sequence. This would ensure only 50 per cent successes in performing the predictive task. Surprisingly the system can do better since it either develops a fully symbolic mechanism or, in the absence of this, it triggers a suitable internal regime which allows the system to capture regularities in the sequence of a higher-order than those implied in the limited input which conveys information only about the current position. It is precisely the action of the genetic and learning algorithms which develop the ability to memorize and thus render the system sensitive to the temporal context. This is primarily due to self-organization in classifier systems whereas it has to be hetero-organized in neural networks which do not have genetic algorithms [51]. In this respect, let us remark that classifier systems embody many of the features previously invoked to qualify intelligent behaviour in biological systems. In particular, one may recall the pertinent observations of Bateson [64] and Edelman [57] on the stochastic character shared by learning and biological evolution. Another distinctive trait of intelligence, which is well reproduced by the dynamical solution to the task of Section 3, is the ability to select autonomously the pertinent context that is needed to deal successfully with the problem at hand [2, 57].

Our analysis leads us to the conclusion that the current orientation of connectionism towards the paradigms of complexity is inextricably linked to the tendency towards a more extensive exploitation of internal dynamics. The extension of dynamics to the reasoning phase requires some kind of forcing term or self-sustained oscillations. Actually, in classifier systems this is provided by the bucket-brigade algorithm which operates in the course of the reasoning phase as well. In the same vein, the most extreme and evocative proposal, not least for the philosophical implications involved, foresees the use of chaotic dynamics to support the fast access to different attractors [44, 50, 52, 53, 54].

Finally, it is noteworthy that learning supported by the self-organizational properties of the system allows a notable minimisation of the a priori knowledge which is needed for the system to work properly. The most drastic reduction is achieved in connectionist systems which can even start from scratch; if this is the case, the internal representation can be absolutely meaningless, at least in the early stages of the learning phase. Therefore, the claim that connectionist systems are 'representationalist' (i.e. necessarily committed with meaningful representations) [42, 46] seems not to apply to the learning phase in self-organizing connectionist systems. But we are also in a position to raise a similar objection with regard to the reasoning phase, on the basis of above results. In fact, while the representational character appears to be preserved in the symbolic solution, it gets lost in the dynamical solution. We have seen that the subsymbolic character of the dynamical solution makes the attendant internal representation more systematic (in the sense outlined in [47]) and this allows the relaxation of the constraint of logical consistency (mutually excluding statements are asserted on the same time step). Put in another way, the semantic labels of the active rules are no longer sufficient to account for the overall meaning of the state the system is in. The emergence of dynamical regulatory processes causes part of the meaning to be coded in subsymbolic features.

A final comment on the points made in Sections 2 and 3.1 is in order as to the parallel development guided by similar paradigms of the different disciplines that converge in the connectionist approach to AI. What is more interesting for the analysis of the process of scientific discovery is the 'diffusion' of paradigms in neighbouring areas of research. A notable example is provided by the evolutionist paradigm that has originated from the studies of macroscopic biological populations, has subsequently been used as a tool for simulating the performance of cognitive systems and has eventually been incorporated in the theoretical foundations of modern immunology [55, 56] and brain theory [57]. In this connection a related phenomenon has been described in the recent history of mind theories. It has given rise to the so-called 'tools-to-theories' heuristics that consist in the change of status of tools (e.g. metaphors) that happen to be raised to the rank of theoretical models [58]. More far-reaching reflections of such concept dynamics are expected to be conducive to substantial revision of the current epistemological views. More precisely, it has been argued that the transition from control-centred to emergence-centred theories of cognition has a relevant bearing on the birth of a 'naturalized epistemology' or 'epistemology of participation' [27].

REFERENCES

[1] Papert, S., 'One AI or many?', *Daedalus*, 117/1 (1988), 1–14.

[2] Putnam, H., 'Reductionism and the Nature of Psychology', in J. H. Haugeland (ed.), *Mind Design*, Bradford Books, Montgomery, Vt., 1981, 205–19.

[3] Churchland, P. M., 'On the Nature of Explanation: A PDP Approach', *Physica* D 42: 281–92 (1990).

[4] Smith Churchland, P., *Neurophilosophy. Toward a Unified Science of the Mind-Brain*, MIT Press, Cambridge, Mass., 1986.

[5] Morin, E., *La Méthode, I. La Nature de la Nature*, Editions du Seuil, Paris, 1977.

[6] Gardner, H., *The Mind's New Science*, Basic Books, New York, 1985.

[7] Serra, R., Zanarini, G., Andretta, M., and Compiani, M., *Introduction to the Physics of Complex Systems*, Pergamon Press, Oxford, 1986.

[8] Prigogine, I., and Stengers, I., *La Nouvelle Alliance. Metamorphose de la Science*, Gallimard, Paris, 1979.

[9] Piaget, J., *Biologie et Connaissance*, Gallimard, Paris, 1967.

[10] Popper, K. R., *Objective Knowledge. An Evolutionary Approach*, Clarendon Press, Oxford, 1972.

[11] Chomsky, N., 'Review of Skinner's "Verbal Behavior"', *Language*, 35/1 (1959), 26–58.

[12] Watson, J. B., 'Psychology as the Behaviorist Views it', *Psychological Review*, 20 (1913), 158–77.

[13] Wertheimer, M., *Productive Thinking*, enlarged edn. Harper & Bros., New York, 1959.

[14] Serra, R., and Zanarini, G., *Complex Systems and Cognitive Processes*, Springer-Verlag, Heidelberg, 1990.

[15] Steels, L., 'Artificial Intelligence and Complex Dynamics', paper delivered at the IFIP Workshop on Concepts and Tools for Knowledge-Based Systems, Mount Fuji, Japan, 1987.

[16] Serra, R., 'Dynamical Systems and Expert Systems', in R. Pfeifer, Z. Schreter, F. Fogelman-Soulié, and L. Steels (eds.), *Connectionism in Perspective*, North-Holland, Amsterdam, 1989, 265–76.

[17] Compiani, M., Montanari, D., Serra, R., and Simonini, P., 'Dynamical Systems in Artificial Intelligence: The Case of Classifier Systems', in R. Pfeifer, Z. Schreter, F. Fogelman-Soulié, and L. Steels (eds.), *Connectionism in Perspective*, North-Holland, Amsterdam, 1989, 331–40.

[18] Lamettrie, J. O. de, *L'Homme Machine*, 1747.

[19] Braitenberg, V., *Vehicles: Experiments in Synthetic Psychology*, MIT Press, Cambridge Mass., 1984.

[20] Dennett, D. C., 'Intentional Systems', in J. H. Haugeland (ed.), *Mind Design*, MIT Press, Cambridge, Mass., 1981, 220–42.

[21] Perrin, J., *Les Atomes*, Editions Gallimard, Paris, 1970.

[22] Bachelard, G., *Le Nouvel Esprit Scientifique*, Presses Universitaires de France, Paris, 1934.

[23] Monod, J., *Le Hasard et la Nécessité*, Editions du Seuil, Paris, 1970.

[24] Eigen, M., and Winkler, R., *Das Spiel*, R. Piper & Co., Munich, 1975.

[25] Musil, R., *Skizze der Erkentnis des Dichters*, Summa, Hellerau, 1918.

[26] Steels, L., 'Self-Organization through Selection', in M. Caudill and C. Butler (eds.), *IEEE First International Conference on Neural Networks*, ii, San Diego, Calif., 1987, 55–62.

[27] Varela, F. J., *Principles of Biological Autonomy*, Elsevier-North-Holland, New York, 1979.

[28] Kauffmann, S. A., 'Metabolic Stability and Epigenesis in Randomly Constructed Genetic Nets', *Journal of Theoretical Biology*, 22/437 (1969).

[29] Kauffmann, S. A., and Smith, R. G., 'Adaptive Automata based on Darwinian Selection', *Physica*, 22D (1986), 68–82.

[30] Kauffmann, S. A., and Levin, S., 'Towards a General Theory of Adaptive Walks on Rugged Landscapes', *Journal of Theoretical Biology*, 128/11 (1987).

[31] Burks, C., and Farmer, J. D., 'Towards Modeling DNA Sequences as Automata', *Physica*, 10D (1984), 157–67.

[32] Holland, J. H., 'Escaping Brittleness', in R. S. Michalski, J. G. Carbonell and T. M. Mitchell (eds.), *Machine Learning. An Artificial Intelligence Approach*, ii, Morgan Kaufmann, Los Altos, Calif., 1986, 593–623.

[33] Holland, J. H., Holyoak, K. J., Nisbett, R. E., and Thagard, P. R., *Induction. Processes of Inference, Learning and Discovery*, MIT Press, Cambridge, Mass., 1986, ch. 4.

[34] Farmer, J. D., 'A Rosetta Stone for Connectionism', *Physica* D 42 (1990), 153–87; repr. in *Emergent Computation*, S. Forrest (ed.), MIT Press, Cambridge, Mass., 1991, 153–87.

[35] Compiani, M., Montanari, D., Serra, R., and Valastro, G., 'Classifier Systems and Neural Nets', in E. R. Caianiello (ed.), *Parallel Architectures and Neural Networks*, World Scientific Publishers, Singapore, 1989, 105–118.

[36] Farmer, J. D., Packard, N. H., and Perelson, A. S., 'The Immune System, Adaptation, and Machine Learning', *Physica* D 22 (1986), 187–204.

[37] Schaffer, J. D., Caruana, R. A., and Eshelman, L. J., 'Using Genetic Search to Exploit the Emergent Behavior of Neural Networks', *Physica* D 42 (1990), 244–8.

[38] Montana, D. J., and Davis, L., 'Training Feedforward Neural Networks using Genetic Algorithms', Proceedings of the IJCAI, 1989.

[39] Harp, S. A., Samad, T., and Guha, A., 'Towards the Genetic Synthesis of Neural Networks', *Proceedings of the Third International Conference on Genetic Algorithms*, Morgan Kaufmann, San Mateo, Calif., 1989, 360–9.

[40] Wilson, S. W., 'Perceptron Redux: Emergence of Structure', *Physica* D 42 (1990), 249–56; repr. in *Emergent Computation*, S. Forrest (ed.), MIT Press, Cambridge, Mass., 1991.

[41] Koza, J., *Genetic Programming*, MIT Press, Cambridge, Mass., 1992.

[42] Fodor, J. A., and Pylyshyn, Z. W., 'Connectionism and Cognitive Architecture: A Critical Analysis', *Cognition*, 28 (1988), 3–71.

[43] Rostand, J., *Les Origines de la Biologie Expérimentale et l'Abbé Spallanzani*, Fasquelle Editeurs, Paris.

[44] Harth, E., 'Order and Chaos in Neural Systems: An Approach to the Dynamics of Higher Brain Functions', *IEEE Transactions on Man, Systems and Cybernetics*, 13/5 (1983), 782–9.

[45] Smolensky, P., 'Connectionism and Constituent Structure', in R. Pfeifer, Z. Schreter, F. Fogelman-Souliè, and L. Steels (eds.), *Connectionism in Perspective*, North-Holland, Amsterdam, 1989, 3–24.

[46] Fodor, J. A., 'Methodological Solipsism Considered as a Research Strategy in Cognitive Psychology', in J. H. Haugeland (ed.), *Mind Design*, MIT Press, Cambridge, Mass., 1981, 307–38.

[47] Haugeland, J., 'The Nature and Plausibility of Cognitivism', in J. H. Haugeland (ed.), *Mind Design*, MIT Press, Cambridge, Mass., 243–81.

[48] Compiani, M., Montanari, D., Serra, R., and Simonini, P., 'Asymptotic Dynamics of Classifier Systems', *Proceedings of the Third International Conference on Genetic Algorithms*, Morgan Kaufmann, San Mateo, Calif., 1989, 298–303.

[49] Compiani, M., Montanari, D., and Serra, R., 'Learning and Bucket Brigade Dynamics in Classifier Systems', *Physica* D 42 (1990), 202–12; repr. in *Emergent Computation*, S. Forrest (ed.), MIT Press, Cambridge, Mass., 1991, 202–12.

[50] Skarda, C. A., and Freeman, W. J., 'How Brains Make Chaos in Order to Make Sense of the World', *Behavioral and Brain Sciences*, 10 (1987), 161–73.

[51] Elman, J. L., 'Finding Structure in Time', Cognitive Science, 14 (1990), 179–211.

[52] Guevara, M. R., Glass, L., Mackey, M. C., and Shrier, A., 'Chaos in Neurobiology', *IEEE Transactions on Man, Systems and Cybernetics*, 13/5 (1983), 790–8.

[53] Tsuda, I., 'A Hermeneutic Process of the Brain', *Progress of Theoretical Physics* (Supp.), 79 (1984), 241–59.

[54] Nicolis, J. S., and Tsuda, I., 'Chaotic Dynamics of Information Processing: The Magic Number Seven Plus-Minus Two Revisited', *Bulletin of Mathematical Biology*, 4/3 (1985), 343.

[55] Jerne, N. K., 'The Immune System', *Scientific American* (1973), 52–60.

[56] Jerne, N. K., 'Towards a Network Theory of the Immune

System', *Annales d'Immunologie (Institut Pasteur)*, 125 C (1974), 373–89.

[57] Edelman, G. M., *Neural Darwinism. The Theory of Neuronal Group Selection*, Basic Books, New York, 1987.

[58] Gigerenzer, G., 'From Tools to Theories. A Heuristic of Discovery in Cognitive Psychology', *Psychological Review*, 98 (1991), 254–67.

[59] Wittgenstein, L., *Philosophical Investigations*, Macmillan, New York, 1968.

[60] Hirst, J. D., and Sternberg, M. J. E., 'Prediction of Structural and Functional Features of Proteins and Nucleic Acid Sequences by Artificial Neural Networks', *Biochemistry*, 31 (1992), 7211–18.

[61] Compiani, M., Fariselli, P., and Casadio, R., 'Neural Networks and Prediction of Protein Structures', in F. Masulli, P. G. Morasso, and A. Schenone (eds.), *Neural Networks in Biomedicine*, World Scientific, Singapore, 1994: 313–32.

[62] Compiani, M., Fariselli, P., and Casadio, R., 'The Statistical Behaviour of Perceptrons: The Case Study of the Prediction of Protein Secondary Structures', *International Journal of Neural Systems*, 6 (Suppl. 1), (1995), 195–9.

[63] Compiani, M., Fariselli, P., and Casadio, R., 'Noise and Random-like Behaviour of Perceptrons: Theory and Application to the Prediction of Protein Structures', in S. K. Rogers, and D. W. Ruck (eds.), *Proceedings of the SPIE Applications and Science of Artificial Neural Networks VI*, SPIE-The International Society for Optical Engineering, Bellingham, Wash., 1996.

[64] Bateson, G., *Mind and Nature*, Fontana, London, 1985.

3
Remarks on the Impact of Connectionism on Our Thinking about Concepts

JOOP SCHOPMAN AND AZIZ SHAWKY

In this paper attention will be given to the incentive which the revival of connectionism has had on the ideas about the nature of concepts. Therefore, we will start with a short description of the prevailing position in this problem. Then a sketch will be presented of connectionism as far as is needed to sketch the consequences its reintroduction has for our thinking about concepts. Finally, an evaluation will be given which in its turn might lead to suggestions for future research.

1. THE PREVAILING THINKING ABOUT CONCEPTS IN COGNITIVE SCIENCES

Notwithstanding recent developments in several disciplines and fields one must acknowledge that prevailing thinking about the nature of concepts is still strongly dominated by positivistic ideas. In linguistics, philosophy, and psychology, for example, there remains a strong inclination to adhere to the so called 'rationalistic tradition'.[1] In this, the underlying assumption is that the world can be divided into a finite set of objects and relations. On their turn, concepts have a content completely determined by their particular reference to one of the members of this set. The referential relation is a purely conventional one. In this approach concepts are understood

---

[1] This term is used in this sense by T. Winograd and F. Flores in their *Understanding Computers and Cognition*, Norwood, NJ: Ablex, 1986.

as formal symbols, which derive all their content from their (conventional) allocation. The penetrative power of this tendency becomes apparent, for example, when one realizes that even such sophisticated thinkers as Fodor and Pylyshyn adhere to it. A careful reading of their attack on connectionism[2] makes clear that their idea of concepts appears to be more applicable to logical than linguistic concepts. They themselves acknowledge that it cannot be simply applied to concepts in natural languages. In their case, one gets the impression that their idea of concepts is much more dictated by their computational metaphor than by the actual properties of natural languages.

The first problem one bumps into is the difference between concepts and their linguistic counterparts. Given the fact that this is a topic in itself, and given the point we want to make, we will here conflate the two. Thus, for the sake of our argument, concepts will be restricted to linguistic concepts, words, or terms in a language. This means that we can rephrase the rationalistic view as: words get their meaning completely from their reference to a particular part of the world or a particular relation. This reference is not an internal property of words, but it has been attributed. As a consequence, the problem arises that language itself becomes a formal system. The well-formedness of any linguistic utterance only depends on a system of rules which is considered to be independent of the meaning of the sentences. On the other hand, to understand a sentence, one only needs to know what meaning has been attributed to each of its words, or to put this differently: sentences have a combinatoric semantics. This picture of language might seem attractive as long as one deals with computers. They can only manipulate formal symbols, the interpretation of which is our task, as their designers. There, meaning has its origin in an external, attributed interpretation. But it is clear that this position poses problems when one wants to apply this model to our own use of natural language, where we attach a meaning to our own utterances.

---

[2] J. A. Fodor and Z. W. Pylyshyn, 'Connectionism and Cognitive Architecture: A Critical Analysis', in *Cognition*, 28 (1988), 3–71.

2. CONNECTIONISM WITH REGARD TO CONCEPTS

Due to the problems which the research in Artificial Intelligence (AI) encountered, and to a different idea about the nature of human intelligence, several researchers have revived since the mid-1970s the hardware metaphor which dominated the 'intelligence' scene before 1956.[3] In their opinion, intelligence cannot be characterized as a formal manipulation of symbols. Intelligence appears to be the outcome of an extremely complex process of neural interactions. The main difference with the original hardware metaphor is that the functioning of the neural network does not occur serially, according to the rules of logic, but that it is carried out massively parallel, according to the dynamics of self-organizing systems. To simulate their characteristics mathematical calculations are applied to simplified models of neural networks. This is not the place to go into detail, but it is important to stress that these networks have the ability to learn by organizing their internal connections. This learning happens in interaction with external inputs. Thus, during the course of learning the neural structure reorganizes itself, so that the result is a changed internal structure.[4] This structural change cannot be called a representation of the original input, because the restructuring is the outcome of an interactive process between the state of the organism and the input. That means that the changed structure does not represent the external world, but it represents—if one wants to stick to the term—the interactive process: input-organism's or environment-organism's interaction. Thus, one can say that it has a relation with the input, the external world. The important difference, as we see it, that this relation is a 'natural' one. It does not reflect a designer's intervention in the system. The changed structure has a meaning for its owner: it means something to its owner although never in an absolute sense, but only in relation to the organism's actions in its environment. So, one can say that the learned structure-change has its own intrinsic semantics; nothing has to be ascribed to it and it requires no external interpretation. The important consequence for our

---

[3] For details, cf. J. Schopman, 'Frames of Artificial Intelligence', in Brian P. Bloomfield (ed.), *The Question of Artificial Intelligence*, London: Croom Helm, 1987: 165–219.

[4] This process is beautifully described by Maturana and Varela in their *The Tree of Knowledge*, Boston: New Science Library, 1988.

story is that the problem of how to find the semantic relation has evaporated.

The connectionist point of view does not mean that no problems are left, perhaps even new ones have been introduced. The main problem we are confronted with is the explanation of higher-level structures such as concepts; or, to state it differently, a central issue has become: what is the relation between the altered structure and what is usually called 'the conceptual level'? Recently several efforts have been made within different disciplines to solve this problem.

The first was made by Paul Smolensky.[5] Between the so-called cognitive level and the level of the neurons, he introduces an intermediate 'subconceptual' level which is 'built up of entities that correspond to *constituents* of the symbols used in the symbolic paradigm [and whose operations are] much finer-grained (numerical) operations'[6] than in the symbolic paradigm. From this one gets the impression that the subconcepts, or micro-features as he also calls them, greatly resemble the (symbolic) concepts. The main difference is that they are 'sliced' thinner. Thus a concept such as 'bachelor' might be thought to correspond to a vector in a space of features including MALE, HUMAN, ADULT, MARRIED, whereby a value of + or − is assigned to each feature. These assignments to micro-features are assumed to be derived automatically via learning procedures from the statistical properties of samples of stimuli. The resemblance to symbolic concepts gets confirmed when one reads his statement about the subsymbolic semantics. Although subsymbolic semantics is intrinsically situated, 'in the subsymbolic case, the internal processing mechanisms (which can appropriately be called inference procedures) do not, of course, directly depend causally on the environmental state that may be internally represented or on the veridicality of that representation. In that sense, they are just as formal as syntactic symbol manipulations.'[7] Somewhat earlier in his paper he explicitly says that semantically the subconceptual level resembles more the conceptual level, but syntactically it stands closer to the neural one. From such remarks one gets the impression that in fact the subconceptual level becomes the hypostasis of all the problems of

[5] P. Smolensky, 'On the Proper Treatment of Connectionism', in *Behavioral and Brain Sciences*, 11 (1988), 1–74.

[6] Ibid. 3.   [7] Ibid. 16.

the concept–neural substrate relation. So that in the end, nothing has really been solved as regards the problem of the semanticity of neural structures.

Another more interesting suggestion has been made by Adrian Cussins.[8] He, too, introduces a distinction within cognitive content. In his opinion, there is not only the traditional conceptual content, but *non-conceptual content* as well. Interestingly, his view allows him to recognize the fact that cognition is not a static property, but a dynamic one, because for him it is possible that a certain type of cognition starts as non-conceptual. That means that for that particular subject there exists a knowledge of the world, but that knowledge is not articulated. The subject can act properly in its environment, but it has no intellectual grasp of that environment. In Cussins's terms, the subject's knowledge lies completely in his subject-domain (or s-domain) which allows it to act, but it does not know in the literal sense of the word. This situation can and will be changed by the intellectual growth of the subject. Thereby it creates and increases its task-domain (or t-domain). In this process a transition takes place from experience to (explicit) knowledge. That process can be seen as an objectivation of the experience. One can also explain it as a transition from the s- to the t-domain. It is this transition which gives the subject a much larger freedom of action because the subject is—so to speak—no longer completely bound by its direct environment, but by the distance it has obtained, it gets more ways to go about it.[9]

The question, however, arises whether Cussins uses the conceptual–non-conceptual distinctions as poles of thinking, or that they represent 'real' states in the subject. In our opinion, this is a very important point, because in the first case there is the possibility that the subject can be only in its s-domain, there is no conceptual cognition at all. This might be the case for very young children or animals. On the other hand, it would be possible to get knowledge which is completely objective, or perspective-independent as he also calls it. In the second case, knowledge is always a mixture of

---

[8] In a paper 'The Connectionist Construction of Concepts', in M. A. Boden (ed.), *The Philosophy of Artificial Intelligence* (Oxford University Press, 1980), 368–440.

[9] In this sense it can be compared with the difference between scientific research which is devoid of any insight, and thus completely trial-and-error on the one hand; and research which can provide theoretical insight.

conceptual and non-conceptual contents; of explicit and implicit knowledge. Then, intellectual growth means a shifting of the balance between the two in the direction of explicitness without ever reaching a state of completely explicit or context-free knowledge. We ourselves prefer the latter option, because we are convinced that knowledge can indeed become very abstract, very far from the original experience, but that it can never cut its original ties. From Cussins's text one gets the impression that he favours the first option.

But whatever option one prefers, there remains a real problem, namely the fact that both models allow mixtures of conceptuality and non-conceptuality, and the question cannot be avoided how far these two can be mixed. Or even stronger, how is it possible that conceptuality arises from—even the term 'emerges' is used by Cussins—the non-conceptual. This picture is very attractive, and we can go along with it completely. Nevertheless, the problem has not been solved: how can experience be translated into explicit knowledge? What happens to it during the necessary process of 'translation'?

Finally, we would like to draw attention to the position taken by Mark Johnson[10] because he deals with the same problem. He does that in much the same way; he too is looking for 'embodied cognition' but he starts from a completely different angle. This approach is based on his co-operation with the linguist George Lakoff.[11] In his book Johnson describes the process Cussins is referring to: the emergence of conceptual content of knowledge. According to Johnson, as soon as we start our life, we are exposed to all kinds of experiences: our own body, gravity, objects which hinder our movements, etc. These events are not completely chaotic for us. We are able to organize them, to experience them as meaningful events. Thus, we experience them not as pure multitude but as highly organized occurrences, as 'Gestalts'. For this, we need 'image schemata' as he (and Lakoff) calls them; a terminology derived from Kant's *Kritik der Urteilskraft*. These initial experiences are extended to other domains as our exploration of the world continues. This process of extension is possible by our amazing ability to find analogies between quite different

[10] *The Body in the Mind*, Chicago: University of Chicago Press, 1987.
[11] Cf. G. Lakoff, and M. Johnson, *Metaphors We Live by*, Chicago: Chicago University Press 1980.

situations.[12] He presents several examples of such cases in which experiences gained and named in initial, simple situations get extended to more sophisticated ones, even to the domain of human reasoning as such. Using linguistic examples he demonstrates how these primitive experiences as the meeting of resistance when we try to move about are collected in the Gestalt 'force'. This allows us to extend the original experience to completely different domains, e.g. that of social interactions, so that we can now experience and name social forces. As we said, the range of extensions is not restricted to such direct experiences. Our Gestalt 'force' can even be applied to such abstract levels as epistemology. This allows us to speak about the 'forcefulness' of arguments. The consequence of Johnson's exposé is that ability to articulate even our most abstract experiences is made possible by our initial ones, our ability to organize experiences in Gestalts, and our capability to draw analogies. In his opinion knowledge always remains attached to the original experiences; it never becomes separate, context-free. Or to state it differently, there only exists embodied knowledge but there are degrees of embodiedness. So, he chooses the first of the two above-mentioned alternatives.

3. EVALUATION AND DIRECTION OF FUTURE RESEARCH

Moving from Fodor via Smolensky to Johnson we notice a remarkable shift in the status of concepts. In the case of Fodor, and most of cognitive science (and beyond), knowledge is an ability which is quite specific for humans. But it does not only divide humans from non-human organisms, but within humans it divides cognitive abilities from all the other ones. That makes cognitive activities context-free and syntactic by nature. On the other hand, for Johnson (and ourselves) cognitive abilities are intrinsically connected with the experiences of organisms; they always are contextual and thus semantic by nature.

These two positions with regard to 'concepts' are related to different ways of practising Artificial Intelligence. Fodor's ideas

---

[12] A fact which has also astonished D. R. Hofstadter, cf. his 'Analogies and Roles in Human and Machine Thinking', in *Metamagical Themas: Questing for the Essence of Mind and Pattern*, Harmondsworth: Penguin, 1985: 547–603.

are clearly inspired by the metaphor of the computer software, and Johnson's position is similar to that of neo-connectionism. We don't want to reduce the positions to the impact of computer technology because we are well aware that many more factors have contributed to the difference in perspective of the nature of cognition.[13] But we want to stress that in both cases the computer metaphor has contributed to the positions taken.

It will be evident that the *agenda of future research* strongly depends on which position one takes in this dispute. Because we favour the vision of an embodied knowledge, as expressed by Johnson and many others, we think that the research agenda should consist of two topics which need to have priority in the study of the nature of concepts. The first one is the emergence of concepts out of initial experiences; the origin and developments of image schemata as Johnson calls them. The second item is the extension of the original experience to other domains of our existence. Such studies have been undertaken, namely the study of what determines the analogy between situations. What is urgent is the connection of both types of study. We would prefer to start with one particular type of situations which allows a thorough study of both topics, e.g. three-dimensionality, or perspective. For our purpose, however, this agenda will be incomplete when the question will be left out what properties the neural network should have to allow the properties to be studied to appear. And, conversely, the feasibility of the network properties should have its impact on the solutions proposed in the first two cases mentioned. This means that this research requires the co-operation of psychologists, linguists, philosophers, and people working on neural networks.

[13] This might be evident because the position taken by Lakoff and Johnson has its origin in developments in the study of language.

4

Causation in the Philosophy of Mind

FRANK JACKSON AND PHILIP PETTIT

———— • ————

Causation has come to play an increasingly important role in the philosophy of mind, reaching its apotheosis in the doctrine that to be a mental state of kind K is to fill the causal role definitive of that kind of mental state: the typology of mental states is a typology of causal roles. However, ironically, there is, from this very functionalist perspective, a problem about how to understand the causal role of mental properties, those properties which make a mental state the kind of mental state that it is. This problem surfaces in one way or another in the debates over the language of thought (for instance, in the argument that only if intentional states have syntactic-like structure can they play the required causal roles); over the explanatory role of broad content (for instance, in the argument that broad content is explanatorily irrelevant to behaviour because doppelgängers behave alike while possibly differing in broad content); and over the eliminativist implications of connectionism (for instance, in the argument that certain versions of connectionism falsify the propositional modularity component of the folk conception of the causes of behaviour). We wish, however, to reverse the usual order of discussion. Instead of entering directly into one or another of these fascinating debates, we want to raise the problem of how to understand the causal role of mental properties as an issue in its own right. We will then offer a solution to the problem which seems to us plausible independently

This paper arose out of discussions engendered by the notion of a program explanation in 'Functionalism and Broad Content'. In addition to the acknowledgements already made, we can remember the changes forced by talking to Martin Davies and Robert Pargetter. No doubt there are more than we can remember. The main article appeared in *Philosophy and Phenomenological Research*, 50 (1990), 195–214.

of those debates. The final stage of our discussion will be a brief application of the proffered solution to argue that connectionism does not have the eliminativist implications sometimes associated with it.[1]

THE PROBLEM

How things were at some earlier time is succeeded by how things are at subsequent times, and we distinguish the way and extent to which how things were is causally responsible or relevant to how they are or will be. For instance, one aspect of how things were a little while ago is that there was a sharp drop in atmospheric pressure, and another aspect of how things were a little while ago is that a man with an odd number of freckles scratched his nose; the first aspect of how things were is causally relevant to the fact that it is now raining, the second is not.

But how things were, are, or will be at a time is a matter of which properties are instantiated at that time. So our common-place observation amounts to noting that we can and must distinguish a relation of (positive) causal relevance among *properties*. Those who hold to a fine-grained or relatively fine-grained conception of events, which broadly places them in the category of property instances, or of property instances of some favoured class of properties, will see this as really nothing more than the familiar doctrine that (singular) causation relates events.[2] But for those

---

[1] For the application to how broad content can explain see e.g. Martin Davies, 'Individualism and Supervenience', *Proceedings of the Aristotelian Society* (Supp.), 60 (1986), 263–83; Frank Jackson and Philip Pettit, 'Functionalism and Broad Content', *Mind*, 97 (1988), 381–400, and the references therein. The bearing of the issue about the causal role of mental properties, and of content properties especially, to the debate over the language of thought is central in Jerry A. Fodor, *Pyschosemantics*, Cambridge, Mass.: MIT Press, 1987. See also D. R. Braddon-Mitchell and J. B. Fitzpatrick, 'Explanation and the Language of Thought', *Synthese*, 83 (1990), 3–29.

[2] For different versions of this approach see e.g. Jaegwon Kim, 'Events as Property Exemplifications', in M. Brand and D. Walton (eds.), *Action Theory*, Dordrecht: Reidel, 1976: 159–77, David Lewis, 'Events', in *Philosophical Papers*, ii, Oxford: Oxford University Press, 1986: 241–69, and David H. Sanford, 'Causal Relata', in Ernest LePore and Brian P. McLaughlin (eds.), *Actions and Events*, Oxford: Blackwell, 1985: 282–93. But note that property instances in these approaches need to be distinguished from property instances in the sense of the tropes of Donald C. Williams, 'The Elements of Being', in *Principles of Empirical Realism*,

who hold to a coarse-grained conception of events which places them in the category of concrete particulars which have or instantiate properties, but are quite distinct from, and much more sparse than, properties or their instances, our commonplace must be seen as an addition to the story about causation being a relation between events. In addition to asking which events are causally relevant to which other events, we can and must ask which properties of events are causally relevant to which other properties. But surely this must, or should, have been an implicit ingredient in the story about singular causation all along.[3] Surely not even the most robust defender of a concrete conception of events supposed that *featureless* events might do some causing. Their events caused what they did because of how they were—that is to say, because of which properties they possessed.

Accordingly, we are going to take as a datum the idea that we can distinguish among properties in respect of their causal relevance to the obtaining of some effect or other. Exactly how to fit

---

Springfield, Il.: Thomas, 1966: 74–109. For in these approaches, when one and the same person at one and the same time says hullo loudly and thereby says hullo, the instance of saying hello is distinguished from that of a saying hello loudly—that is essential to allowing them to stand in different causal relations. Whereas Williams's tropes are absolutely specific; and so, if the saying hullo is a property instance in his trope sense, it is identical with saying hullo in some absolutely specific manner, and, therefore, in the case in question, to saying hullo loudly. On the absolutely specific nature of property instances on the Williams scheme, see Keith Campbell, *Metaphysics*, Belmont, Calif.: Dickenson, 1976, ch. 14. As a result of this point, a trope approach to the relata of the causal relation will, like the Davidsonian approach discussed next in the text, need to regard our commonplace as something to be added to the story about causation.

[3] And is, we think, though under a different guise, in Donald Davidson's adumbration of the view that causation is a relation between events concretely conceived in his 'Causal Relations', *Journal of Philosophy*, 64 (1967), 691–703. For, first, he holds that singular causal relations hold in virtue of causal laws (while holding that exactly how to spell this out is no easy matter), and, secondly, in discussing the kinds of examples which lead other writers to make events property-like, he admits in effect that we can, when dealing with what is in his view one and the same event, discriminate which properties of the single event play a special role in a causal explanation: although the bolt's giving way is one and the same event as its giving way suddenly in his view, the special place we may well give the latter in explaining the tragedy is accommodated by giving the correlative property a special place in the causal explanation of the tragedy. Davidson may well wish to urge that this special place is a place in a causal *law*, not in a singular causal relation. But for our purposes what is central is the partition of properties into causally relevant and causally irrelevant ones with respect to some effect, not whether this partition is a topic in the theory of singular causation or the theory of causal laws. We are indebted here to a discussion with Peter Menzies.

this fact into an event metaphysics of causation is left as a question for another time. We should emphasize that by 'causal relevance' in what follows we mean positive, actual causal relevance. We mean what might best have been called 'causal responsibility' except that 'relevance' has become somewhat entrenched in the literature, and 'responsibility' perhaps carries a connotation of sufficiency, whereas we are talking about the idea of a property being *a* factor, and typically one factor among many, in the causing of something.

We are now in a position to state our problem. Perhaps we can say a priori that a number's being prime cannot be causally relevant to any physical occurrence, but most often the question of whether a property is causally relevant to some effect is an a posteriori one. It was, for example, an empirical discovery that the mass of a body is irrelevant to its rate of acceleration under gravity in a vacuum, and that the density of a medium is relevant to the speed of light through that medium.

How do we establish that some property or set of properties is causally irrelevant to some effect? An attractive answer is that we do so by completely explaining the effect in terms of properties distinct from that property or set of properties. This is the point behind the familiar argument—sometimes referred to as 'the shadow of physiology' argument—against dualist interactionist theories of mind.[4] It is observed that it is very plausible that in principle a complete explanation of each and every bodily movement of a person can be given in terms of their internal physiology, with their neurophysiology playing a particularly important role, along with interactions of a physical kind between their physiological states and their environment. There are no mysterious, unclosable-in-principle gaps in the story medical science tells about what makes a person's arm go up. The conclusion then is that the sort of properties that feature in the dualist story are causally irrelevant to behaviour, and we are led to the familiar objection to dualism that the interactionist variety of dualism has to give way to an epiphenomenalist variety—and so much the worse for dualism![5]

Our problem is that if the popular functionalist approach to mental properties is correct, the very same style of argument appears

---

[4] See e.g. Keith Campbell, *Body and Mind*, London: Macmillan, 1971, ch. 3.
[5] But see Campbell, *Body and Mind*, and Frank Jackson, 'Epiphenomenal Qualia', *Philosophical Quarterly*, 32 (1982), 127–36, for reservations about the decisiveness of this argument when (and only when) directed at qualia.

to be available to cast doubt on the causal relevance of mental properties. The shadow of physiology seems to raise a problem for functionalists as well as for dualists despite the fact that functionalism is compatible with a purely materialistic view of the mind. Take, for instance, content and our common-sense conviction that content is causally relevant to behaviour, our conviction that the fact that a certain state of mind has the property of being the belief *that p* or of being the desire *that q* is causally relevant to my arm moving in a certain way. (We will stick with this example from now on in order to avoid the difficult problem of *qualia* or raw feels. We take it for granted that a materialistic account of an essentially naturalistic variety can be given of intentional states and their contents.) How can that be, given the just-discussed fact that a complete explanation in principle entirely in physiological terms of my behaviour is possible? For the kind of property content that is identified within the functionalist story will not appear anywhere in that story. What will matter at the various points in that story will be the physiological, and particularly neurophysiological, properties involved, whereas, as has so often been emphasized, what matters from the functionalist perspective for being a certain kind of mental state is not the nature of the state neurophysiologically speaking but rather the functional role occupied by that state. One way of putting the point is by saying that what drives behaviour is the physiological nature of the various states, not the functional roles they fill. How then can functional role, and so content according to functionalism, be a causally relevant property?

Some have concluded from considerations like these—so much the worse for functionalism as an account of content, in somewhat the same way that an earlier generation of philosophers concluded—so much the worse for dualism.[6] We think, however, that there is

---

[6] Most recently, Ned Block, 'Can the Mind Change the World?' in George Boolos (ed.), *Meaning and Method: Essays in Honor of Hilary Putnam*, Cambridge: Cambridge University Press, 1990: 137–170. See also Hartry H. Field, 'Mental Representation', repr. in Ned Block, *Readings in Philosophy of Psychology*, ii, London: Methuen, 1981: 78–114, see esp. 88–96; Jerry A. Fodor, 'Introduction: Something on the State of the Art', in his *Representations*, Brighton: Harvester, 1981: 1–31, but see his *Psychosemantics*, Cambridge, Mass.: MIT Press, 1987: 140 for what we take to be something akin to the supervenience approach we describe below. The problem and the associated issues would, of course, be much the same for views which regard functional role as a major ingredient, along with evolutionary history or whatever, in determining content. To keep things simple, we will set these hybrid views to one side.

an important error in the line of thought that suggests that functionalism makes content (and mental properties in general) causally irrelevant or epiphenomenal. Before we say what it is, we need to say why, as it seems to us, two initially attractive responses to our problem fail. The first response appeals to a type-type version of mind-brain identity theory based on functionalism; the second to the fact that functional role is supervenient on physiology plus physical environment.

THE IDENTITY THEORY RESPONSE TO OUR PROBLEM

The identity theory as originally presented was a type-type identity theory. Mental properties, including the possession of some particular content, were identified with neurophysiological properties.[7] Functionalists sometimes speak as if the familiar and correct point that the kind of functional role definitive of content (to stick with that example) can be, and most likely is, variously realized in different sentient organisms refuted this theory.[8] We agree, however, with the unrepentant type-type theorists that the point about the possibility of different neurophysiological states realizing a given content in different species, or even in different members of the same species, or even in a given individual at different times, only shows that different properties may be a given content in different species, or in different members of the same species, or in the one individual at different times.[9] Does this mean that we should espouse a simple answer to our question about the causal

[7] See e.g. J. J. C. Smart, 'Sensations and Brain Processes', *Philosophical Review*, 68 (1959), 141–56, D. M. Armstrong, *A Materialist Theory of the Mind*, London: Routledge & Kegan Paul, 1968, and, most explicitly, David K. Lewis, 'An Argument for the Identity Theory', *Journal of Philosophy*, 63/1 (1966), 17–25.

[8] See e.g. Hilary Putnam, 'The Mental Life of Some Machines', repr. in his *Mind, Language and Reality*, Cambridge: Cambridge University Press, 1975. Putnam is, of course, no longer a functionalist, see e.g. ch. 5 of *Representation and Reality*, Cambridge, Mass.: MIT Press, 1988, but the point is widely accepted, see e.g. Daniel Dennett, 'Current Issues in the Philosophy of Mind', *American Philosophical Quarterly*, 15/4 (1978), 249–61.

[9] See e.g. David Lewis, 'Review of Putnam', repr. in Ned Block (ed.), *Readings in Philosophy of Psychology*, i, London: Methuen, 1980: 232–3, and Frank Jackson, Robert Pargetter and Elizabeth W. Prior, 'Functionalism and Type-Type Identity Theories', *Philosophical Studies*, 42 (1982), 209–25.

relevance of being in a state with a certain content—namely the answer that being in that state is precisely as causally relevant to the action it putatively explains as is the neurophysiological property the relevant content property is identical with?

We think that this reply evades the crucial question of concern. When I explain your behaviour by citing your belief that it is about to rain, I am surely explaining your behaviour in terms of something I know about you, or at least that I think that I know about you. I am not saying that there is some internally realized property, I know not what, which is causally relevant to your behaviour. That would be hardly more than a declaration that your action is not a random occurrence. I am rather explaining your behaviour in terms of something I know about you; and as I do not know, and know that I do not know, about the nature of your internal physiological states, it can only be the relevant functional role which I am citing as the property which you instantiate which is causally relevant to your behaviour. When we explain behaviour in terms of the contents of beliefs and desires, the properties we are invoking must be the known or guessed about functional roles, not the unknown nature of the occupiers of those roles. Moreover, even though type-type theorists identify a given belief content in a given organism on a given occasion with a neurophysiological state (type) rather than a functional state, they must and do hold that it is the functional role the state occupies, not the kind of neurophysiological state it is, which gives that state the belief content it has. Functional role is the final arbiter. The upshot is that we need to vindicate the causal relevance of functional role—it is what we know about and what in the final analysis matters—in order to justify the common-sense attitude to causal explanations in terms of content.[10]

THE SUPERVENIENCE RESPONSE TO OUR PROBLEM

Our problem was framed in the following terms. The whole causal story about the origins of behaviour can be told in terms of the neurophysiological nature of our internal workings combined with

---

[10] We take it that our objections here are essentially the same as Block's, 'Can the Mind Change the World?'.

environmental considerations—where then is there room for functional properties to do any causal work? Ergo, functional properties are causally irrelevant. Our model was the familiar argument which forces dualists into embracing an epiphenomenalist position on the mind.

There is, however, a major difference between dualism and functionalism. Although both see properties other than neurophysiological ones as what is crucial to being minded, the properties functionalism sees as crucial *supervene* on physiology, or at least on physiology together with the relevant laws and, if we are dealing with broad functional roles, certain environmental and historical factors, whereas the properties dualists see as crucial are *emergent* ones. There is a sense, that is, in which the crucial properties according to functionalists, namely the functional properties, are not *wholly* distinct from the neurophysiological ones. Although no functional property is identical with any neurophysiological one, enough by way of neurophysiological properties when combined with environmental facts (and perhaps laws of nature) fully determines the functional properties. The supervenience reply to our problem, thus, is the observation that from the fact that the whole causal story can be told in neurophysiological terms, and that no functional property is any neurophysiological property, it does not follow that the functional properties do not appear in the story. They appear in the story by supervening on the neurophysiological properties (in the same way though less transparently, that you and I being the same height appears in a story that includes your being 182 cm. and my being 182 cm. in height).

This reply wins the battle but not the war. Our problem is not how to reply to scepticism about whether functional properties are instantiated, but how to reply to scepticism about their causal relevance. Some philosophers have worried about whether we should acknowledge truth and reference as features of the world on the ground that neither the fact that some sentence is true nor the fact that some word has a certain reference plays a role in explaining the causal order of the natural world.[11] The reply to this worry is that truth and reference supervene on what does feature in the best explanations of the natural world. Similarly, the fact that a person's behaviour can be explained in full without explicit reference to the functional properties as such of their internal

---

[11] See e.g. Michael Devitt, *Realism and Truth*, Oxford: Blackwell, 1984, ch. 6.

states does not show that we should be sceptics about their states instantiating functional properties. The functional properties supervene on the properties we do explicitly invoke in our explanations. It is, though, one thing to be reassured about the presence of certain properties, and another to be reassured about their causal relevance. The point about supervenience leaves open the question of the causal relevance of the functional properties.

It might be thought easy to close this question by appeal to the following principle: If being F is causally relevant to some effect E, and being G supervenes on being F, then being G is causally relevant to E. The idea would be that we solve our problem by observing (*a*) that physiological properties are non-controversially causally relevant to behaviour, (*b*) that functional properties supervene on them, perhaps in combination with other matters, and then (*c*) use the principle to obtain the desired result that functional properties, and so, contents, are causally relevant to behaviour.[12] The principle is, however, false. In general for any property or property complex which is causally relevant to the obtaining of some effect E, there will be indefinitely many properties which supervene on that property or property complex, and it would be absurdly generous to count all and sundry as causally relevant. Examples bear this general observation out.

Consider a machine with two weighing platforms set up to respond whenever the weight on one platform is half that on the other. In that case alone a circuit in the machine closes causing a bell to ring, and further suppose that on some particular occasion a weight of 3 grams is placed on one platform and a weight of 6 grams on the other causing the bell to ring. Clearly none of, one weight's being a prime number of grams, one weight's being one less than 7, or one weight's being divisible by three or the weight of the Prime Minister is causally relevant to the bell's ringing. And yet all these properties supervene on the properties that on the occasion were causally relevant—namely one weight's being 3 grams when the other was 6 grams. As we might naturally say it, one

---

[12] The principle would be a kind of converse of that espoused by Jaegwon Kim, see e.g. 'Epiphenomenal and Supervenient Causation', *Midwest Studies in Philosophy*, 9 (1984), 257–70, and, for a recent critical discussion of the surrounding issues to which we are indebted, Peter Menzies, 'Against Causal Reductionism', *Mind*, 97 (1988), 551–74. The 'perhaps in combination with other matters' is included in (*b*) to cover the possibility that the functional properties are broad ones tailored to capture broad content. Also, a full specification of the supervenience base should include the relevant laws.

weight's being 3 grams and the other being 6 grams was relevant because three is half six and not, for instance, because three is a prime number, or because six is one less that seven. Or again suppose that the fact that someone lives in a particular suburb on the north side of town is causally relevant to their being happy about where they live. Their living *somewhere* on the north side of town supervenes on their living in the particular northern suburb that they do live in, yet it need not be the case that their living somewhere on the north side of town causally explains their contentment. Perhaps they particularly dislike all the other northern suburbs apart from the one they live in—in this case it would not be their living somewhere on the north side, but only their living just where they do in fact live which would be causally relevant. Or again, going to twenty committee meetings may be causally relevant to Jones's sorry state of mind in a way in which going to at least two is not, yet going to at least two supervenes on going to twenty.[13]

A SOLUTION TO OUR PROBLEM

We can think of functional properties as a more complex and general case of dispositional properties, and as our problem has a simplified analogue in the case of dispositional properties, we will start with them.

Dispositional properties are causally relevant: a glass breaks because it is fragile; Fred is saved because his seat-belt has the right degree of elasticity; Mary dies because the ladder she allows to touch power lines is a good conductor of electricity; a kingdom is lost because a monarch is intemperate; and so on and so forth.[14]

[13] Examples such as these abound in the literature, but the focus is most often not so much on whether causal relevance among properties is transmitted over supervenience, but rather on whether it is events concretely conceived or whether it is property-like entities (be they called 'events' or not), which are the relata of the causal relation. See e.g. Kim, 'Events as Property Exemplifications', Lewis, 'Events', Alvin I. Goldman, *A Theory of Human Action*, Englewood Cliffs, NJ: Prentice-Hall, 1970, and Sanford, 'Causal Relata'.

[14] Why does the first example in this list have so much less force than the others? Because being fragile is in part defined in terms of a certain relation to breaking; in consequence, being told that a glass broke because it is fragile is not particularly informative. Some have gone further and held that being fragile is no explanation. We disagree but do not pursue the point because the other examples will serve.

And yet a full account of how these various events come about can be given in terms of the dispositions's categorical bases rather than the dispositions themselves. It is this point that lies behind the familiar doctrine that dispositions are, as it is sometimes put, causally impotent.[15] How then can they be causally relevant?

It can be tempting to think that there is a simple solution to this puzzle.[16] A dispositional property may be properly invoked in a causal explanation despite its impotence provided that its categorical basis is causally relevant to what is being explained.[17] This is the analogue for dispositions to the identity solution to our problem discussed above, and we could simply repeat, suitably modified, our objections to that solution. However, there happens to be a simple and decisive counter-example to the solution as applied to dispositions. It is the case of conductivity.[18] The categorical basis in metals of the different dispositional properties of electrical conductivity, thermal conductivity, ductility, metallic lustre, and opacity is essentially the same, namely the nature of the cloud of free electrons that permeates the metal. Nevertheless, the person who dies because she allows her aluminium ladder to touch power lines does not die because her ladder is a good conductor of heat, or because it is lustrous or ductile or highly opaque; she dies because her ladder is a good electrical conductor. Although one and the same property is the categorical basis of all these dispositions, out of these dispositions it is only being a good electrical conductor which is causally relevant to her death. This is a contingent fact, of course. It might have been the fact that the ladder obscured someone's view which was crucial, in which case the ladder's opacity would have been the causally relevant property;

---

[15] See e.g. Roger Squires, 'Are Dispositions Causes?' *Analysis*, 29/1 (1968), 45–7, and Elizabeth W. Prior, Robert Pargetter, and Frank Jackson, 'Three Theses about Dispositions', *American Philosophical Quarterly*, 19/3 (1982), 251–7.

[16] One of us was tempted, see Prior, Pargetter, and Jackson, 'Three Theses about Dispositons'.

[17] We agree with D. M. Armstrong, *A Materialist Theory of the Mind*, London: Routledge & Kegan Paul, 1968: 85 f, though for reasons different from his, that it is necessarily true that a disposition has a categorical basis. However, the argument needs only the weaker doctrine that there is in fact a categorical basis. Moreover, we can regard the term 'categorical basis' as a tag phrase, and so do not need to buy into the debate about exactly how 'categorical' it must be.

[18] We owe the example to Peter Menzies, 'Against Causal Reductionism', who owes it in turn to David Lewis. We are much indebted to them for it. They should not be held responsible for the use we make of it.

or it might have been the opacity together with the good electrical conductivity which was the real problem, or . . . The point of importance for us is that the fact that there is one categorical basis for the various dispositions does not mean that the various dispositions are alike in causal relevance.

We propose in place of an 'identity theory' that the causal relevance of dispositions can be captured in terms of what might be called invariance of effect under variation of realization. Here is a simple non-dispositional example to illustrate the central idea. Smith takes 10 grains of arsenic which causes him to die about 10 minutes later. Jones takes 10 grains of arsenic which causes him to die in about 10 minutes also. When is it right to say that the fact that they both died in about the same time is explained by the fact that they both took the same amount of arsenic? Well, suppose the time to die after taking a given dose of arsenic is given by a complicated formula involving body weight, and that this formula gives in the case of Smith and Jones very different times to die for a given identical dose *except* when the dose is 10 grains. In that case the explanation of their taking the same time to die would be their both taking 10 grains, and not their taking identical doses. After all, if the one and only case where the same dose is followed by the same time to die is the single case where the doses are both 10 grains, it is a fluke—the fluke that the sameness in doses happened to be constituted or realized by their both taking 10 grains— that the sameness in dose was followed by their taking the same time to die. Only if its being 10 grains in both cases does not matter to their dying in about the same time, that is if they would take about the same time to die after the same dose pretty much regardless of the dose provided it was lethal, is it correct to explain their dying in the same time as being due to the doses being the same. We can view the matter in terms of realizations. There are many ways of realizing taking the same doses—by both taking 10 grains, by both taking 9 grains, . . . If any of a good range of these realizations, including the actual one, would lead to death in the same time for each person, then it is correct to explain the sameness in times to die in terms of the sameness of doses, and taking the same dose is causally relevant to dying in the same time. For then the doses each being 10 grains is not what is crucial for Smith and Jones dying in the same time, but rather the doses each being the same number of grains.

We suggest a similar approach to causal explanation by citing dispositional properties. The reason being a good conductor of electricity is causally relevant to Mary's death is that it did not matter (within reason) what the categorical basis of that disposition was, for provided the causal role definitive of good electrical conductivity was occupied by a state of the ladder she would have died. We move from the non-contentious causal relevance of the categorical basis to the causal relevance of the disposition via the facts that (*a*) the actual categorical basis was causally relevant to the death by electrocution, and (*b*) had the good electrical conductivity of the ladder had a different categorical basis, then that basis would have been causally relevant to the death. And, of course, the reason opacity, say, is not causally relevant to her dying is that it might easily have been realized without her dying—as would, for instance, have been the case had the ladder been wooden.

The explanatory interest of an explanation in terms of a dispositional property is now clear. We are often interested not merely in how something in fact came about but also in how it would have come about. That is why, paradoxically, we can sometimes improve an explanation by, in a sense, saying less. An elevator has a safety device which holds it at a given floor if more than ten people step into it at that floor. Twenty people step into it on the ground floor and as a result it does not move. In explaining what has happened to the disappointed customers, it will be better for me to say that the reason that the elevator is not moving is because more than ten people stepped into it than to say that it is not moving because twenty people stepped into it. How so—after all, that twenty people stepped into the elevator entails, but is not entailed by and so is logically stronger than, that at least ten people stepped into it? The answer, of course, is that in giving the explanation in terms of at least ten, I tell the customers what would have happened had, say, fifteen people stepped into the elevator.

Our account of how functional properties, and so in particular content, can be causally relevant to behaviour will by now come as no surprise. A certain piece of behaviour will have a certain property, say that of being in the direction of a certain cup of coffee, as a result of the concatenation of very many neurophysiological states which will have given rise to that piece of behaviour by virtue of their natures, that is, by virtue of the neurophysiological properties they instantiate. But, of course, there will be other ways that behaviour with the property of being towards the coffee could have been caused, other neurophysiological ways, or even, other non-neurophysiological ways if we allow ourselves Martian speculations. Is there anything interesting that we can say about resemblances between these various actual and possible ways of getting behaviour towards the coffee? The answer is that it may be that many of these ways, including the actual way, are united by the functional properties they realize, and in particular by the functional properties definitive of contents that they realize. In that case, an explanation in terms of content-bearing states will apply and its explanatory interest will lie in the fact that it tells us about what would happen in addition to what did happen. That is how the content properties may be causally relevant.

HAVE WE REALLY LAID THE DEMON TO REST: THE METAPHYSICS OF CAUSATION?

The intuition that functionalist accounts of content make content epiphenomenal is a strong one.[19] We have encountered the following response to our defence of the causal relevance of content properties. 'You have shown how the fact that a certain piece of behaviour follows the instantiation of certain content properties need not be a fluke. For (a) it is not a fluke that the behaviour follows a certain concatenation of neurophysiological states, (b) this concatenation is, at the least, a major part of what the relevant functional properties supervene on, and (c) it may be that many different complexes of neurophysiological states alike in having the relevant functional properties supervening on them would also be followed by behaviour exemplifying the feature we are seeking to explain. (Often the behaviours will count as different under some natural taxonomy, but this is, of course, consistent with their being alike in the respect of interest.) But all that that shows is the non-flukey nature of a certain sequence, and the explanatory value of content ascriptions. It does not show that content properties conceived functionally do the *driving* of behaviour. The fact remains that that is done by neurophysiological (or

---

[19] As Ned Block and Paul Boghossian convinced us.

least relatively intrinsic structural or syntactic) properties; yet surely the common-sense intuition that cries out for vindication is that content drives behaviour.'

Now of course it is true that some non-flukey sequences are not causal. That possibility lies at the heart of classical epiphenomenalism. According to epiphenomenalism, a certain kind of mental event regularly precedes a certain kind of brain event which leads on to the behaviour we associate with that mental event; but this is not because the first event causes the second but because both are caused by a third, earlier brain event. But it is essential to this story that according to classical epiphenomenalism the mental event is indeed caused by the earlier brain event. But if caused then distinct, whereas a key part of our account of how content properties are causally relevant to behaviour is that they are not completely distinct from the relevant neurophysiology; they instead supervene on it. We would be in trouble if our story was that the neurophysiological properties are causally relevant both to the content properties and to the behaviour. But our view is rather that the connection between neurophysiology and content is that the latter supervenes on the former, and supervenience is incompatible with causation. More precisely, enough by way of neurophysiology and the relevant laws together possibly with environmental setting and history (how much of the latter two you need to include depends on whether and to what extent the content is broad) *logically* fixes the content, and therefore is not *causally* responsible for it. Accordingly, as the neurophysiology is a proper part of what the content logically supervenes on (we might put this by saying that the content contingently supervenes on the neurophysiology), the neurophysiology is not causally relevant to the content. This is why the content is not possessed a moment after the relevant neurophysiological facts obtain, as would have to be the case were the connection causal.

Nevertheless, there is more to say about the objection, for behind it lies an attractive view about the metaphysics of causation.[20] Suppose that in a laboratory in Russia electron A is acted on by a force of value four and accelerates at rate seven (all in some suitable units). At the same time in a laboratory in America electron B is also acted upon by a force of value four and as a result

---

[20] One author (F.J.) finds it more attractive than does the other (P.P.).

it too accelerates at rate seven. Suppose that the sameness of the resultant accelerations is in no way dependent on the fact that the impressed forces were of value four. All that mattered (within limits, of course) for the sameness of the accelerations was the sameness of the impressed forces. Then clearly the sameness of the impressed forces is causally relevant to the sameness of the resultant accelerations. The sameness of the first causally explains the sameness of the second. (The situation is in essentials the same as in the arsenic example described earlier.)

Suppose, however, we think of causation as a matter of production or efficacy which does not reduce sooner or later to nothing move than nomological sequence: according to this view, a sequence is nomological because of underlying causal productivities, not conversely.[21] Then it is plausible that in some sense the sameness of the impressed forces does not actually *produce* the sameness of the resultant accelerations.[22] Consider electron A. It is acted upon by a force which both has the property of taking the value four and the relational property of being the same in value as the force acting on electron B. Does the latter fact actually have any influence on the way the electron moves off under the impact of the force? Surely not. All the work is done by the force acting on A taking the value four, how things are with B, which after all is a very long way away, is surely in *some* sense irrelevant. Perhaps the sharpest way of putting the point is the Occamist one. Supposing that the force taking the value four produces the acceleration of value seven in both cases is enough to explain (because it entails) the fact that sameness of impressed force on A and B is in fact followed by sameness of acceleration by A and B. There is no need in addition to give the property of having the same impressed force *per se* a productive or efficacious role with respect to the sameness of the resultant accelerations.[23]

The idea then is that we can distinguish as a special case of

[21] This is a view forced on us if (but *not* only if) we accept the non-Humean idea that there can be strongly singularist causation in the sense of one event causing another which does not fall under a law, either deterministic or indeterministic. For defences of strongly singularist causation, see G. E. M. Anscombe, 'Causality and Determination', in E. Sosa (ed.), *Causation and Conditionals*, Oxford University Press, 1975: 63–81, and Michael Tooley, 'The Nature of Causation: A Singularist Account', *Canadian Journal of Philosophy* (Supp.), 16 (1990), 271–322.

[22] Of course, from a purely nomic point of view, and provided the details are sufficiently filled out, the sequence: same forces, same accelerations, may be just as 'good' as the sequence: force four, acceleration seven.

[23] We are here in agreement with Block, 'Can the Mind Change the World?'

causal relevance among properties, causal efficacy. Every case where an instance of F is causally efficacious with respect to an instance of G is a case of causal relevance, but some cases where an instance of F is causally relevant to an instance of G are cases of relevance without efficacy.[24] The objection under discussion can now be put as follows: our defence of the explanatory role of content from the functionalist perspective only shows causal relevance (and indeed we used that very term to describe matters earlier); it does not show that content properties are causally efficacious with respect to behaviour, and it is the latter which is integral to the common intuition about content's role with respect to behaviour.

Our reply turns on the point that the Occamist thought that lies behind distinguishing causal efficacy as a special case of causal relevance has far-reaching ramifications. It has been widely noted how plausible is the idea that everything about the way our bodies move, including everything by way of the causal relations involved, supervenes on how things, including the laws, are at the most fundamental micro-physical level. If this is right, then the Occamist attitude combined with the view of causation which does not reduce it to nothing more than nomological sequences, enjoins us to restrict relations of causal efficacy to certain properties in fundamental physics—which properties exactly is a matter for empirical science—and to see all the causal relevancies 'higher up' as, strictly speaking, non-efficacious.[25] For we do not need to believe in any fundamental efficacies over and above those between properties at the micro-level in order to explain the regularities, actual and counterfactual, all the way up, because supervenience tells us that they are fixed by how things are at the bottom (*if* there is a bottom). But then the neurophysiological properties are not causally efficacious in the special sense any more than are the content properties. And more generally there will not be a contrast between the causal relationship that content and functional properties generally have to behaviour, and the causal relationship that taking arsenic has to death, that lying in the sun has to getting hot, that

---

[24] Elsewhere, we refer to cases of causal relevance without causal efficacy as cases of causal programming, see 'Functionalism and Broad Content'; see also 'Program Explanation: A General Perspective', *Analysis*, 50 (1990), 107–17.

[25] For a defence of the view, to put it in our terms, that the answer science delivers is that causal efficacy is a relation between forces, see John Bigelow and Robert Pargetter, 'Metaphysics of Causation', *Erkenntnis*, 33 (1990), 89–119.

rising inflation has to falling living standards, and so on and so forth. These cases will be all alike in being cases of causal relevance without causal efficacy. Ergo, the functionalist account of content does not downgrade its causal role, rather it leaves it in the excellent company of everything except for certain members of that most exclusive of clubs, the properties of fundamental physics.[26]

We suspect that the thought behind the view that we functionalists have made content epiphenomenal is that we have somehow taken the 'push' out of content. But consider someone being torn apart by an imbalance of forces acting on him (as happens if you step into space without a space suit on). The imbalance of forces has plenty of push but plausibly is not efficacious, for the simple reason that it is a 'convenient fiction'. It is plausible that the resultant force in the familiar parallelogram of forces is a convenient fiction. It is the component forces which really exist (or rather certain of the component forces, the component forces in a parallelogram of forces can of course themselves be resultants in some other parallelogram of forces), and so it is they at most which can stand in relations of causal efficacy.[27]

APPLICATION TO AN ARGUMENT FOR ELIMINATIVISM

We can now see the mistake in an interesting and initially appealing line of argument for eliminativism about the propositional attitudes.

---

[26] We are not, of course, saying that most of our common-sense convictions about causal connections expressed in everyday language are false. When we use terms like 'efficacious' and 'productive' in everyday talk, they mean roughly what we are using 'causal relevance' for (perhaps restricted to causal relevance between relatively intrinsic properties, see Lewis, 'Events'). Our thesis is a thesis in (a posteriori) metaphysics which holds, not that most of our convictions are mistaken, but rather that what makes the true ones true is a relation between properties in fundamental physics. We take this general way of looking at the matter to be consonant with D. M. Armstrong's species of realism about universals, as expressed for instance in his *A Theory of Universals*, Cambridge: Cambridge University Press, 1978, see particularly vol. 2, ch. 24 for the connection with causality. What becomes of the doctrine that dispositions are causally impotent on this metaphysics of causation? *If* 'causally impotent' is given the special sense given to 'causally inefficacious', then the doctrine is true; but it is also true that a disposition's categorical basis is impotent unless specified micro-physically.

[27] On the existence of component forces, see John Bigelow, Brian Ellis, and Robert Pargetter, 'Forces', *Philosophy of Science*, 55 (1988), 614–630.

Eliminativists see the apparatus of beliefs and desires with their associated contents as part of an ancient (and so prima facie suspect, but that is another story) theory—dubbed 'folk psychology'—which we invoke to explain and predict *inter alia* and especially behaviour. But to explain behaviour is to say something about the causes of behaviour and, runs the argument we wish to reply to, what folk psychology says about the causes of behaviour may turn out as a matter of empirical fact to be mistaken in an important respect, a respect important enough to justify describing what has happened as a refutation, rather than, say, an elaboration, of folk psychology. What is meant here by 'as a matter of empirical fact' is not as a matter of abstractly possible empirical fact—it is common ground (or ought to be) that it is logically possible that the causal story about our behaviour be incompatible with folk psychology. What these eliminativists have in mind is the causal story implied by certain connectionist views about information-processing in the brain, which they take to be very much live options. Eliminativists see folk psychology as committed to beliefs and desires being properly described as propositional attitudes. This combined with the idea that folk psychology is an explanatory theory leads to the doctrine that the folk are committed to the idea that the internal causes of behaviour can be illuminatingly divided up in terms of the propositions which are the objects of our beliefs and desires. Folk psychology carries with it its own way of taxonomizing the causes of behaviour in terms of contents given typically by indicative natural language sentences prefixed by 'that'—propositional modularity, as it is sometimes called. The eliminativist argument is that if developments in neuroscience confirm certain connectionist views, then this will show that propositional modularity is false, and so will be nothing less than an empirical refutation of the folk taxonomy of the causes of behaviour, and so of folk psychology with its apparatus of beliefs and desires.[28]

One might quarrel with one or another detail of the eliminativists's account of folk psychology, but the general picture is highly

---

[28] The most explicit development of this argument that we know is in William Ramsey, Stephen P. Stich, and Joseph Garon, 'Connectionism, Eliminativism, and the Future of Folk Psychology', in *Philosophy and Connectionist Theory*, W. Ramsey, D. E. Rumelhart, and S. P. Stich (eds.), Hillsdale, NJ: Erlbaum, 1991: 199–228; but see also Paul M. Churchland, *Scientific Realism and the Plasticity of Mind*, Cambridge: Cambridge University Press, 1979, §§ 18 ff, and 'Eliminative Materialism and the Propositional Attitudes', *Journal of Philosophy*, 78 (1981), 67–90.

plausible. For consider Jill, who believes that a book relevant to her current research has arrived in the library and also believes that it will rain later today. We folk do distinguish these two beliefs precisely because they differ in content, and that is a matter at least very closely connected with the propositions expressed by the embedded sentences.[29] And further we do distinguish the causal role that the two beliefs play with respect to her behaviour. Unless we have reason to attribute somewhat bizarre desires to Jill, the belief that a book relevant to her current research is most likely to be appealed to in order to explain her going to the library, and the belief that it will rain later is most likely to be appealed to in order to explain her taking an umbrella to work.

Our reply to the eliminativist argument takes this general picture for granted. We grant that we folk distinguish the two beliefs by distinguishing their propositional objects and that we folk give the distinguished beliefs distinct causal roles in explaining Jill's behaviour precisely in accord with their distinct propositional objects (and the same goes for desires, of course). Our quarrel is with the claim that there is an incompatibility between this picture and certain connectionist views about information-processing in the brain.

Why do eliminativists see an incompatibility between connectionism and folk propositional modularity? Well, if beliefs are anything like stored sentences in the brain, then it is plausible that there will be in Jill's brain two distinct bits of storing, one of the sentence about the book, the other of the sentence about the rain, and eliminativists observe that consequently in this case we can sensibly suppose that the first bit of storing has a special causal relationship to Jill's movements towards the library that the second lacks, and that the second bit of storing has a special relationship to her umbrella-taking that the first lacks. But, runs the argument, if certain versions of connectionism are correct, it will be impossible to isolate in any way one part of the brain or its activities and see this as one of the beliefs, at the same time as isolating something else in the brain and seeing that as the other belief. Information-processing is a completely holistic and distributed matter on these versions of connectionism. There will be nothing in the brain, at the neurophysiological level or at the level

---

[29] See David Lewis, *On The Plurality of Worlds*, Oxford: Blackwell, 1986, for arguments that the connection between the objects of beliefs and the embedded sentences in our reports of belief is more complicated than one might have hoped.

of cognitive architecture, to be isolated as one belief as opposed to the other.[30] How then can the folk hypothesis about distinctness of causal roles be true?

Our reply is that our approach to the causal relevance of content properties in terms of invariance of effect under variation of realization of that content, shows how one and the same underlying state (be it widely distributed or localized) can realize two different contents, one of which is, and the other of which is not, causally relevant to a given piece of behaviour. We do not need to find distinct states at, say, the brain level—distinct encodings, or whatever—to be the two beliefs in order to vindicate the common-sense conviction that my belief that p may differ in its causal relevancies from my belief that q. For on our approach, a certain content is causally relevant to a certain effect if (*a*) a state occupying the role definitive of that content is causally relevant to that effect, and (*b*) had that content been differently realized, then other things being equal the counterfactual realizer state would have been causally relevant to that effect. Now it is clearly a live possibility that a single state S be such that it occupies the role definitive of different contents, C_1 and C_2, and yet for some effect E other ways of realizing C_1 would *ceteris paribus* have been causally relevant to E, whereas other ways of realizing C_2 would not. Indeed, the dispositional correlate of this live possibility actually obtains in the case of conductivity discussed earlier (and remember we noted that it is wrong to conclude from the fact that we cannot pick out distinct underlying states of Mary's ladder to be the bases of the various distinct dispositional properties of her ladder, that all the dispositions are equally causally relevant to what happened to her).

This story fits well with our everyday approach to our case of Jill who believes both that a book relevant to her current research has just arrived in the library and that it will rain. Although she has both beliefs, we take it that it is the first that is causally relevant to her movement towards the library, because we take it that she would have moved towards the library whether or not she had had the belief that it will rain; whereas she would have taken

[30] See Ramsey *et al.*, 'Connectionism, Eliminativism and the Future of Folk Psychology', and Andy Clark, *Microcognition*, Cambridge, Mass.: MIT Press, 1989, and the references therein to the connectionist literature. Clark is with us in denying that connectionism implies eliminativism.

an umbrella whether or not she had believed that a book especially relevant to her research had just arrived in the library, and
so this belief is not why she took an umbrella.[31]

It might well be objected that when we explain Jill's movement
towards the library in terms of her belief that a book especially
relevant to her research has just arrived, we are giving that belief
an active role in the story.[32] It is not a standing condition but
rather a state being activated in the context of a set of standing
conditions. The same point applies when we explain Fred's survival in terms of his seat-belt having the right degree of elasticity.
The seat-belt presumably had that right degree of elasticity from
the day of its manufacture, but something happened at a certain
moment during the accident which brought that degree of elasticity into play in a way which led to his survival. A fair question,
therefore, is whether in the supposed connectionist case where
there is no isolating one belief from the other in different encodings,
we can give Jill's belief that a book especially relevant to her
research has just arrived in the library an active role in explaining
her movement towards the library without at the same time giving
the intuitively irrelevant belief that it will rain the same role? But
consider our ladder example again. Mary's aluminium ladder was
a good conductor of electricity from the day it was made. When
its being so was actively causally relevant to her death by electrocution what happened was that the nature of the cloud of free
electrons in the matter of the ladder occupied the role definitive
of being a good electrical conductor in a special way. The set of
subjunctive conditionals definitive of that role contained a member which, in addition to being itself true, had a true antecedent
and a true consequent. It was true that for some salient-to-being-
an-electrical-conductor conditional 'had so and so happened, then
such and such would have happened' that, not only was it the case
that it obtained by virtue of the nature of those electrons, in
addition, on the occasion in question, so and so actually happened
and, by virtue of the nature of those electrons, such and such
followed in a way which contributed to Mary's death. In brief, the
disposition manifested itself; and the crucial point is that, although
the underlying basis for being a good electrical conductor in the

---

[31] We are supposing that the important problems of overdetermination and
causal pre-emption are separate ones from those under discussion here.

[32] As Andy Clark reminded us.

ladder is one and the same as that for, for instance, being opaque and being a good heat conductor, being a good electrical conductor can, and did in the case we are imagining, manifest itself without the other dispositions manifesting themselves. The same can be said in the case where Jill's belief about the book played an active role in getting her to the library. It did so by virtue of certain of the inputs and outputs salient in the specification of the functional role corresponding to having that belief actually obtaining, and, of course, that can happen without the differently specified inputs and outputs constituitive of having the belief that it will rain actually obtaining.

CONCLUSION

Functionalism specifies mental properties in terms of causal roles. The irony is that it then appears to be the case that functionalism deprives mental properties of causal relevance. It appears that it is the properties in virtue of which the relevant states occupy the relevant causal roles, and not the roles themselves, which are causally relevant to behaviour. Our aim in this paper has been to rebut this beguiling argument, and to do so in a way which shows the flaw in the equally beguiling argument that connectionism supports eliminativism.

POSTSCRIPT

We have elsewhere described the sort of story told in this article as a 'program' model of how properties at different levels can be causally relevant at the same time to one and the same event.[33] As the story has it in the mind case, the beliefs and desires 'program' for the behaviour to which they are relevant to the extent that all their neurophysiological realizers—to go to the simplest case—are of a kind fit to produce that behaviour and the actual realizer does produce it. The article makes clear that the neurophysiological antecedents may program in turn for the behaviour produced, in

---

[33] Functionalism and Broad Content'; see also Frank Jackson and Philip Pettit, 'Program Explanation: A General Perspective', *Analysis*, 50 (1990), 107–17.

that they relate to microphysical realizers in the same way that the intentional antecedents relate to them. That we speak of neurophysiological production rather than programming—or that we say, as well we might, that it is the neurophysiological antecedents which do the causing of the behaviour to which the beliefs and desires are causally relevant—is pragmatically determined; with any two levels of causally relevant properties it is always natural to favour the lower in this terminological way.

The program model has been taken to involve a sort of epiphenomenalism, so far as programming always presupposes production.[34] But the charge is mislaid. The model is meant to explain the preservation of causal relevance across levels and is consistent even with the possibility that there is no bottom level—that levels go on indefinitely—as we have emphasized elsewhere.[35] Consider an analogy. An aggregate-level object is positioned in space in virtue of the spatial position of its parts. But if it turns out that there is an infinite progression downwards in parts that will not mean that there is no such thing as spatial position. It will only mean that we must search in vain for basic or ultimate spatial occupants, as the parallel scenario would mean that we must search in vain for basic or ultimate producers.

As we mentioned in the paper, a possible and perhaps appealing metaphysic would say that there is a bottom level of causally relevant factors. This metaphysic would ensure, then, that those factors enjoy causal relevance in a unique sense: they are the only causally relevant factors that do not presuppose lower-level determinants and, by some accounts, they may be possessed of a special, irreducibilist efficacy.[36] But we are not committed to that metaphysic and we do not think that it implies epiphenomenalism about higher-level causality: after all, under this scenario, higher-level factors will still have the programming sense of causal relevance. The

[34] See e.g. Simon Blackburn, *Essays in Quasi-Realism*, New York: Oxford University Press, 1993: 205; Ned Block, 'Can the Mind Change the World?' in George Boolos (ed.), *Meaning and Method: Essays in Honor of Hilary Putnam*, Cambridge: Cambridge University Press, 1990: 137–70, at 168; Pierre Jacob, 'Externalism and Mental Causation', *Proceedings of the Aristotelian Society*, 92 (1991–2), 203–19; and esp. Graham Macdonald, 'The Nature of Naturalism', *Proceedings of the Aristotelian Society* (Supp.), 66 (1992), 225–44.

[35] Jackson and Pettit, 'Program Explanation: A General Perspective'; Pettit, *The Common Mind*, New York: Oxford University Press, 1993: 164.

[36] See Philip Pettit, 'The Nature of Naturalism', *Proceedings of the Aristotelian Society* (Supp.), 66 (1992), 245–66.

point of the program model is not to identify some uniquely privileged level of basic causality but rather to insist that higher-level causality is not emergent in relation to lower. There are higher-level as well as lower-level causal factors, not in virtue of higher, autonomous orders of causal power, but only in virtue of the programming architecture. The denial of the emergence of higher-level causality is no more the denial of higher-level causality than is the denial of the emergence of tables and chairs a denial of tables and chairs.

5
Altered States and Virtual Beliefs

JON OBERLANDER AND PETER DAYAN

1. INTRODUCTION

Functionalism derives its explanatory force from its firm grounding in the certainties of Turing machines (TMs) and their practical approximations, the von Neumann machines (vNMs). One branch of cognitive psychology, and its philosophical stablemate, has taken this doctrine seriously, and coupled it with some of the basic notions of folk psychology such as beliefs, desires, hopes, etc. Most of the theories are wedded rather firmly to these architectures, with all their connotations of logicality. They therefore face problems explaining the apparent *illogicality* and obvious *tractability* of human cognition. In desperation, some functionalists, whilst naturally retaining the Turing metaphor at the heart of their theories, have been forced to abandon these folk psychological constructs. The switch is either to instrumentalism, proposing that these constructs are *not* causal in producing behaviour but are still useful for explaining or predicting it [4], or else to a more radical position, holding that they are not even satisfactory for that [23].

Connectionism, for all its many faults, gives the first hint that something may be wrong with this retreat. It demonstrates that, despite essential computational equivalence, the strict analogy with TMs that has survived into vNMs is not the only way of conceiving of the functional mechanisms of thought. Furthermore, on broadening the range of possible mechanisms, it becomes apparent that too simplistic a notion of human competence is potentially dangerous. Unfortunately, connectionism seems rather remote architecturally and representationally from high-level psychological entities, so some *independent* motivation behind alternative functional mechanisms is required.

Section 2 works through some of the reasoning behind instrumentalism, involving such problems as virtual beliefs and inferential tractability, and discusses certain conditions under which the
instrumentalist retreat may be avoidable. Section 3 sketches out a
view of functionalist mechanisms that satisfies these conditions.
Section 4 concludes that the case for abandoning folk psychology,
an unattractive move in the absence of a viable alternative, is not
yet proven.

2. COMPETENCE, PERFORMANCE, AND VIRTUAL BELIEF

The process of 'systematizing' folk psychology involves constructing a functionalist tableau around its basic entities such as beliefs
and desires, and its basic notions of how they interact. In cartoon
form, one such notion might be 'if person A believes that doing B
will result in C, and desires that C, then, all else being equal, A
will do B'. Folk psychology is not systematic in any functionalist
sense, and does not concern itself with mechanism or the causal
efficacy or otherwise of its entities.

The overall tableaux most commonly suggested involve sentential
belief boxes and desire boxes containing the beliefs and desires
respectively, together with central processors that execute the 'rules'.
Although this is but a crude sketch, it has two key features that are
common to most such postulations: the one-by-one consideration
of the folk psychological entities; and the variously expressed commitment to some variety of logic for the rule-processing. As hinted
above, both of these are strongly associated with the traditional
view of the vNM.

It is important to remember that one cannot attack *all* system-
atizations by merely attacking one. In fact, the ongoing debate
about folk psychology between Stich [23], Dennett [5], Fodor [9],
and many others, is conducted *solely* about the kind of model just
outlined. Opponents of the *Language of Thought* (LoT) type doctrine point to various flaws and apparent absurdities in the inferences it suggests. They then either reject folk psychology totally,
or else suggest that its efficacy is merely approximate, and that its
entities are not real, extant, and causal, but merely abstract calculating devices with which one can predict behaviour. The former

view seems a little churlish given that folk psychology seems on the face of it to be the only theory that has any predictive power. The latter view is at root unattractive since it is not accompanied by any compelling alternative causal entities. However, if the problems for folk psychology suggested by Dennett and others are indeed damaging in the way posited, instrumentalism would be the only course open. We shall proceed by establishing and examining the framework within which the objections are cast.

2.1. Competence and incompetence

The first objection comes from a concern about the mechanistic relevance of Chomskian [2] competence theory rather than a performance theory. On the one hand, there is the competence of the undistracted, resource-unlimited ideal thinker. On the other, there is the performance of distracted, error-prone real thinkers. Dennett (1987: 76) has emphasized the significance of the correct choice of competence model for psychological theorizing. If we get the competence model badly wrong, any performance model based on it will be full of artefactual results and *ad hoc* mechanisms. Poor results with this performance model will tend to reflect back on the competence model. Dennett says that:

The fact about competence models that provokes my 'instrumentalism' is that the decomposition of one's competence model into parts, phases, states, steps, or whatever *need* shed no light at all on the decomposition of actual mechanical parts, phases, states, or steps of the system being modeled—even when the competence model is, as a competence model, excellent. (Dennett, 1987: 76)

Any competence model that suggests that human reasoning is fundamentally logical runs up against problems such as those from human conditional reasoning. In some tasks [20, 14], 97 per cent of humans fail to satisfy the logical idealization, so the LoT might in fact rather be called an *In*competence model. This is not in itself destructive of the LoT, since it is always possible to multiply entities to save the phenomena. Further arguments below about virtual belief are more persuasive.

It is important to realize that the truth of the quotation and the unpalatable facts about logical reasoning are not arguments against *all* possible systematized folk psychology, only against the LoT version. Of course, competence theories may say nothing about performance mechanisms, but that does not absolve them from empirical and theoretical study. If, as in the case of purely logical inference, incompetence is found to be rife, and furthermore achieving competence is known to be computationally intractable, it follows that the competence model is incorrect. Note also a possible lacuna made apparent by this; if the competence model is too far divorced from performance, it is useless even for instrumental theorizing, since its predictions will be invalid.

2.2 *Virtual belief*

Dennett does not reject the LoT view on account of conditional reasoning data. He prefers rather to look at the more complex case of virtual beliefs. They provide an interesting test case in view of the alternative explanation available from the memory machine picture that will be established in Section 3.

When describing what someone believes, we can distinguish at least three significantly different cases. Take Neil. He believes that Margaret is Prime Minister. No doubt he also believes that 30001 > 30000. And we judge, watching him play chess, that he believes that you should get the queen out early. In making these ascriptions, we have traded on three different kinds of belief. The belief about Margaret is probably something that Neil has actively considered and has stored (after the 1987 general election, perhaps). As such, it is perhaps an *explicit* belief. The belief about the numbers he probably never entertained before, but would assent to immediately if asked. It's something that his other beliefs, about numbers and arithmetic, commit him to. Indeed, it could perhaps be inferred, via a laborious logical proof, from what he explicitly believes. Let's call this an *implicit* belief. Given this ostensive definition, it should be obvious that Neil is committed to an infinite number of such implicit beliefs. Finally, his belief about chess is something he has never entertained before, that he might not admit, and perhaps cannot infer from his explicit beliefs. It too is implicit in the way he behaves. But to distinguish it from the second case, let us call it an *emergent* belief. Implicit and emergent beliefs are sometimes known as *virtual* beliefs.

Now, if we assume the LoT model of inferential behaviour, we must constrain our theorizing about possible performance models to be compatible with both the competence model, and with some of the hard facts about explicit and virtual belief. Since reasoning is fundamentally logical, but humans rarely seem to believe all the consequences of their beliefs, it is tempting to build a performance model of reasoning along the following lines.

Explicit beliefs form a core library of axioms. A logical inference device, commonly called the 'extrapolator-deducer' (XD), derives implicit beliefs from these axioms by applying the internal rules of inference [9, 4]. If you ask Neil about the number 30001, he will be able to derive the belief in question very rapidly. Emergent beliefs don't quite fit into this picture, and proposals have been made that they are not really represented, either statically (as explicit beliefs) or on demand (as implicit beliefs), but are really 'there' as properties of the architecture of the belief retrieval system [16].

This is a performance model made in hell. Various problems with it are well known. The XD must have its own stock of beliefs in order to know which beliefs to use in deduction. The power of the XD will vary from person to person. The number of inference steps the XD can take in (say) 100ms is arbitrarily fixed at (say) 15—but we can't tell which logical system the XD is using. There are some implicit beliefs that the XD should be able to infer that it can't, and vice versa. Further, it is really not at all obvious that an account of emergent beliefs can be grafted onto the XD. In what sense does the 'Get the queen out early' belief reside in the activity of the XD?

Dennett expresses these problems with performance models of virtual belief effectively in his description of a machine designed to get jokes about Newfoundlanders. He supplies a joke (but attributes it to Pylyshyn), and lists various propositions we have to believe if we're to get the joke, and states:

Not only do these beliefs not 'come to mind' . . . but it is also highly implausible to suppose that each and every one of them is consulted, independently, by a computational mechanism designed to knit up the lacunæ in the story by a deductive generation process. . . . The list of beliefs gives us a good general idea of the information that must be in the head, but if we view it as a list of axioms from which a derivational procedure deduces the 'point of the joke,' we may have the sketch of a performance model, but it is a particularly ill-favored performance model. (Dennett, 1987: 77)

Following this argument leaves only two options to those who insist on rejecting all systematized folk psychology on the basis of the performance inadequacies of the LoT; one can either retain folk psychology (and *a fortiori* its entities such as belief) as an instrumental, non-causal theory, or one can reject it altogether. A third option, which is followed below, is to suggest an alternative systematization.

It bears notice that Dennett's preferred option, the first of the above, involves a certain prestidigitation. If folk psychology is to be useful to us in predicting and explaining other people's behaviour, we must have a way of using *their* assertions of beliefs and desires appropriately. If the theory is so incoherent, intractable, or implausible, that these entities cannot be implicated in *causing* the behaviour, how can they be implicated in *explaining* or *predicting* it? Dennett also faces criticism from the radical anti-folk psychologists such as Stich [23], who argue that having rejected causality, to retain beliefs and desires, etc., in explaining behaviour is like explaining planetary motion in terms of Ptolemaic epicycles whilst rejecting their entire basis.

Ruling systematized folk psychology out of court is a fundamentally unattractive course, since there is no equally predictive, let alone better, replacement. Such a move can be avoided if some alternative XD theory can be developed, particularly one that has independent motivation. This is the aim of the next section.

3. ALTERED STATES

In searching for new and fruitful analogies with which to extend and defend their models of cognition, functionalists continually find their writing room limited by fundamental Turing equivalence. Despite the possibilities of reimplementation and simulation of one such computational system by another, properties that have natural explanations in the one may seem mysterious in the other. By applying, and then extending, one such transformation, we will attempt to demonstrate this constructively, and to produce a model of memory that can be used in an alternate extrapolator-deducer theory.

The obvious evolutionary path from the TM architecture to

the vNM architecture is to leave unchanged the nature and role of the central processor (the reader) and its states, but to regard the memory of the vNM as a *finite* tape. Arbitrary locations on this virtual tape can be accessed in $O(1)$ rather than $O(N)$ time, where N is its virtual length. The ability easily to write to, or read from, arbitrary locations makes a vNM considerably easier to program than a TM, and the (almost) size-independent read/write times, makes a large class of algorithms computationally feasible. However, the recent debate pitting Reduced Instruction Set (RISC) against Complex Instruction Set (CISC) microprocessors points to an obvious trade-off that, as described, is rather hidden in the detail of Turing universality. Specifically, there is a balance between the complexity of the set of states and state transitions of the central processor on the one hand, and the complexity and length of the programs that perform a task, on the other.

Since the memory of a vNM is finite, one can take this view on complexity further. We can draw the 'state versus tape' boundary around not only the central processor, but also some or all of the memory. Under the new description, states represent not only the contents of the internal flags and registers of the microprocessor, but also the entire contents of memory—roughly, all the transistors that comprise the operation of the machine. This new description is precisely that of the entire computer as a finite state machine (FSM), which of course is exactly what its finite memory permits it to be. State transitions are instigated just as before by the operation of the central processor, but *now* the state transition diagram is extremely rich and complex. The way that von Neumann machines are designed has the effect of enforcing what might be described as *locality* in this state transition diagram. That is, if the states were 'ordered' in an appropriate way,[1] most of the possible next states themselves would be local.

The new complexity and richness of the set of states and state transition diagram in this alternative viewpoint accounts for the infrequency of its adoption. But it is precisely the *attraction* for us. The distinctions between program and storage appear considerably eroded, and we will go on to erode them even further. Note that at this stage this is only an alternative perspective of exactly

[1] By the 'invisible' values of the program counter, the registers and flags, the possible values of the memory location pointed to by that program counter and then all the other possible values of all the other memory locations.

the same machine, which is condemned to traverse exactly the same states and execute in the same way exactly the same programs.

Various key properties of computation look very different on this alternative picture of the vNM, particularly symbolic representation and the potentially holistic influence of memory. What could previously be identified as separate contents of memory can only be found, if at all, in the *labels* of a whole set of states; and the labels, of course, have no causal role in engendering the behaviour of the system. It is therefore no longer even sensible to try to isolate out particular symbol structures stored at particular places in memory, or to determine the nature and provenance of their logical effects. The symbol-processing properties of the whole machine are entirely emergent from the dynamics of the simple low-level entities.

In addition, the whole of memory is wrapped up in a state, so moving from one state to another could correspond to a radical change in its entire contents. Of course, the vNM architecture prevents such transitions from happening. Memory is like tape, inviolate except serially. A rational explanation for this severe constraint is that such radical changes are potentially dangerous in the absence of any well-founded method of policing them. However, different mechanisms for state transition need not necessarily labour under such constraints.

Removing another such bar could allow the whole contents of memory not only to be changed by such a state transition, but also to determine which state transition occurs. This new picture naturally encompasses a much richer theory of the interaction between memory and inference, mediated in a complex fashion by the hardware of the machine. It would also appear to be more commensurable with the views on cognition of Maturana and Varela [18]. They consider the nervous system less as a machine responding as a program to a set of inputs with a set of outputs, and more as a system whose states and dynamical state transitions are affected by all its components. Some of these will have characteristics partly determined by events in the external world.

We do not have, and indeed to respond to Dennett do not need, a sophisticated picture of how to develop from the above picture a complete XD. The naïve mechanism which will suffice may best be imagined as some form of PROLOG system whose inferences are executed on one computer, but whose database and short-term memory are stored on another. The first requests rules and facts from the second, and demands that changes be made in the light of its inferences. Although continuing to view the first computer, the inference engine, in a traditional way, though not of course as a PROLOG machine, we will investigate the consequences of considering alternative mechanisms underlying the function of the second computer, the memory machine, by further developing the above picture. This general view of the relationship between memory and inference in an XD has a number of defenders, e.g. Anderson [1].

Consider now the memory machine (MM). Under a traditional description it would contain symbols, and would be searched (subject to a request from the inference engine) according to some criteria, such as 'find a script containing doctors', or 'what is the capital of France?', or the like. Under the new description, the answers to such queries can be determined from the state the MM occupies, and its own searching procedure for finding the required information can be seen in the set of states traversed. However, on this picture, it is natural to contemplate altering the hardware of the machine, the complex system that applies the rules for moving from one state to another, and consequently changing the whole *modus operandi* and output of the MM.

One such change is to consider the states as the local minima of some function (perhaps an *energy function*, for want of a better term), and the state transitions as movements from one local minimum to another (*cf.* [13, 10]). The hardware can be considered as moving the system around the energy surface, according to its principles, landing up in states at the local minima. Learning changes the energy surface so as to alter either the minima, or the traversable paths from one minimum to another, and consequently the states actually entered (roughly the memories recalled) by the MM under given conditions. This, as advertised, licenses state transitions *other* than those allowed by the vNM. Now, the whole contents of memory are causally implicated in every move.

The appeal of making this change is that it's much easier to see how to build a human-like memory (if not actually to do so). Contextual flexibility, associational memory, and inferential error, can all be given natural explanations on this model. Of course, we are not able to specify either the energy function, or the mechanisms that are sensitive to it, but in that respect we are no worse off than other functionalists, and need only demonstrate possible Fodorian 'floating straws'.

The evolutionary sequence has been as follows. First we had the Turing machine. Then we had the von Neumann machine as the implementation of a finite TM. Then we had the vNM as a finite state machine. And finally we reached alternative mechanisms for state transition in an FSM, and consequently alternative state transitions. This motivates and locates a (connectionist) dynamical picture of the mechanisms of mind. It also neatly demonstrates the difficulties connectionists are bound to have in talking about symbolic representation in their models. Even when we know that the symbols are explicitly emergent, as in the FSM description of the vNM, they are elusive, to say the least.

We have previously [3] linked related notions of local *max*imization (reversing the sign) with those of Elster [7], Doyle [6], and Simon [21]. Very briefly, the suggestion was that global maximization based on predictions of the future, which Elster claims to be criterial for rationality, is too difficult for mere machines (including us) in interesting domains. However, not all local maxima are as high as others, and one can understand Simon's satisficing, and consequently Doyle's ideas of rational psychology as utility maximization, in these terms. These maxima are actually on a longer and larger scale than the ones on which we concentrate in this paper, since here, the local maxima just define the raw material for the inference engine. However, large-scale *global* maximization cannot be based on small scale *local* maximization, which is the basis for our claim about the difficulty.

It is worth very briefly comparing the possible alternative views on representation. Symbols can vary on two dimensions: hard versus soft, and active versus passive. Hard symbols are like those to be found on a tape of a TM, in the memory of a vNM, or indeed in the localist models of Hofstadter [11, 12] or Feldman and Ballard [8]. They are hard in the sense that their semantic (and usually syntactic) boundaries are fixed at 'compile' time and do not vary during the course of a computation. Soft symbols are more like those of distributed connectionist models, or (hopefully) the emergent symbols of the MM described above. Their mutual semantic boundaries vary in a context-dependent way, and indeed are usually learnt during the operation of the system. The distinction between passive and active symbols is rather less precise, since it gets unhelpfully entangled with the differences between declarative and procedural representations. Passive symbols are like those in a typical frame-type system [19], in that they are more 'processed over' than 'processing' entities. Active symbols are just the reverse, as in Hoftstadter's fluid concepts or the holistic MM above. Adequate context-dependency and learning seem to require soft, active symbols, since all attempts at passive symbols seem to falter on the former criterion, and hard ones on the latter.

This section has attempted to motivate a significant move away from the traditional model of computation by taking seriously the obvious fact that a von Neumann machine has only finite memory. The reconceptualization involved can lead to an architecture where states are actually large dimensional vectors upon which soft symbols are emergent, and whose state transitions correspond to movements along some form of energy surface defined by the interactions between the various components in the system. The hard symbols of Turing-machine tapes and the active symbols of Hofstadter's and Feldman and Ballard's models are both rejected.

We are now in a position to evaluate the consequences for the behaviour of the overall XD, like Dennett's joke-getting system. We have changed the functioning of the MM, which of course stores both the rules consulted by the IM, and the memories used in executing the rules. The contextual flexibility built into the MM derives from the implication of the entire contents of memory in state transitions. Even in the naïve picture which has only those entities 'come to mind' that are passed from the MM to the IM, it is apparent that the implicit Newfoundlander-joke beliefs that gave Dennett so much trouble need never be passed into the IM. Instead, they can be causally implicated in the overall XD process by helping to determine which consciously 'observable' beliefs are selected during the non-von Neumann search.

Implicit beliefs generally gain a more natural explanation on this picture, since an intractable search amongst rules or memories is not necessary. Indeed, explanations can be imagined for more complex cocktails of repressed beliefs and their apparent effects in terms of modifications to the energy surface determining the search. Of course, this story is incomplete in the absence of an exact specification of the requisite 'all-singing, all-dancing' state-transition system, but work on connectionist memory systems demonstrates at least its potential feasibility, and that is all that is required.

4. CONCLUSIONS

In endorsing functionalism, it has traditionally been too easy to adopt a narrow view of computational mechanisms. The fact that two architectures may be equivalent in the Turing sense does *not* imply that the functional properties that can naturally be ascribed to one can naturally be ascribed to the other. Attempts to systematize folk psychology based on the narrow, logical view have failed. They have failed because of the obvious illogicality and tractability of human reasoning, and because of the implausibility of the inferences which the narrow view insists on. Instrumentalists with the *same* narrow view of mechanism conclude from this failure that the entities and notions of folk psychology are inherently wrong, and that all they can do is provide an abstract, non-realistic tool for computation.

An alternative conclusion is that it is not the entities and notions of folk psychology that are at fault. It is their *particular* systematization under the narrow view. A broader perspective can be adopted, one that can be motivated directly by two moves. First, we draw an alternative boundary between the central-processing unit and the memory of a von Neumann machine regarded in finite state terms. Secondly, we modify slightly the state-transition rules. Instrumentalism was at best unattractive because of its non-causal entities. With richer functional mechanism to hand, we can now reject it as an *un*necessary evil.

REFERENCES

[1] Anderson, J. R. (1983), *The Architecture of Cognition*, Cambridge, Mass.: Harvard University Press.

[2] Chomsky, N. (1965), *Aspects of the Theory of Syntax*. Cambridge, Mass.: MIT Press.

[3] Dayan, P., and Oberlander, J. (1989), *Maximal Mechanical Rationality*, Centre for Cognitive Science, Edinburgh.

[4] Dennett, D. C. (1978), *Brainstorms: Philosophic Essays on Mind and Psychology*, Cambridge, Mass.: MIT Press/Bradford Books.

[5] —— (1987), *The Intentional Stance*, Cambridge, Mass.: MIT Press/Bradford Books.

[6] Doyle, J. (1983), *Some Theories of Reasoned Assumptions: An Essay in Rational Psychology*, Tech. Rep. No. CMU-CS-83-125, Pittsburgh, Pa.: Carnegie Mellon University, Dept. of Computer Science.

[7] Elster, J. (1984), *Ulysses and the Sirens: Studies in Rationality and Irrationality*, revd. edn., Cambridge: Cambridge University Press.

[8] Feldman, J. A., and Ballard, D. H. (1982), 'Connectionist Models and Their Properties', *Cognitive Science*, 6: 205–54.

[9] Fodor, J. A. (1975), *The Language of Thought*, Hassocks, Sussex: Harvester Press.

[10] Hinton, G., Sejnowski, T., and Ackley, D. (1984), *Boltzmann Machines: Constraint Satisfaction Networks that Learn*, Tech. Rep. No. CMU-CS-84-119, Pittsburgh, Pa.: Carnegie Mellon University, Dept. of Computer Science.

[11] Hofstadter, D. R. (1979), *Gödel, Escher, Bach: An Eternal Golden Braid*, New York: Basic Books.

[12] —— Mitchell, M., and French, R. M. (1987), *Fluid Concepts and Creative Analogies: A Theory and its Computational Implementation*, FARG DOC 87-1, Ann Arbor, Mich.: University of Michigan.

[13] Hopfield, J. J. (1982), 'Neural Networks and Physical Systems with Emergent Collective Computational Abilities', *Proceedings of the National Academy of Sciences, USA*, 79: 2554–8.

[14] Johnson-Laird, P. N., and Wason, P. C. (1972), *Psychology of Reasoning: Structure and Content*, Cambridge, Mass.: Harvard University Press.

[15] Lycan, W. G. (1981), 'Form, Function, and Feel', *Journal of Philosophy*, 78: 24–50.

[16] —— (1988), *Judgement and Justification*, Cambridge: Cambridge University Press.

[17] Marr, D. (1982), *Vision*, San Francisco: Freeman.

[18] Maturana, H., and Varela, F. (1972), *De Maquinas y Seres Vivos*, Editorial Universitaria, Chile; published in English (1980), *Autopoiesis and Cognition: The Realization of the Living*, Dordrecht: Reidel.

[19] Minsky, M. (1975), 'A Framework for Representing Knowledge', in P. H. Winston (ed.), *The Psychology of Computer Vision*. New York: McGhaw-Hill, 211–77.

[20] Oaksford, M. R. (1988), *Cognition and Inquiry: An*

Investigation into the Psychosemantics of Conditional Reasoning, PhD thesis, Centre for Cognitive Science, Edinburgh.

[21] Simon, H. A. (1955), 'A Behavioral Model of Rational Choice', *Quarterly Journal of Economics,* 69: 99–118.

[22] Smolensky, P. (1988), 'On the Proper Treatment of Connectionism', *Behavioural and Brain Sciences,* 11: 1–23.

[23] Stich, S. (1983), *From Folk Psychology to Cognitive Science: The Case Against Belief,* Cambridge, Mass.: MIT Press.

[24] Winograd, T., and Flores, F. (1986), *Understanding Computers and Cognition: A New Foundation for Design,* Norwood, NJ: Ablex Publishing.

6

The Relation between Philosophical and Psychological Theories of Concepts

CHRISTOPHER PEACOCKE

———————◆———————

What should be the relation between our philosophical and our psychological theories of concepts? I will be outlining an answer to this question, and tracing out some of its consequences. It is impossible to answer the question without taking a stand on some fundamental issues about the nature of content, meaning, and understanding. The answer I will be giving also suggests an agenda for psychological and computational studies.

My excuse for discussing the issue at a conference which celebrates Turing's work is twofold. My lesser excuse is that what I have to say on meaning and content supports Turing's own position on these issues. When Turing attended Wittgenstein's lectures in Cambridge in the 1930s, he was a vigorous participant in the discussion, and objected to some of the claims that I will also be rejecting.[1] My major excuse for discussing these issues is that the view I will be defending can be seen as squarely supporting the realizability of Turing's broad vision of a computational explanation of human mental capacities.[2] The computational conception

My thanks to Paul Churchland, Martin Davies, and Michael Morris for helpful comments.

[1] See *Wittgenstein's Lectures on the Foundations of Mathematics: Cambridge, 1939*, Cora Diamond (ed.), Hassocks, Sussex: Harvester, 1976.

[2] See his paper 'Computing Machinery and Intelligence', *Mind*, 59 (1950), 433–60. He emphasized those 'functions of the mind' which are 'operations which we can explain in purely mechanical terms', and clearly held that 'the whole mind is mechanical' (454–5). His conception of what mechanism has to involve is now superseded. He identified machines with digital computers. I take it as clear that there is a sense in which the explanations appropriate for a connectionist system are still 'mechanical'. It would be an illuminating task to say exactly what is required for an explanation of psychological capacity to be mechanical. However,

would hardly be compelling if it had to exclude conceptual thought from its purview. If what I have to say is right, no such exclusion is necessary.

1. The first step in answering our question about the relation between philosophical and psychological theories of concepts is to form a clear conception of the goals and nature of a philosophical theory of concepts. I use the term 'concept' in such a way that concepts C and D are distinct if a rational thinker can believe a given content containing the concept C without believing the corresponding content which results from substituting D for C in the given content. By this test, *now* and *9.45 p.m.* as employed in thought by you now are distinct concepts; so are *I* and *Descartes*, even as employed by Descartes; so are the relatively observational concepts *square* and *regular-diamond-shaped*, even though they are true of things of exactly the same shape. So, in very broad terms, these concepts are at Frege's level of sense rather than his level of reference. This is not the only meaning given to the term 'concept' in the cognitive science literature, and certainly not the only legitimate meaning.[3] In that literature, the term 'concept' is sometimes used to mean a prototype, and sometimes used for the mental representation of either a concept or a prototype. Concepts as intended here are distinct from prototypes and from mental representations, and I believe they are indispensable.

It should be a goal of a philosophical theory of concepts to explain all those cognitive, epistemological, and semantical phenomena displayed by a concept (or a family of concepts) which are dependent only upon the identity of that particular concept (or family of concepts). We want an explanation of why a rational subject while he must believe that now is now, can fail to believe that now is 9.45 p.m.; of why Descartes can, when engaged in radical doubt, doubt that Descartes is thinking but not doubt that he is thinking; of why thoughts built up from particular concepts can be true though unverifiable; and so forth. It is plain then that

for my excuse for discussing these issues to be a good one, only this has to be true: on any plausible way of elucidating the notion of a 'mechanical' explanation, if the views for which I am arguing are false, some capacities of the mind will not have a mechanical explanation.

[3] This will be rapidly apparent to any reader of the various papers and discussions in the issue of *Mind and Language*, 4/1–2 (1989) devoted to concepts.

a philosophical theory of concepts must address many of the central classical questions of philosophy. The theory will aim to say what is distinctive of the identity of particular concepts, and to derive an explanation of the cognitive, semantic, and epistemological phenomena from this statement of what individuates the particular concepts in question.

The philosophical treatment of the individuation of concepts must fall into two parts. There will be a statement of the general form which must be taken by any account of what individuates a particular concept. There will then be statements, of that specified general form, of what individuates various particular concepts. My own view is that a concept is to be individuated by an account of what it is for a thinker to possess the concept: that is, the concept is individuated by its *possession condition*. If this is correct, then the general form to be taken by any account of what individuates a particular concept *F* would be this:

> the concept *F* is that concept *C* to possess which a thinker has to meet the condition *A*(*C*).

The 'is' which occurs in this form is identity. It is also required for non-circularity that the concept *F* not be mentioned as the concept *F* within the scope those propositional attitudes of the thinker which occur in '*A*(*C*)'. In a true statement of this form, what replaces '*A*(*C*)' is a statement of the possession condition for the given concept *F*. I refer to this general form as 'the *A*(*C*) form'.[4]

So, to take a maximally trivial case, a plausible possession condition for the logical concept of conjunction is this:

> conjunction is that concept *C* to possess which a thinker must find transitions of the following forms primitively compelling, and must do so because they are of these forms:
>
> $$\frac{A \quad B}{ACB} \qquad \frac{ACB}{A} \qquad \frac{ACB}{B}.$$

This statement of a possession condition does not use 'and' or any of its synonyms within the scope of the thinker's propositional attitudes. What is meant by saying that transitions of these forms

---

[4] There is further discussion of this form and its role in a theory of concepts in my paper 'What are Concepts?', *Midwest Studies in Philosophy*, 14 (1989), 1–28.

are found 'primitively' compelling is that the thinker finds them compelling, and does not do so because he has inferred them from anything else, and is not required to take them as answerable to anything else in order to possess the concept in question.

It is arguable that the possession condition for any concept must make use at some point of the notion of what the thinker finds primitively compelling. I take this to be one of the conclusions to be drawn from Wittgenstein's discussion of rule-following, if it is correct. It is the point Wittgenstein emphasizes when discussing the sense in which someone who has grasped a particular rule or a particular concept has already settled how to apply it in some future case. Wittgenstein wrote:

'All the steps are really already taken' means: I no longer have any choice. The rule, once stamped with a particular meaning, traces the lines along which it is to be followed through the whole of space—But if something of this sort really were the case, how would it help?

No; my description only made sense if it was to be understood symbolically. I should have said: *This is how it strikes me.*

When I obey a rule, I do not choose.

I obey the rule *blindly*.[5]

Of course, it is important to remember that one way in which the notion of what is primitively compelling can enter a possession condition is by way of a requirement that a concept be applied to an object if a theory involving that concept, and which meets specified conditions, entails that the concept applies to that object.

A wide variety of different kinds of condition can instantiate the $A(C)$ form. For some concepts, the possession condition will speak of the commitments incurred in judging certain contents containing the concept. It is plausible that the concept of universal quantification should be treated in this way. For relatively observational concepts, by contrast, a possession condition should anchor mastery of the concept in a level of non-conceptual representational content of perceptual experience. For instance, someone with the perceptually based concept *regular-diamond-shaped* will meet the following condition. Suppose he is taking his experience at face value; suppose too that something is presented to him in perception as occupying a regular-diamond-shaped region of the space in his environment; and suppose finally that he perceives the object

---

[5] *Philosophical Investigations*, sect. 219.

as symmetrical about the bisectors of its angles. Then he must find it primitively compelling that the object so presented falls under the concept *regular-diamond-shaped*. For this as for other possession conditions, there must also be another clause which explains what is involved in having the capacity to judge of an unperceived object that it falls under the concept.

The $A(C)$ form can accommodate the all-pervasive phenomenon of families of concepts which can be grasped only simultaneously. For such a family, a possession condition should be given simultaneously for all the concepts in the family by giving something of this form:

> concepts $F_1, \ldots, Fn$ are those concepts $C_1, \ldots, Cn$ to possess which a thinker must meet the condition $A(C_1, \ldots, C_n)$.

Finally, to emphasize the scope of the $A(C)$ form, I should note that nothing in this conception of possession conditions as so far expounded precludes the possibility that a possession condition should mention the thinker's relation to his environment; or properties of any society of which he is a member; or features of his use of a certain expression he may have for the concept. Whether this is necessary or possible will turn on further argument about the particular concept in question. The same applies to the question of whether the concept must be expressed in the thinker's language, and to whether the thinker has to have a language.

A philosophical theory of concepts must also incorporate an account of the relations of concepts to the level of reference. After all, concepts are constituents of complete contents which are evaluable as true or false. The truth-value of a complete content is a function of the semantic values of its constituents. The philosophical theory has to explain how a semantic value can be determined from a possession condition, together with the world (in all but the logical and a few other cases). For the example of conjunction, the semantic value is that truth-function which makes inferences of the forms cited always truth-preserving. This is the classical truth-function for conjunction. If the semantic value for the concept is fixed this way, it is guaranteed that transitions of the form mentioned in the possession condition are *correct*, in the sense of never leading from true premises to a false conclusion.

The preceding is just about the briefest possible overview that could be given of a philosophical theory of concepts. A full philosophical treatment has to put to work the possession conditions it proposes and explain the phenomena specific to particular concepts and to particular types of concept. It has also to deal with a range of objections and queries about the framework itself, including queries about the ontology of concepts. However, I think we have enough in this overview to raise the question of how we should conceive of the relation between a philosophical theory of concepts and psychological theories.

2. One view is that philosophical and psychological theories of concepts should be relatively independent of one another. On this view, philosophers and psychologists have no professional reasons, beyond such incidental matters as intellectual stimulation, for reading each others' journals. A holder of this view will urge the distinctness of the goals of the philosopher and the psychologist when each theorizes about concepts. The possession conditions supplied by the philosopher have a relatively a priori character. The psychologist, by contrast, will give empirical accounts of such matters as the acquisition of a concept; of how attitudes involving the concept are formed; of the influence of the desires and the emotions on attitudes; and so forth. Like any other theories we accept, we will want our philosophical and psychological theories of concepts to be jointly consistent. But, according to this view of their relative independence, there is no closer connection between the two theories. In particular, to attain the goals of each theory, we do not need to make use of the results of the other theory.

I will be disputing that view. Here is a very simple account of one relation which should hold between a philosophical theory of a particular concept and a psychological theory of the same concept: when a thinker possesses a particular concept, an adequate subpersonal psychology should explain why the thinker meets the concept's possession condition.[6] We can call this 'the Simple Account'. On the Simple Account, one of the goals of a psychological theory makes reference to something which is the concern of a

---

[6] 'Sub-personal theories proceed by analyzing a person into an organization of subsystems ... and attempting to explain the behavior of the whole person as the outcome of the interaction of these subsystems', D. C. Dennett, *Brainstorms*, Montgomery, Vt: Bradford Books, 1978, 153. For the way the term 'subpersonal' is used in the present paper, 'behaviour' in Dennett's characterization should be replaced by 'behaviour and psychological properties'. (The resulting characterization remains within the spirit of Dennett's approach.)

philosophical theory, viz. a concept's possession condition. So the Simple Account denies the relative independence of philosophical and psychological theories of concepts. I will be endorsing this Simple Account.

In defending the view, we must distinguish between explaining why a thinker meets the possession condition for a concept and explaining how the thinker came to acquire the concept. We can compare the case with explaining why some object is a reflector. An explanation of why an object is a reflector will proceed by stating that light consists of a stream of photons, and stating how the physical properties of the surface of the object affect the behaviour of photons which strike it. Such an explanation of why the object reflects light is neutral on how the object came to acquire the surface properties which make it a reflector. Many different explanations of its acquisition of this property are consistent with the correctness of this explanation of why, now, it reflects light. Though for reasons I will touch upon later, the case of the reflector lacks many of the complexities of psychological cases, one further similarity of structure exists. For an object to be a reflector, it has to have the capacity to play a certain role in transitions (involving light). When a thinker meets the possession condition for a concept, there will be, in given circumstances, specified transitions he makes between mental states some of which involve the concept. It is a task for a subpersonal psychology equally to say why, now, he makes those transitions in the given circumstances.

A proposed psychological explanation has to meet various requirements if it is to explain why a thinker meets the possession condition for a given concept. The first requirement is that the subpersonal psychological properties it mentions do not presuppose that the thinker possesses the concept in question. If it does presuppose such possession, the putative explanation will be circular.

This requirement of non-circularity is by no means a general requirement on subpersonal psychological explanations. On the contrary, when for instance we are considering the different topic of the psychological explanation of linguistic understanding, it is important to mention states which *do* presuppose that the thinker has the concepts expressed in the language. Consider those theories which explain a thinker's understanding of an utterance by citing subpersonal mechanisms which draw on information about

the semantic properties of the constituent words of the utterance.[7]
On these theories, the meaning of the utterance is computed from
subpersonal information about the meaning of its parts. It is essential for such theories that at least some of the constituents of
the information drawn upon be concepts possessed by the thinker
at the personal level. The subpersonal information that an object
satisfies 'is square' just in case it is square must involve the same
concept *square* as is used in giving the meaning of sentences containing the public predicate 'is square'. If it did not, the mechanisms would not compute the right meaning for an utterance
containing 'is square'. This presupposition of concept possession
by the explanatory subpersonal states is in order as long as what
we are out to explain is why the thinker understands sentences in
a particular way. For that purpose, we can take for granted his
possession of the concepts in question. We cannot do so, however,
when our concern is with the explanation of concept mastery
itself.

It is probably true that there is no concept for which we know
the full subpersonal psychological explanation of why humans
meet its possession condition. But we do have partial subpersonal
explanations of how humans can be in some of the states mentioned in some possession conditions. We also have accounts of
hypothetical subpersonal mechanisms which could explain a thinker's meeting a possession condition. I will consider two examples,
one of each of these sorts.

As an example of the first sort, consider the concept possessed
by the mature English speaker-hearer of the (spoken) word *vat*.
The speaker-hearer can recognize utterances of the word on particular occasions, and has such beliefs as that the word means in
English a certain kind of container. As is well known, there is no
straightforward correlation of the acoustic properties over time
with the way an utterance is heard. No acoustic property is common to the middle of one-syllable words we perceive as containing
a short vowel *a* sound. It is not a temporal sequence of three
acoustic properties of an utterance which cause it to be heard as
an utterance of the word *vat*. At any given time in an utterance

---

[7] See M. Davies 'Tacit Knowledge, and the Structure of Thought and Language',
in C. Travis (ed.), *Meaning and Interpretation*, Oxford: Blackwell, 1986: 127–58,
and my 'Explanation in Computational Psychology: Language, Perception and
Level 1.5', *Mind and Language*, 1 (1986), 101–23.

of the word, several properties, which contribute to the identification of more than one of the constituent phonemes, may be instantiated.[8]

The possession condition for this concept of the word *vat.* will mention the sensitivity of the thinker's judgements that an utterance falls under this concept to his perceptions of it. A subpersonal psychology must explain how the subject is able to perceive the word in this way. It is a widely accepted hypothesis that devices in the subject subpersonally compute the sequence of three sets of phonological features of the acoustic event, viz.:

$$
\begin{bmatrix}
+\text{consonant} \\
-\text{stop} \\
+\text{voiced} \\
-\text{nasal} \\
\text{labial}
\end{bmatrix}
\begin{bmatrix}
-\text{consonant} \\
-\text{high} \\
+\text{front} \\
-\text{round}
\end{bmatrix}
\begin{bmatrix}
+\text{consonant} \\
+\text{stop} \\
-\text{voiced} \\
-\text{nasal} \\
\text{dental}
\end{bmatrix}
$$

This is certainly the beginning of an explanation. It is only the beginning, because we also need an account of how these features are computed, and a more philosophical or constitutive account of what it is for these features, rather than some others, to be computed. It is also important to note that it is the assigned phonological features themselves which contribute to the explanation of the way in which the utterance is heard. Had the '-voiced' feature been assigned in the first segment, all else remaining the same, then the utterance would have been heard as the word *fat* instead.

The phonological features computed in the perception of the word *vat* do not presuppose that the subject has the concept of the word *vat*. The subpersonal account can contribute to an explanation of the thinker's meeting the possession condition for the relevant concept of the spoken word. It should also be emphasized that the subpersonal contents—the phonological features—which the subpersonal account here relies upon are not to be taken as themselves concepts possessed by the thinker. A final point about this example is that it illustrates that a subpersonal explanation which contributes to an account of why a thinker meets a possession condition is not necessarily exclusively 'internalist'. It may invoke states which are individuated in part by their relations to matters outside the subject. What makes it the case that the content of a

---

[8] For a survey, see 'Phonetic Perception' by A. Lieberman and M. Studdert-Kennedy, in R. Held, H. Leibowitz, and H.-L. Teuber (eds.), *Handbook of Sensory Physiology* viii, Berlin: Springer, 1978.

given state involves the feature 'labial' rather than something else is presumably a complex function of its relation to perceived utterances in which the tongue is used in a certain way.

The second example I want to consider is concerned with a hypothetical explanation—it aims to illustrate the possibility of explanations of a certain kind. Consider the possession condition given earlier for the concept of conjunction. It contains the requirement that the thinker find inferences of certain forms compelling in part *because* they are of those forms. What could explain the thinker's meeting this condition, and indeed how is it possible at all? After all, what is here called a 'form' is a form of transition between contents. Whether these contents are Fregean Thoughts or neo-Russellian propositions, it is far from clear how the form of such a thing can causally influence a thinker. This implies that it is unclear how one part of the possession condition for conjunction can be true of a thinker.

There is a familiar type of subpersonal psychology which could explain how and why this part of the possession condition can hold of a thinker. (There is no commitment here to the claim that it is the only type of theory capable of such explanations.) First, the psychology gives a description of how the state of finding something primitively compelling is subpersonally realized. It will do this in tandem with whatever notion of mental representation it employs. It will say, for a given thinker, what property has to be possessed by a mental representation with a certain content for the thinker to find that content primitively compelling. Second, the theory states that there are types of mental representation corresponding to particular concepts, and which can be combined in some subpersonal functional analogue of concatenation to form mental representations of complex contents. That is, it endorses the hypothesis of a language of thought. If the theory meets these two conditions, then a mental representation of an inference will involve a mental representation of its premiss and a mental representation of its conclusion. Such a theory can postulate a mechanism which ensures the following: the mental representation of an inference is assigned the subpersonal property which realizes the property of being found primitively compelling if the mental representations of premiss and conclusion are themselves of certain forms. Since *these* forms are forms of token representations, rather than forms of abstract objects or something in Frege's third realm, there is no problem of principle of how they can be causally influential.

As a hypothetical explanation of how and why the possession condition holds, this description of course presumes upon the correctness of several philosophical accounts underwriting its assignment of particular contents to mental representations. None the less, it does seem that if a psychological theory of this sort were correct, it would offer a genuine empirical explanation of why the thinker fulfils one part of the possession condition for conjunction. Again, the explanation is not one which presupposes that the thinker already has the concept of conjunction.

Having some subpersonal realization (for our thinker) of the property of finding a given content primitively compelling is an essential part of this account. We would lose explanatory power if there were mental representations of the premiss and conclusion of the inference, but no subpersonal realization of the property of finding something primitively compelling. For in those circumstances there would be no subpersonal explanation of why the thinker finds inferences mentally represented in a certain way primitively compelling. It would be a brute fact, and we would be without any explanation of why the thinker goes on one way rather than another when presented with a new inference of the forms in question.

So much for the requirement that the explanation not presuppose possession of the concept in question. A second general requirement on a psychological explanation of a thinker's meeting a possession condition is actually already illustrated by the most recent example. An adequate psychological explanation of a thinker's meeting a possession condition must give some subpersonal account of what is involved in his finding a content primitively compelling. When a theory does give such an account, I call it *response-absorbent*.

A subpersonal account of a thinker's state of finding something primitively compelling must involve describing that state in other, non-folk-psychological ways. Of course, both connectionist models and non-connectionist versions of language-of-thought models are potential sources of such non-folk-psychological characterizations.

For a subpersonally characterized state to realize a content-involving personal-level state stringent conditions must be met. Suppose it is constitutively required for something to be a particular personal-level content-involving state that it stand in a network of actual and possible causal relations to certain other personal-level states and external events. Then any subpersonal realization of that state must stand in the same network of actual and possible causal relations to those other states and events. It is this requirement which allows the Simple Account to respect the distinction between explaining why a certain transition takes place between two subpersonally characterized states, and explaining why some component of a possession condition holds. The latter is our target; and we achieve it only if the subpersonal states we mention stand in the required network of relations to realize the personal-level content-involving states mentioned in the component of the possession condition.

Does the statement that a subpersonal state realizes the property of a thinker's finding a content primitively compelling commit us to the possibility of some subpersonal reduction of any concept involved in the content which is found primitively compelling? Far from it. Finding some content primitively compelling involves judging that content. The possession conditions for the concepts in that content will determine what in turn is involved in something's being a judgement with that content. In general, those possession conditions may require that something is a judgement involving a concept, of *fairness*, for instance, only if it displays some specified sensitivity to whether decisions or institutions are fair. Such a requirement applies *a fortiori* to a primitively compelling judgement that something is fair. A subpersonal realization of some state described at the personal level must stand in the same actual and counterfactual relations as the state it realizes. It would follow that we cannot even say what it is for something to be a subpersonal realization of a primitively compelling judgement that something is fair without including conditions which relate that state to what *is* fair. Subpersonal reductions of concepts are then not in the offing here, and are not required for present purposes.

Non-folk-psychological characterizations of a state need not be completely free of any use of a notion of content. In fact they involve some notion of content in the phonological example. But it does seem to be true that, if a fully explanatory psychology is to be possible, transitions between content-involving states must ultimately be explained by transitions which are not characterized in content-involving terms. Suppose two suggestions were made:

(i) that some event α say, with content A explains the occurrence of an event β with content B, and (ii) that also there is no further explanation of why this holds. This would be highly problematic. The event α will have the content A because of a complex network of relations in which it stands. The event β will similarly have the content B because of some different network of relations in which it stands. These relational properties may, for example, have to do with the causal antecedents of α, if α is an event in a subpersonal visual computation. Or they may have to do with the inferential or computational behaviour of some type of representation in α within transitions other than the one presently in question. In general it seems that whatever the relevant relational properties of α are, they are not the ones which are efficacious in the production of the event β. Here I assume that the events α and β are not themselves individuated in content-involving terms, but are (for example) neurophysiological events. It should be emphasized that this point continues to apply with full force if the content A is 'narrow'—not involving matters outside the subject's head—rather than 'broad'.[9] The conceptual component *or*, for instance, is narrow if anything is. But what (say) makes it the case that a belief's state has a content *A or B* is in part that in suitable circumstances the subject would move into it from the belief that A alone and equally from the belief that B alone. These are relational facts about this narrow component of the content. Yet (overdetermination and pre-emption aside), the description of the case involving α and β still commits us to the counterfactual: if there had not been an event with content A, then there would not have been an event with content B. Like any other counterfactual, it is not plausible that this one can be barely true, i.e. true but not true in virtue of any feature of the actual world.[10] One way for it not to be barely true is for there to be some locally causally influential property of the event α, a property which in the organism represents the content A. It is this locally causally influential property which, in the context, causally explains the occurrence of β. β will

[9] This point is noted also by F. Jackson and P. Pettit, in 'Functionalism and Broad Content', in *Mind*, 97 (1988), 381–400, at 392. On narrow and broad content more generally, see the papers in P. Pettit and J. McDowell (eds.), *Subject, Thought, and Context*, Oxford: Clarendon Press, 1986.

[10] See M. Dummett, 'What is a Theory of Meaning? (II)', in G. Evans and J. McDowell (eds.), *Truth and Meaning*, Oxford: Clarendon Press, 1976: 67–137.

also have some local property, instantiation of which is caused by the local property of α, and which in the organism represents the content B.[11] But to say this is to admit that there is after all some further explanation of why in this organism events with content A produce events with content B in the organism. So it seems that anyone who denies that such further explanations must be possible has either to admit barely true counterfactuals, or at least to offer some alternative account of why they are not barely true.[12]

A different approach would be to suggest that a content-bearing event can causally explain an effect provided that the effect would occur under all the ways (or under all but very unlikely ways) in which the content-bearing event could be realized.[13] It seems to me, though, that this is not a necessary condition of the possibility of explaining by reference to an event with content. Suppose a person has a visual perception as of an elephant and that its occurrence causally explains his judgement that an elephant is passing by. The experience is realized by some subpersonal state with a complex representational content. We can also suppose that there are two different ways in which visual experiences can be realized in this subject. Perhaps various subpersonal resource-allocation decisions determine that now one, now the other, system of states is put online to the visual system for the production of visual experiences. These two systems may, for instance, not have the same associative connections to other psychological states. We can write into the example that one of the systems, when activated, makes the subject much more cautious in accepting the veridicality of certain experiences—such as one of an elephant passing by—than he is when the other system is activated. In this example, then, it is not true that had the actual visual experience been differently realized, the subject would still have judged that an elephant is passing by. He would not. This does not seem to me to undermine the point that, as things actually are, his having

---

[11] Note that we cannot without some elaboration use a realization relation here instead of a representation relation, at least if the realization of one state by another is explained in terms of their having the same causes and effects. The discussion has been motivated precisely by the fact that it is problematic whether something's having a certain content can be causally efficacious.

[12] On the importance of counterfactuals to claims of causal relevance, see 'Mind Matters' by E. LePore and B. Loewer, *Journal of Philosophy*, 84 (1987), 630–42.

[13] This is the approach of Jackson and Pettit's 'Functionalism and Broad Content', developed in their idea of a 'programme explanation'.

a visual experience with a certain content causally explains his judgement. The counterfactual 'If he had not had the experience, he would not have made the judgement' can also remain true in this example. Actually the point made in this example seems to apply not just to content-based explanation, but to explanation by higher-level or relational states quite generally. We explain the plane crash by saying that its wing was vulnerable to disintegration at high speeds. The basis of this disposition was, let us say, cracks in its wing. The disposition to disintegrate at high speeds could also have had the looseness of bolts as its basis. It may be that this and alternative bases would not have led to a crash, because they are factors that are checked before the aircraft is permitted to take off. But this does not undermine the actual explanation of the crash which cites the vulnerability to disintegration at high speeds.

So far I have been arguing that a subpersonal psychology can explain why a thinker meets a possession condition. The question arises of whether there *must* be an explanation of why a thinker meets a possession condition, when in fact he does. I note very briefly that the reasoning so far seems to contain the materials for constructing such an a priori argument. In general, possession conditions mention judgements made in certain specified circumstances. These circumstances always comprise other content-involving states, including sometimes the non-conceptual representational content of experience. Possession conditions should also be understood as requiring that the relevant judgements are made *because* the subject is in these other content-involving states. (The possession conditions would not be sufficient otherwise.) Now the same problem that was raised for explanation by subpersonal mental representations with content can also be raised here too at the personal level. The relational properties in virtue of which a state has its content are not normally causally efficacious in producing the judgements mentioned in the possession condition. So again the question arises of how the content-involving states can be explanatory of the judgements mentioned in the possession condition. And again, we can give an answer in terms of subpersonal representational properties which are locally causally efficacious.[14]

If the conception I have been defending is right, then a

---

[14] A more general treatment should consider analogues of this requirement in the other special sciences.

subpersonal psychological explanation of why a thinker meets a certain possession condition is not precisely analogous to an advanced physical explanation of some phenomenon characterized in folk physics. According to the present account, the ultimate subpersonal psychological explanation of the fulfilment of a possession condition must be undergirded by an explanation which does not use the notion of content. In this respect, we have a radical discontinuity with the folk psychology in which talk of concepts is embedded, for there mention of content is pervasive. By contrast, a serious scientific physics can be seen as reached by a series of improvements in attaining the same kinds of goal as those of folk physics. There is no requirement in advance that there exist in scientific physics a level of explanation which makes less use than does folk physics of a certain notion, in the way that such a requirement holds for subpersonal psychology.[15]

The agenda for psychology suggested by the general approach I have been advocating is this: for each type of thinker and for each concept possessed by a thinker of that type, a subpersonal explanation should be given of why the thinker meets the concept's possession condition. While some of the psychological work which has already been carried out is relevant to this agenda, there is surely an immense amount we do not understand at present. Carrying out this agenda is also in its very nature an interdisciplinary enterprise. For any particular concept, the task for the psychologist is not fully formulated until the philosopher has supplied an adequate possession condition for it.

3. I now turn to address the bearing of what I have said on some fundamental issues about meaning, content, and understanding.

Wittgenstein's arguments about rule-following have sometimes been taken in a way which would exclude the possibility of giving a psychological explanation of why a thinker meets a possession condition. I have already said that on one central issue, that of the need to mention what is found primitively compelling—how we 'naturally go on'—in the possession condition, it seems to me that

---

[15] There is here an obvious parallel, and a connection, with Dennett's discussion of the way in which Artificial Intelligence accounts can explain the presence of intelligence and comprehension by positing devices of lesser intelligence and lesser understanding. See his paper, 'Artificial Intelligence as Philosophy and as Psychology', repr. in *Brainstorms*, 109–26.

Wittgenstein's insight is consistent with the Simple Account. But the fact is that Wittgenstein's rule-following considerations comprise a battery of arguments, some of them independent of the others. It would be quite wrong to represent all of these arguments as equally consistent with the Simple Account. Let me start by considering the arguments that are consistent with the Simple Account.

The Wittgensteinian points summarized by saying that rule-following has 'no essential inner epistemology' are consistent with the Simple Account.[16] The fact that my justifications when following a rule or applying a concept come to an end does not imply that the explanation of my reaction to a case comes to an end at the same point. The subpersonal states and computations which explain the thinker's fulfilment of the possession condition are unconscious. They lie below the bedrock at the bottom of reason-giving explanation.

For some philosophers, these comments will serve only to increase the tension between the Simple Account and Wittgenstein's insights. It is, they will say, internal to the nature of a concept that it involves a distinction between correct and incorrect applications. The norms that are somehow grasped in possessing a concept must surely have to do with the conscious level at which the notion of justification can get a grip.[17] These are entirely correct observations. They do not, however, undermine the Simple Account. The normative dimensions of a concept should be accounted for by citing various properties and relations of its possession condition, which involves notions at the personal and conscious level. It would be quite inappropriate to try to explain the normative dimension of concepts at the subpersonal level.

This is no place for an extended discussion of the complex and fascinating topic of the normative character of concepts.[18] I will confine myself to the following remark. I would defend all of the following views: concepts (senses) are individuated by their

---

[16] The quoted phrase is Crispin Wright's, from his 'Wittgenstein's Rule-following Considerations and the Central Project of Theoretical Linguistics', in A. George (ed.), *Reflections on Chomsky*, Oxford: Blackwell, 1989: 233–64.

[17] For an expression of this concern, see G. Baker and P. Hacker, *Language, Sense and Nonsense*, Oxford: Blackwell, 1984, esp. 297–9 and 309 ff.

[18] I attempt a preliminary discussion in 'Content and Norms in a Natural World', in E. Villanueva (ed.), *Information, Semantics and Epistemology*, Oxford: Blackwell, 1990: 57–76.

possession conditions; concepts (senses), together with the world, determine reference (perhaps relative to a context); and truth-value is determined by reference (of the components of a thought). So the truth-value of a thought is determined by the possession conditions for its various constituents, together with the world. But we surely have the materials for building an account of one important normative dimension of a concept when we can elucidate what is involved in aiming at the truth of thoughts containing it. It is the possession condition, rather than the empirical subpersonal explanation of a particular thinker's meeting it, which supplies these materials. Properly understood, the normative dimension of concepts is no obstacle to the Simple Account. If the normative is elucidated with materials at the personal level, we can still give an explanation at the subpersonal of why the thinker meets the possession condition.[19]

If the possession condition for a concept gives the requirements for mastery of the concept, then we must acknowledge that often we attribute attitudes to others using a concept even though the other does not meet its possession condition. In a case of partial grasp of a concept, there is a further kind of norm to which the thinker is answerable: that he defer to the correct judgements of those with greater mastery of the concept. This phenomenon certainly undermines any identification of possession conditions with attribution conditions. It also undermines the view that all norms characteristic of the attribution of concepts are somehow fixed directly just by the possession condition. But it does not undermine the core of the Simple Account. When a thinker has an incomplete or incorrect grasp of some concept, there will be a specification of what it is to have such an incomplete or incorrect grasp. A subpersonal psychology can still explain why the thinker makes the transitions involved in meeting that specification of an incomplete or incorrect grasp.

What Wittgenstein's rule-following arguments do exclude is a certain kind of platonism, characterized by Crispin Wright as 'the view that the correctness of a rule-informed judgement is a matter quite independent of any opinion of ours'.[20] On one understanding of the phrase 'quite independent', the general framework within

---

[19] For some discussion of the normative dimension of concepts, see my 'Content and Norms in a Natural World'.
[20] 'Wittgenstein's Rule-following Considerations.'

which I am working here is not platonistic in Wright's sense. Whether a rule-informed judgement is correct depends on the semantic values of its conceptual constituents. In the framework I am using, the account of what makes one object, function, or whatever, the semantic value of a concept will show how it is fixed from the concept's possession condition (together with the world). Since the possession condition in turn mentions what thinkers find primitively compelling, there is one clear sense in which correctness is not in the present framework 'quite independent of any opinion of ours'.

Making this point does not commit one to verificationism, nor to any kind of subjectivism. Universal quantification over the natural numbers can illustrate the point for us. The possession condition for universal quantification will state, roughly, that the thinker finds the transition from such a quantification to an arbitrary instance primitively compelling, and does so because the transition is of that form.[21] This possession condition manifestly mentions what is found primitively compelling. The natural way to fix a semantic value from this possession condition is to say that the quantification *All natural numbers are F* is true just in case all its commitments are true, where its commitments are the singular numerical instances *Fi*. This truth condition is one which can obtain without our being able to know that it does. In general, a possession condition can be response-mentioning without our being able to respond affirmatively and reliably to the question of its truth in every case in which the concept applies. Consequently we can, without any commitment to verificationism, respect this aspect of Wittgenstein's rule-following arguments as long as our subpersonal explanation of concept-possession is response-absorbent.

There is however a second, more radical, way of understanding the doctrine that the correctness of a rule-informed judgement is not independent of our opinions. On this reading, the doctrine is taken to be what I shall call the *Ratification Thesis*.[22] I use this label for the thesis that when someone possesses a particular concept, the correctness of his judgement of whether a given object falls under the concept is not determined by any of the circumstances

---

[21] This form can be instantiated for inaccessibly large numbers.

[22] In formulating the Ratification Thesis, I have been much helped by the discussion in ch. XI, 'Anti-Realism and Objectivity', of Crispin Wright's *Wittgenstein on the Foundations of Mathematics*, London: Duckworth, 1980.

surrounding his judgements of whether other objects fall under it. The thesis gets its name because if it is true, then there is a sense in which the correctness of a judgement in which a concept is applied to a previously unencountered object involves some ratification on the thinker's part, a ratification which is not settled by anything in the circumstances of his previous judgements involving the concept.

The Ratification Thesis is to be distinguished from this claim: that from the fact that all the objects in a given set each fall under a concept it does not follow that some new object outside the set also falls under the concept. That claim should command unhestitating assent, since it would be generally agreed that for any set of examples, we can find two concepts which agree on objects in that set but diverge on an object outside it. What distinguishes the Ratification Thesis is its claim about a failure of determination of correctness in a new case by anything in the circumstances surrounding the thinker's application of the concept in question in previous cases.

The Ratification Thesis is a denial of a certain kind of objectivity of meaning and content. It would clearly undermine the idea that new judgements are responsible to a meaning already grasped. It was in fact the consequences of this idea for the notion of a proof in mathematics which provoked Turing's opposition at Wittgenstein's lectures.[23]

We ordinarily think that it can be determinately true or determinately false of some unencountered object that it falls under a concept. That is, we think of the concept as *investigation-independent* in Crispin Wright's sense.[24] As Wright has emphasized, anyone who believes in the possibility of such investigation-independence of concepts is committed to rejecting the Ratification Thesis. Conversely, belief in the Ratification Thesis for a particular concept provides a major motivation for those who wish to reject investigation-independence for that concept. In fact, we have here one of several points at which a metaphysical problem turns on issues in the philosophical theory of concepts.

Given the theory of concepts I have been outlining, we ought to draw a principled distinction between two kinds of case when

---

[23] See *Wittgenstein's Lectures*, esp. 62–7.
[24] *Wittgenstein on the Foundations of Mathematics*, ch. XI, sect. 3, 206.

assessing the Ratification Thesis. In the first kind of case, there is a particular clause of the possession condition for the concept in question, a clause with this property: the hitherto unencountered object falls (or fails to fall) under the concept because of its relations to this clause, while all the other objects about which the thinker has made judgements fall (or fail to fall) under the concept because of their relations to some other clause in the possession condition. In a case of this first kind, we would expect just the sort of failure of determination which the Ratification Thesis asserts to be the general case. Suppose someone has perceived a number of objects, and classified them, on the basis of his perceptual experience of their shape, as falling under a certain shape concept. We can include in the description of our information that he classifies them as falling under this concept because he experiences them as square—this is a specification of the non-conceptual representational content of his experience—and because he is taking his experience at face value. We cannot infer from this information the correct answer to the question of whether some currently unperceived object falls under the concept he has applied in these previous cases. For in addition to the concept *square*, there is a legitimate concept, *perceived by the subject to be square*, for which the subject's circumstances in previous examples will be quite appropriate for the judgements he made, but for which a different answer will be correct in the new case. This is true even when the 'circumstances' are taken to include detailed information about the causal explanation of the subject's previous answers. Given that the possession condition for the concept *square* will comprise two clauses, one dealing with a canonical kind of case in which an object is perceptually presented, and the other dealing with that in which it is not, this is precisely what we should have expected.

The second kind of case is that in which the given, new object falls under the concept by virtue of its relation to the *same* clause of the possession condition as objects about which the thinker has already made judgements involving the concept. In this case the Ratification Thesis seems to me to be false. Suppose the explanation of a subject's judging something to fall under a given concept is that certain conditions hold, and that it is part of the possession condition for the concept that those conditions should explain the subject's judgement. Suppose also that the account of how the semantic value of the concept is determined from the possession condition entails that the object does fall under the concept in such circumstances. Then, first, we should expect the same conditions to explain a corresponding judgement in the case of a new object if the subject continues to possess the concept. This much generality is implicit in the idea of a non-probabilistic explanation.[25] Second, given the supposition about how the semantic value of the concept is fixed, the judgement about the new object will also be correct.

It is sometimes objected that anyone who rejects the Ratification Thesis must be attributing to a thinker some kind of privileged first-person knowledge of his meanings and concepts, of a sort such that there is no more to an application of a concept being correct in a new case than its seeming so to the thinker. This line of thought is attributed because, once it is agreed that the fragment of the extension of a concept fixed by responses to previous examples by itself settles nothing about a new case, there may seem nothing else for knowledge of meaning and concepts to consist in.[26] On the account I have been developing, however, what makes it the case that someone is employing one concept rather than another is not constituted by his impressions of whether he is. It is constituted rather by complex facts about the explanation of certain of his primitively compelling judgements. This is a position which leaves room for something which is a major desideratum in the theory of content: an epistemology which makes possible privileged first-person knowledge of one's meaning and concepts without also making it vacuous, and whilst also leaving the content of the knowledge accessible to others too.

In so far as the Ratification Thesis is one strand in Wittgenstein's rule-following considerations, the account I have been developing is indeed incompatible with that part of them. This is not the place for detailed exegesis, but there are certainly some passages in Wittgenstein which are most naturally read as relying upon the

---

[25] I do not mean that when the explaining conditions are met, the corresponding judgement will be made, without exception. Anything from sudden distraction to neural failures can produce a gap. I take it, though, that there are apparently explanatory principles in psychology. What matters here is that the explaining conditions obtained from a possession condition can function as the explaining conditions in such an explanatory principle. How such explanatory principles work, however, remains in need of a great deal of clarification: see Stephen Schiffer, 'Ceteris Paribus Laws' (forthcoming).

[26] See e.g. C. Wright, *Wittgenstein on the Foundations of Mathematics*, at 216 ff.

Ratification Thesis. One example is his treatment of the statement 'The sequence 770 occurs in the decimal expansion of π'. He rejects the idea that this statement must have a determinate truth-value, and his grounds appear to involve his views on rule-following.[27] If Wittgenstein had not held the Ratification Thesis, but only the weaker claim that the notion of what is found primitively compelling must enter the possession condition of any concept, then there would be no good reason for his denying determinacy of truth value to such statements. The statement in question can be taken as a universal quantification over natural numbers: for any natural number n, the $n$the number in the decimal expansion of π is not the first of a sequence 770 in the expansion. Suppose we endorse the possession condition given above for such universal quantification. This stated that the thinker finds the transition from such a quantification to an arbitrary instance primitively compelling, and does so because the transition is of that form. The truth condition of the universal quantification 'For all n $F(n)$' is that all contents of the sort which are conclusions of the inferences of the form mentioned in the possession condition—that is all the instances $F(i)$—be true. This can have a determinate truth-value in advance of any suitable ratification.

A second, closely related, respect in which the views developed here are in tension with Wittgenstein's emerges from his own descriptions of what is involved in understanding an expression. *Philosophical Investigations* section 209 starts:

'But then doesn't our understanding reach beyond all the examples?'—A very queer expression, and a quite natural one!

But is that *all*? Isn't there a deeper explanation; or mustn't at least the *understanding* of the explanation be deeper? Well, have I myself a deeper understanding? Have I *got* more than I give in the explanation?

The theorist of possession conditions should answer 'yes' to this last question. The 'explanations' Wittgenstein is talking about here are those given to a pupil learning an expression, and they will consist fundamentally of giving examples. The understanding of the teacher will involve more than any examples he can give, because

---

[27] See *Remarks on the Foundations of Mathematics*, iii (3rd edn., Oxford: Blackwell, 1978). See also Wright's discussion of this passage in *Wittgenstein on the Foundations of Mathematics*, ch. 8.

the teacher's verdicts on examples have to have a certain kind of explanation if the teacher is to understand.[28]

These are not the only respects in which Wittgenstein would disagree with the position I have been outlining. His general distaste for causal accounts of psychological concepts would reinforce his rejection of the possession-condition account. As he said, his view was rather that use flows from meaning as behaviour flows from character.[29] It seems to me, however, that Wittgenstein's most powerful arguments—the rejection of mythological and regressive accounts of understanding and concept-mastery—are already taken on board once we recognize that possession-conditions can mention what is found primitively compelling. The dispute with Wittgenstein is over the further step to the Ratification Thesis and its associated claims. In endorsing a theory of concepts which rejects the Ratification Thesis, we restore the kind of objectivity Turing wanted to conceptual contents.[30]

---

[28] In the arithmetical case, they have to be answerable to certain forms of inference: for more on this see 'Content and Norms in a Natural World'.

[29] *Remarks on the Foundations of Mathematics*, i. 13.

[30] This essay is included here at the volume editors' special request; for further elaboration and development, see *A Study of Concepts* (MIT Press, 1992) and 'Content, Computation, and Externalism', *Mind and Language*, 9 (1994), 303–35. For some further thoughts, including a defence of the idea that finding something primitively compelling may on occasion have a personal-level explanation by the thinker's implicit knowledge of a semantic rule, see my essay 'The Philosophy of Language', forthcoming in a volume of essays edited by Anthony Grayling (Oxford University Press, 1997).

7

How Simple is the Simple Account?
Comment on Peacocke

MICHAEL MORRIS

———◆———

Christopher Peacocke proposes what he calls 'the Simple Account' of the proper relation between philosophical and psychological theories of concepts. A philosopher will characterize the possession conditions for concepts. A subpersonal psychology ought then to explain why a subject who has a concept meets the possession condition for that concept—just as a physical theory ought to explain why a particular object is a reflector.

I think this claim needs some clarification before we can see exactly what its commitments are.

First, what is a possession condition? Nothing generally reductive is intended: Peacocke is not here concerned with the question of what it is in general for someone to possess a concept (any concept). Rather, the project is one of individuation. The idea is to explain what is special about each concept in terms of what is special about the requirements for possessing *it* rather than any other concept. You give the possession condition for a particular concept by saying what's special about possessing *it* in particular.

Characteristically, the possession condition for a concept C will be given by specifying necessary conditions for possessing it, of at least one of these two forms:

(i) *a* possesses the concept C only if, when *p*, *a* will judge that . . . C . . . (and will do so *because p*);

(ii) *a* possesses the concept C only if, when *a* judges that . . . C . . . , then *p* (and it is true that *p because a* judges that . . . C . . .).

We may say that form (i) gives a possession condition in terms of *grounds* for judgements involving a concept, and form (ii) does it in terms of the *commitments* of judgements involving a concept. Some concepts may have possession conditions of a combined form, involving both grounds and commitments. The possession conditions will only give *necessary* conditions in this form, but this will still enable us to pick out each concept uniquely, since for each concept we will look for a necessary condition which has the following property: only *this* concept has this as a necessary condition for its possession.

With this laid out, we can now make clear what I think is the crucial point for the proposed relation between philosophical and psychological theories of concepts. The replacements for '*p*' in conditions of the form of (i) or (ii) will naturally vary between different concepts, but they will *always* involve reference to other mental states of the subject. (These other mental states won't themselves involve deployment of the concept in question, of course: that would be circular.)

The upshot of this is that in general you will only count as possessing a certain concept if, in certain circumstances, you do, or would, make certain transitions between your mental states. The view of concepts therefore has some affinities with a functionalist or inferential role conception of concept possession.

What, then, does Peacocke expect a subpersonal psychology to do? I think he demands two things:

(a) For each subject who possesses a concept, it should explain each of the transitions that are made when the possession condition requires them to be;

(b) For each subject who possesses a concept, it should explain what it is about that subject *now* in virtue of which *all* those transitions will or would be made.

It's (b) which is crucial; for it is only by meeting the demand of (b) that a subpersonal psychology will explain why a subject meets the possession condition for a concept.

Peacocke insists on several constraints on a subpersonal psychological account which meets the demand of (b). I'll note just two of these.

The first requirement is that the account be non-circular. This means that the subpersonal explanation of a subject's meeting the possession condition for a concept should not be couched in terms which themselves presuppose that the subject possesses that concept.

The second requirement arises, I think, from a special case of a general feature of possession conditions. It will not in general be enough to say that in certain circumstances certain transitions will occur in one who possesses a concept: we will need also to insist that the transitions occur in the right way, that they are the right kind of transitions. In particular, some transitions for any given concept will need to be found primitively compelling by the subject: the transitions will not be due to an *inference*. Peacocke seems to take this to require that a subpersonal psychology should explain what is involved in a given subject's finding a content primitively compelling.

There are other details, of course, but I think this now provides us with the essence of Peacocke's view of the proper relation between philosophical and psychological theories of concepts.

My difficulty is that I still don't find the *shape* of Peacocke's position clear. I don't see its commitments clearly enough to be able to locate this view in philosophical space. So in order to push the debate a little further, I'll raise four questions about Peacocke's view, as I understand it. My hope is that readers will be able to use them to understand Peacocke's position better for themselves, and to focus their own intuitions about the issues he addresses.

The first question is this: Why exactly *should* a subpersonal psychology explain what is involved in a given subject's finding a transition primitively compelling? The official reason seems to be just that this follows from the fact that the *possession conditions* for concepts will need to state that certain transitions are found primitively compelling. But I don't see *why* it follows. It's just not obvious why the fact that something needs to be mentioned in a philosophical, personal-level account means that it needs to be explained by a subpersonal psychology.

There might, however, be an independent, and more direct, reason for the requirement. Take Peacocke's example, of someone who possesses the concept of conjunction. If such a person judges that A and judges that B they will find the thought that A *and* B primitively compelling, immediately and without further inference. Now is it not reasonable to ask *why* that person finds the thought that A *and* B primitively compelling? And is this not evidently a psychological question? Moreover, since the only answer we seem able to give at the personal level is just 'Because they understand conjunction', the question seems to be one for a *sub*personal psychology.

But if a subpersonal psychology is to be able to answer such a question, it must be able to cash out in its own terms what is involved, for a given subject at least, in that subject's finding something primitively compelling. So we get Peacocke's requirement.

How good is this reasoning? I don't find it compelling: it seems to me to depend in the end on just the argument I found unobvious in the official reason for this requirement. Suppose that the personal-level answer to the question why this person finds the thought that *A and B* primitively compelling is just the one suggested. That is, all we can say at this level is that this is required for possessing the concept of conjunction and this person *does* possess the concept of conjunction. Why should we then expect a subpersonal psychology to tackle more than just the general task of giving an account of what is involved in this person's possessing the concept? Why should that account contain a particular feature corresponding to the particular personal-level property of finding something primitively compelling?

A third line of argument for the requirement might be suggested by reflecting on the Wittgensteinian reasoning which is cited for it. We might take Wittgenstein as holding that someone's finding a thought primitively compelling is a function of three factors:

(i) Their training.
(ii) The epistemological suitability of the circumstances to the exercise of the concepts involved.
(iii) The fact that they are, e.g. human, with a distinctive range of basic sensibilities and predispositions.

The task of a subpersonal psychology might then be thought to be to give an account of that third factor in such a way as to explain in more fundamental causal terms how it can combine with the other two to produce a certain kind of response.

The difficulty here is to see why we should expect to be able to isolate the third factor in terms which Peacocke could count as fundamentally causal in the appropriate way. That third factor is no more than the extra that is required to yield primitive compulsion, once we've got the first two. But the first two are characterized in essentially *normative* terms ('training', 'epistemological suitability'). It is then hard to understand the crucial third factor in a normatively neutral way. But Peacocke himself says 'it is a mistake to think that the materials for elucidating the normative dimensions of a concept can be found at the subpersonal level.'

In fact we should have been worried about this all along. For Peacocke only characterizes the notion of finding something primitively compelling in the normative terms which he takes to belong distinctively to the personal level: finding a transition *primitively* compelling is finding it compelling for some reason other than because it has been *inferred* from something else, and without taking it as *answerable* to something else.

In short, I see no good reason for Peacocke to insist that a subpersonal psychology should explain what's involved in someone's finding certain transitions primitively compelling.

My second question raises a similar kind of worry about Peacocke's whole conception of giving a subpersonal account of a thinker's possessing a concept. The crucial demand on a subpersonal psychology is the one I labelled '(*b*)' earlier:

> For each subject who possesses a concept, a subpersonal psychology should explain what it is about that subject *now* in virtue of which *all* of the relevant transitions will or would be made.

My question is this. Why should we expect *any* interestingly unified account of the full range of these transitions, apart from the one couched in terms of the relevant concept itself? There might be good reason, deriving ultimately from the generality of physics, for expecting to be able to say something about *each* transition in more fundamental terms. But this would not yet be good reason for expecting an interestingly unified account of *all* the transitions taken together.

Peacocke should expect, but does not meet, opposition from those who believe in the explanatory autonomy of the special sciences. These people hold that the identity of the special sciences is precisely determined by the fact that they pick out and explain uniformities which cannot be characterized or explained at any more fundamental level. This opposition, it should be noted, does not depend upon supposing that an interestingly unified account at the fundamental level would offer a *single* fundamental-level property as the correlate of each higher-level property. 'Interestingly unified' means just what it says: interestingly unified. Nor need the opposition suppose that Peacocke is demanding a general reduction of what it is for *anyone* to possess a given concept. The problem remains even when we're dealing with what it is for a particular given individual to possess a given concept. Why should there be an interesting uniformity, characterizable independently of the terms of the concept itself, in what explains all the relevant transitions which even one individual would make?

In the light of this, it seems question-begging for Peacocke to cite a Language-of-Thought model as a possible way of meeting his requirements on a subpersonal account of concept-possession, as if this showed the requirements to be reasonable. One of the things which is most controversial about Language-of-Thought models is their assumption that there are non-semantically characterizable uniformities ('syntax') which correspond precisely to semantic uniformities. The opposition I have in mind would question whether syntax *can* be characterized non-semantically, even for the case of a particular given individual.

My first two questions express in different ways the worry that Peacocke is demanding an excessive correspondence between the shape of theories stated in personal and subpersonal terms. My third question addresses the analogy from which this springs. Peacocke likens the demand that a subpersonal psychology should explain why a given thinker meets the possession condition for a concept to the demand that physics should explain why a given object is a reflector.

The question is this: Is the relation between possessing a concept and subpersonal psychology *really* analogous to that between being a reflector and physics? There is at least this disanalogy. It seems to be a matter for physics to determine what it is in general for an object to be a reflector; but, on Peacocke's own account, it is not a matter for a subpersonal psychology to determine what it is in general for someone to possess a given concept (his view is that *philosophy* sorts that out).

Peacocke might respond to this by saying that it is not the *physical* account of what it is to be a reflector which is being compared to the philosophical account of concept possession, but the conception of being a reflector which is afforded by a naïve proto-scientific conception of the world around us. But this response doesn't seem adequate. For the naïve conception of being a reflector is surely *correctable* by properly scientific physics, whereas Peacocke does not appear to hold that a philosophical account of concept possession is correctable by a subpersonal psychology. (His view seems to be that psychologists should read philosophical journals, but not vice versa.)

This is part of what strikes me as a general tension in Peacocke's view of the relation between philosophy and psychology. He appears at times to be drawn towards the view that the property of possessing a given concept is a natural kind of subpersonal psychology, whereas at other times (for example, when he insists that the normative is outside the sphere of subpersonal psychology) he seems keen to resist that view. Thus, in his discussion of Crispin Wright (and Wright's view of Wittgenstein), he envisages appealing to subpersonal psychology for an independent determination of the extension of a concept, which is not easy to understand unless concept possession is a natural kind of subpersonal psychology; but he is generally very wary of the reductionism such a view would suggest.

My fourth (and last) question expresses a worry that's likely to be felt by psychologists and cognitive scientists. An agenda is set for a science called subpersonal psychology, but very little is said about what that science looks like. The question is this. Is Peacocke appealing to a science of which we have some independent conception, with a recognizable range of terminology, an identifiable range of relevant data, and a familiar conception of its own explanatory goals—or is subpersonal psychology simply stipulated to be that science, whatever it is, which answers Peacocke's questions in the way he wants them answered?

If it is the first, we might expect some practising psychologists and cognitive scientists to be a little surprised to find a philosopher intervening with these demands: Why should *their* science do what Peacocke wants? If it is the second, we need convincing that there really is a science of the kind Peacocke is looking for.

I'll conclude by making three critical remarks, which summarize my worries about Peacocke's paper as I understand it. First, it is not an entirely simple matter to see what the Simple Account is. At times it seems to veer towards an *excessively* simple correspondence between personal-level uniformities and subpersonal uniformities; but the picture is complicated by the insistence that the subpersonal level cannot explain the normative aspects of concept possession. Secondly, it is not clear what subpersonal psychology is. Thirdly, I have not found a convincing argument against what I take to be the obvious opposition to what I take to be Peacocke's view. But this might just mean that there is no simple correspondence between what I take to be Peacocke's view and what Peacocke actually believes.

Note: This is an expansion of some informal introductory remarks I made as chairman of the session at which Christopher Peacocke presented his paper. I raised then the four questions I raise here. Christopher Peacocke replied briefly to them at the time; I have tried to take those replies into account in the way that I've presented the questions here.

8

Modularity and Logical Cognitivism

BEATRICE DE GELDER

———◆———

Since the late 1950s philosophy of science and psychology have each gone their own way. Psychology need no longer restrict itself to behaviourism as it would have had to if the regime of empiricist philosophy of science had been successfully imposed upon it. In any case, it would seem that in philosophy an empiricist approach to science has been largely abandoned just as in psychology behaviourism now belongs to history. But the interest philosophers take in the proper conduct of psychological research has remained and become more intense over the last two decades. Among the few milestones marking the road away from empiricism and behaviourism is J. A. Fodor's *Psychological Explanation* (1968) making a convincing anti-behaviourist case defending mentalism and the scientific study of mental processes as the building-blocks of proper psychological explanations. In other words, whatever the shape of things to come, a future 'entente' between philosophy and psychology would no longer be negotiated among empiricists and behaviourists.

One is therefore surprised to hear J. A. Fodor remark that 'cognitive science is philosophy of science writ small' (Fodor, 1983: 217). Prima facie, such a remark suggests a number of readings. Maybe, at its most general level, it just reflects the regain of interest in psychology among philosophers of science and vice versa. Alternatively, it brings out that in Fodor's view cognitive science addresses many of the same issues discussed at length in philosophy of science. Indeed, Fodor presents a comprehensive picture of the agenda of post-behaviourist psychology. Moreover, he shows the impact of cognitive psychology for central issues in philosophy of

Thanks to S. Bromberger, R. Held, and R. van Baaren for helpful discussions and to the latter also for assistance with the final preparation of the manuscript.

science and epistemology. Yet, these readings are pushed in the background by one specific aspect of the close link between the two disciplines. In fact, Fodor (e.g. 1984) argues that present-day cognitive psychology vindicates the distinction between observation and theory, a distinction which is generally agreed to have been the cornerstone of logical empiricism became its Achilles' heel (Suppe, 1974).

This is a puzzling statement. If the observation–theory distinction was thoroughly criticized and has contributed to the abandonment of logical empiricist ideals (e.g. Suppe, 1974) one must have new motives to want to rescue it and solid arguments to succeed in doing so. The case of the defence is complicated by the fact that apparently Fodor's motives are not philosophical but relate to his views on what ought to be the proper way of conducting psychological inquiry. Specifically, in the course of reconstructing the rationale and the proper explanatory project behind cognitive psychology, Fodor argues for the view that information-processing in the human mind has a peculiar architecture which he calls modular. The argument for modularity is a blend of facts and a forecast of future findings. The picture is incomplete but already clear enough for the facts about modularity to lend support to the old if not obsolete philosophical distinction between observation and theory. It thus would seem that with the views expressed by Fodor we have come full circle. From a situation where philosophical distinctions led the way to safe empiricist science we have come to a situation where hitherto unsafe mentalist science rescues philosophy. Since the entry of mentalism was welcomed as a cognitive revolution, the view of the mind as modular might be taken by some as something like a contra-revolution in psychology.

The present analysis focuses on the role the thesis of the modularity of mind plays in linking logical empiricism to cognitivism, but its scope is much more limited than those notions suggest since only very specific aspects of modularity and of logical empiricism matter for the present purpose. As concerns modularity, no systematic analysis of this notion will be tempted. Still, it is clearly and unsurprisingly the case that the notion of a module builds upon existing traditions and incorporates Chomsky's notion of a module as a unit of analysis of language competence, a psychological and neuropsychological notion of a module as cognitive structure as well as the notion of a module familiar from research in artificial intelligence. One might argue that the notion that is central for the thesis of modularity and its epistemological message incorporates all these contexts and rationalizes their conceptual links. As far as logical empiricism goes, the present analysis is concerned with Carnap's project of a rational reconstruction of scientific theories. The continuity with Fodor's analysis of cognitivism does not imply any claims about the empiricism vs. realism or for that matter, instrumentalism debate, about cognitivism being the one or the other. Such matters are outside the scope of this project.

The present paper examines the continuity between logical empiricism, as it is taken to be the received view in philosophy of science and cognitivism, as taken to be the received view in cognitive science. I analyse some of the assumptions that figure prominently in logical empiricism and in cognitivism, e.g. the distinction between observation and theory, the role of formalism in the representation of knowledge, and the syntactic and semantic aspects of representation. Finally, I look at similarities between the difficulties logical empiricism faced and those cognitive psychology might be confronted with as a consequence of the way Fodor presents it and which I propose to label 'logical cognitivism'.

COGNITIVISM

The notion of 'cognitivism' is widely used and does not have a clear meaning. Knowledge and representation are relied upon to pin down what is characteristic of a cognitive approach are themselves notoriously vague concepts and cover a wide spectrum of meanings. Sometimes talk about knowledge refers to the intelligent design of a biological or artificial system (e.g. Dennett, 1978, 1988). At the other end of the spectrum one finds a notion of knowledge dressed in its full folk regalia and referring to subjective epistemic ability. At the same time there is the habit to identify knowledge with cognition as information-processing. This raises questions about the intentionality of thought, about the relation between cognition and rationality, and the link between information-processing and conscious experience (de Gelder, 1992). And then also all these meanings get confounded. For example, Haugeland

(1978) believes that: 'intelligent behaviour is to be explained by appeal to internal "cognitive processes"—meaning, essentially, processes interpretable as working out a rationale' (p. 260–1). But it is doubtful whether it is entirely appropriate to put all the age-old philosophical riddles about the mind on the agenda of cognitive science.

To move closer to the sense of 'cognitive' that will concern us here it is useful to mark the contrast with what was presumably at stake in the cognitive revolution overtaking behaviourism. As it has been used the expression 'cognitive revolution' refers to the paradigm shift that took place in psychology in the late 1950s and early 1960s (Palermo, 1971; Weiner and Palermo, 1974). There is a good deal of consensus about the original cognitive revolution. The central thesis of the cognitive view is that all information-processing whether taking place at lower perceptual levels or involving symbolic processes such as language understanding is mediated by an organism's internal representation of its environment. Fodor (1984) mentions the popularity of this cognitive view with philosophers like Kuhn, Hanson, and Goodman, all of them quoting the findings from cognitive or the so-called 'New Look' psychologists of the 1950s and 1960s. However, the cognitive paradigm as it has been understood since the 'New Look' is the target of the attack Fodor launches and which must lead to new support for dogmas of logical empiricism.

Before expanding on this attack we need to clarify our use of the notion of cognitivism in this context. The term 'cognitivism' has at least three meanings possibly relevant here. Cognitivism is often used to refer to a particular focus of a number of disciplines that each study different aspects of cognition and are brought together as cognitive science. At other times the term cognitivism refers to a mode of explanation that some disciplines have in common, e.g. cognitive sociology (Cicourel, 1973), cognitive biology (Goodwin, 1978), or more recently, cognitive linguistics (Langacker, 1987). A third meaning is that of cognitivism as a specific meta-theory or a foundational theory or an interpretation projected upon the study of cognition or upon cognitive science just mentioned. I shall argue that for Fodor's position the third meaning is the most relevant and that Fodor defends cognitivism in the sense of a metatheory and one which is intimately related to its precursor in philosophy of science, logical empiricism.

*Cognitivism as a foundationalist metatheory for
cognitive science*

In the third and most controversial meaning, 'cognitivism' refers
to a specific metatheoretical and foundationalist analysis of human cognitive activity which Fodor discovers to be the backbone
of the empirical research done by cognitive scientists, foremost in
cognitive psychology. The views amounting to this approach have
become familiar under the label of 'representational theory of mind'
(e.g. Fodor, 1975, 1980, 1987). The most comprehensive picture of
the psychological implications of it is presented in *The Modularity
of Mind* (Fodor, 1983). Before turning to this, it is worth pointing to
some of the intuitions that may have paved the way for a logical
cognitivist picture of human cognition. Among others this was
typically achieved by presenting an inquiry into the foundations of
human cognition as an undertaking very similar to a study on the
foundations of scientific theories.

Foundational cognitivism states that human cognitive processes
are a matter of mental representations of the external and internal
world of the organism. From a foundationalist perspective like
Fodor's the notion of 'symbolic representation' is the cornerstone
of cognitive theorizing and is a direct descendant of the Cartesian
notion of 'idea'. There are some doubts about these pedigree claims.
For example, in the foundational literature one often reads about
neo-Cartesianism (Fodor, 1983) and about Hume's or Kant's problem (Dennett, 1978). At present we can do no more than hint at
the bias introduced by this approach. Hacking (1975) points out
that our present concept of knowledge is a relatively late one.
Nothing in their discourse even means 'knowledge' (p. 161). The
origin of our current notion of knowledge must be traced to the
scientific revolution in the nineteenth century. Therefore, in the time
of 'Descartes or Hume "theory of knowledge" was not an identifiable discipline . . . The emergence of a named study of autonomous knowledge—epistemology—coincides with the differentiation
and naming of different kinds of knowers, e.g. physicists' (1975:
166). Thus it is at least doubtful that the question recently raised
by the scientific study of knowledge is properly modelled along,
for example, Cartesian or Kantian inquiries.

These historical remarks bring to light a perspective on knowledge which is common to many foundationalist cognitivists, e.g.

the bias towards knowledge as theory in the sense of a structured set of propositions or sentences. It would have made little sense for a Cartesian to formulate the problem of knowledge as the problem of finding the answer to the question on the truth of a collection of sentences. Yet, to students of science, physics does appear to be exactly that: it is a theory in the sense of a collection of statements. On the strength of this picture, philosophical reflection on the scientific knowledge of the physicist starts from the suggestion that human knowledge in general is theoretical and consists of a collection of sentences. The historical merit of the sentential approach was that it admitted to the fact that knowledge is not a state of the ego, but is public, communicated, written down in books, etc. In principle it took only reading skills and no superior illumination to decipher what was there.

Recently Fodor's approach to cognition has been attacked as representing the 'sentential view' of cognition (e.g. Churchland, 1986). Fodor's sententionalism represents the inverted-spectrum version of the sentential picture or of scientific knowledge we find in the theory view of human knowledge sketched above. In the sentationalist picture of the cognitivist the human knower is credited with a collection of sentences stored in the mind. For example, on Fodor's view, to believe that p, is to stand in a relation to a representation conceived as a syntactically structured object, expressed in the language of thought (Fodor, 1978). Sentential cognitivism promises to deliver the formula which will allow us to cash in our intuitive notion of a mental representation for that of an internal sentence in the language of thought.

The modularity of mind

In his recent book, *The Modularity of Mind* (1983), Fodor presents a picture of the developments in cognitive psychology and points out their relevance for central issues in epistemology and philosophy of science. Specifically, the modularity thesis has led Fodor to claim that a crucial aspect of the logical empiricist heritage long abandoned by its former champions has now been vindicated by the scientific study of the cognitive apparatus. At the same time Fodor defends a naturalized epistemology. Like others since Quine (1969) he means thereby, crudely stated, the view that epistemological issues can or must profit from trying empirical psychological solutions to them. On this picture a central epistemological issue as naturalized by cognitive psychology is that a belief is justified in case it results from the representation-producing competences of the subject's cognitive system. In this perspective the traditional epistemological burden of justification of beliefs does not rest with a traditional philosophical and normative theory but with a scientific study of subjective cognitive processes. It it thus up to cognitive psychology to tell which beliefs are well founded by identifying in detail how the cognitive system comes to have the beliefs it has. A conclusion might thus be that only those beliefs are justified that are arrived at in a manner which conforms to the representation-producing processes as pictured in cognitive psychology.

While it looks as if much of what Fodor argues for is in line with this general ideal of naturalization, the picture drawn in *The Modularity of Mind* represents a naturalization with a twist. Fodor defends an architecture of the cognitive system which cuts at the roots of earlier naturalizations of epistemology and philosophy of science, e.g. those representing the cognitive approach to knowledge and theory defended in the 1960s by philosophers as well as by psychologists. In his defence of the modular mind Fodor is in fact attacking what many people since Kuhn (1962) have come to call 'the cognitive revolution'.

Fodor's claim is that 'there is a class of beliefs that are typically fixed by sensory/perceptual processes, and that the fixation of beliefs in this class is, in a sense that wants spelling out, importantly theory neutral.' Or, more concretely, 'Two organisms with the same sensory/perceptual psychology will generally observe the same things, and hence arrive at the same observational beliefs, *however much their theoretical commitments may differ*.' Or again, 'the boundary between what can be observed and what must be inferred is largely determined by fixed, architectural features of an organism's sensory/perceptual psychology' (Fodor, 1984: 24–5). Fodor builds his case on the psychological distinction between perception and cognition refuted by the first generation of cognitivists. In his view a second look at the psychological evidence (for example the experiments quoted by Kuhn) shows that the subject's background theory or the scientist's paradigm does not play a role in his perception. Instead, 'how the world looks can be peculiarly unaffected by how one knows it to be' (1984: 34). Yet, the psychological evidence does not carry over to the epistemological distinction between observation and theory, nor does modularism vindicate that distinction outright. Observation is not perception. In some domains perception is indeed saturated with cognition but in other domains this is not so. The notion of a module will allow Fodor to segregate those aspects of perception that correspond to the epistemological notion of observation (and the arguments in favour of it) from the aspects of perception that can more appropriately be called cognitive. The properties of modules most relevant for the present discussion are that modules are special-purpose devices, mini-expert systems, competent question-raisers, extremely knowledgeable in their own domain, yet unable to do more than they are built to do. They cannot learn from others or rely on background knowledge present elsewhere in other subparts or at the central levels of the system.

There is a strong, almost messianic message to modularism. Like Carnap, Hempel or Feigl before him, Fodor announces where salvation must lie for scientific psychology. On a modular conception of the mind the domain of cognitive psychology is that of the modular architecture only. Science has nothing to say about the subject's epistemic states, their etiology, etc. The scope of empirical research is in principle restricted to modular processes and the intermediate levels of cognition postulated between sensory processes and thought. Modules provide thought processes with food but they do not do the chewing. It is not up to the cognitive psychologist to come up with a theory of higher-thought processes. In return, the cognitive psychologist has nothing to say about interference and reasoning in science. But might one not hope then that the study of scientific inference provides a model for the study of central cognitive processes? If this were the case, the relation between philosophy of science and psychology would come full circle. Instead of philosophy legislating how psychology should be done, it would now be the turn of psychology to tell how philosophy of science should be done.

LOGICAL EMPIRICISM

It is common to refer to logical empiricism or neopositivism as what was the 'received' or the 'orthodox view' in philosophy of science between the 1920s and the late 1950s. Over the years the received view has been defended and attacked by philosophers and scientists alike. In many cases, attacks as well as defences rest on a somewhat distorted picture of the original project. For example, logical empiricism as Carnap conceived it, was not intended as a philosophy of science in the sense of a study of the nature of scientific thinking and of the method for discovering scientific truth. At most, recommendations of scientific method and criteria for evaluation are fringe benefits derived from the epistemological analysis. But many scientists have come to expect that philosophy of science should live up to its promises with respect to methodology. This is partly due to a misinterpretation of the original intentions of logical empiricism on the side of its critics and customers alike.

The original intentions of logical empiricism are most forcefully stated by Carnap (1928). In his view the central task of philosophy with respect to science was an epistemological one. Its goal was to understand science in the sense of explaining how scientific theories, as we see them successfully at work, are possible. The goal was also to justify the notions of truth and objectivity that are characteristic of science. This was already Kant's perception of the philosopher's job. The particular way in which Carnap chose to look for epistemological foundations was inspired by Frege and Russell's treatment of mathematics and the role played in it by his notion of language (Proust, 1986). The Frege–Russell approach was ready to be adapted to empirical science. Carnap undertook to formulate the project of providing a logical reconstruction of science. Three aspects of this reconstructivist approach are central to understanding the continuity between logical empiricism and logical cognitivism: the notion of structure, the idea of physicalist language, and the distinction between observation and theory.

To the outsider science appears as a more or less systematic collection of propositions linked to the objects in the world through the scientist's subjective experiences, his perceptions, and cognitions. It is trivial to say that, for example, a particular experience depends to some extent upon language in order to be expressed as a scientific statement. But once this point is granted, it is clear that the capacity of language to express experience is a function of the systematic and structural nature of language, including the language of science. In reflecting upon this intuition (and on Frege and Russell's successes) the epistemological study of science appears as the study of the deeper structure of the language of science which underlies the scientists' familiar statements. The philosopher's task is one of postulating a metalanguage underlying the systematicity of scientific statements and accounting for it. In other words, his job is that of a logical reconstruction of the propositions made in one or another science. In principle this can be conceived of as a reduction or translation of the scientific propositions into the postulated formal metalanguage.

(i) Language and structure

Carnap (1928) proposes that a scientific theory consists on the one hand of logical notions and on the other of strictly empirical statements. Of course, such a proposal must be put to the test in the course of the logical reconstruction of the scientific theory considered. Its success will give the measure of its feasibility and the validity of the reconstruction appears as a foundational reductionism because it sets out to reduce scientific statements to propositions in a language where the part of the formal and that of the empirical is clearly sorted out. In this perspective all propositions that go beyond empirical statements, are reduced to logical constructions. On that account epistemological problems raised by non-empirical terms are the competence of logic.

(ii) Structuralism and empirical content

In Carnap's view logical reconstruction starts from a given scientific discourse and its systematic description of objects in the world. The goal of logical reconstruction is to articulate the structure of this scientific discourse by showing how its primitive contents—the contents of the naïve propositions about objects in the world one finds in the scientist's discourse—can be reconstructed out of the networks of formal relations between the propositions. In this sense logical reconstruction is a deduction of the empirical content of the scientific propositions.

(iii) Translation and physicalism

The term 'physicalism' owes its notoriety to a convergence of recent discussions on the place of psychology in the picture of a unified science and on the age-old mind–body problem. The physicalist thesis states that all science, including psychology, is built with physical concepts and formulates physical laws. Physicalism is usually associated with reductionism, the view that at the bottom the special sciences reduce to physics. If that is the thesis of physicalism, it represents quite understandably a major challenge for the autonomy of a science of the psychological. But we would misrepresent Carnap's intuitions and underestimate their relevance for cognitivism were we only to look at physicalism in that sense and only in the context of reductionism and unity of science. Certainly, Carnap offers a physicalist solution to psychology (Carnap, 1932/3). Yet, this solution is an integrative part of the project of logical reconstruction. It is not just the application of a recipe that is successful in physics. To perceive this I propose to return to the project of epistemology as logical reconstruction.

As mentioned above, one can look upon logical reconstruction (and empirical deduction or reduction) as an operation of translation between the language of the science considered and the metalanguage to be built. In this sense, translation is equivalent with the epistemological construction itself or with the logical reconstruction of the object language. Yet, there is another problem of translation which is of a somewhat different nature because it appears in the preparatory stages and in the execution of the logical reconstruction more than in the formulation of the program itself. The material of the logical reconstructivist consists of the propositions of science, which Carnap calls the system language. It is the language of the scientific theory. But the scientific system language is not, so to speak, the mother tongue of the scientist. An observer does not 'talk theory' (nor does he 'talk metalanguage') but he speaks about what he sees and hears, about what is given in his experience, about what he perceives, believes, and infers. In other words, the observer expresses himself in ordinary language, saturated with ordinary psychological and mentalist notions ('under such and such circumstances images of such and such sort occur to a person'—examples like these are discussed in Carnap, 1934), referring to mental entities and quantifying over psychological states. Ordinary language is, as it happens, also the language of psychology. Could there then be one and the same solution for the two linguistic problems? Might one give an account of the relation between the protocol sentences of the observer, the system language of science and the logical reconstruction?

Carnap's answer is contained in his proposals for the 'physicalization' of psychology. The central thesis of physicalism is that psychological statements are translatable into propositions about the physical states of persons and in this way Carnap adds a new dimension to reductionism. What goes for the sentences of psychology also goes for the protocol sentences of the observer. We are entitled to claim that subjective protocol sentences are statements about the physical state of the observer. And Carnap goes on:

We are not demanding that psychology formulate each of its sentences in physical terminology. For its own purposes psychology may, as heretofore, utilize its own terminology. All that we are demanding is the production of the definitions through which psychological language is linked with physical language. We maintain that these definitions can be produced, since, implicitly, they already underlie psychological practice. (Carnap, 1959: 167)

Like psychological theory itself, the observer can go on using his own terminology, reporting on his beliefs, etc., for his own purposes. All we demand is that definitions be produced which link his cogitations with physical descriptions of the state he is in when producing them. Carnap's solution eludes the risk of privacy and individualism. We noted that in his view psychology will show that the statements of the scientist correspond to physical states of his organism.

To summarize, in Carnap's perspective there is an intrinsic relation between philosophy and psychology. An account of the psychological states of the observer is an integral part of the epistemological project of logical reconstruction. At the same time the possibility of physicalization of psychology is anticipated by the very logic of Carnap's procedure. We shall see below how these matters are at the heart of Fodor's claim that modularity vindicates philosophy of science.

LOGICAL COGNITIVISM

One may now draw upon some convergences between cognitivism and logical empiricism and why a Fodorean metatheory in the style of Carnap leads to *logical cognitivism*. Carnap stressed the expressive power of language, its role as medium or its capacity for making statements and how he defined epistemology as the study of the language of science. In the same spirit Fodor relates cognitive capacity to the possession of language. Or, more precisely in the spirit of Carnap, Fodor reduces the study of cognitive competence to linguistic competence.

(i) Language and metalanguage

Like Carnap, Fodor forges a distinction between ordinary language (used for everyday and scientific purposes alike) and a hypothetical underlying language, the *language of thought*, or mentalese (Fodor, 1975). Fodor presents the notion of a language of thought as inherent in the logic of the very idea of mental representation and cognitive processes. For example, he typically claims that a psychology, committed to the idea of systems processing information with the aim of representing their environment, is committed to the existence of a language of thought. Yet in pursuing the logic of psychological explanation Fodor is also speaking as an epistemologist. The hypothesis of a language of thought is at the same time defended in the context of the logical reconstruction of cognitive psychology. As a matter of fact, Fodor does not perceive his job as one of describing what psychologists do and why, but as reconstructing why it is that psychological explanations are good. In his view the theorist of psychology must look at a clear case of what scientists take to be a good explanation and analyse what makes it a clear case. Metatheory requires a reconstruction of science. To this Carnapian idea Fodor adds the second Carnapian idea which makes reconstruction a matter of constructing an underlying language. And, Fodor's metalanguage is the language of thought.

(ii) Metalanguage and epistemology

In the logical empiricist project the construction of the metalanguage is at the same time the logical construction of the world as ultimately known by science. Likewise, the study of the language of thought is the study of the world of the cognitive system or the world as known by such and such a cognitive system, underlying and lending consistence to phenomenal experience. Quite naturally then, this view leads to what is the corrolary of Carnapian epistemological constructivism: the postulated metalanguage defines the boundaries of that the individual can know (the thesis of 'epistemic boundedness').

(iii) A formal-syntactical notion of metalanguage

The thesis of a purely formal-syntactical notion of mental representation is the 'hard core' of Fodor's cognitivism. The hypothesis of a metalanguage allows Fodor to claim that mental representations are sentences in the language of thought. But only the formal or the syntactical aspects of the internal sentences matter. Cognitive processes are assimilated to operations over symbols. If this logical, computational or formalist view of mental representations holds, the study of cognitive processes can afford to ignore the content of mental representations. In this perspective Fodor appears entitled to claim that the functional and causal career of symbols is fixed by their formal or syntactical properties together with the rules of the system and not by their semantical properties or their referents.

The formality condition has caused some degree of perplexity even among authors basically in sympathy with the computational view of the mind. To bracket mental content seems counterintuitive from the vantage point of the intuitions of our folk psychology, from the vantage point of professional psychologists, and from the philosopher's perspective of the primacy of the intentionality of the mental. The discussions that have followed Fodor's thesis (for example after Fodor, 1980) have pointed to various unwelcome or implausible aspects of the view. But until recently Fodor's way of framing the fundamental issues was implicitly granted and with it the consequences of that for how psychology must be done given that formalist mentalism is unavoidable. Debates have since raged over Fodor's formality condition, but not much attention is paid to the metatheoretical origin of this view.

(iv) From logical cognitivism to empirical science

As a matter of fact, the cognitivist metatheory is also presented as the empirical psychological theory. Indeed, when speaking as an empirical scientist, Fodor takes the mentalese sentences postulated in the metatheory of cognition as the objects of empirical study. Psychological theory is in the business of studying internal mental formulas. Thus he distinguishes between internal representations in the sense of formulas in an internal language and structural descriptions of internal representations in the vocabulary of an (ideally completed) psychological theory. Yet he does not discuss or clarify the standard relation between a structural theory (for example a psychological theory of mental states) and its object (for example, mental states the theory is about). As Fodor puts it, the idea is that 'internal representations (like, for that matter, English sentences) express the content they do because they satisfy the structural descriptions they do' (Fodor, 1981: 169). Once we have our psychological theory, we will be able to refer to the internal representations with sentences from that theory. In the meantime, English must do.

On closer inspection, this predicament is not as bad as it looks. Our temporary reliance upon natural language does not compromise our chances for doing scientific psychology. As a matter of fact, the English sentences we use, for lack of anything better, do themselves have structural descriptions. 'For, on current views, structural descriptions are normally (among) the ones that speakers intend their utterances to satisfy and that hearers recover in the course of construing the utterances of speakers. That is: in the theoretically interesting cases, the internal representation of an English sentence *is* its structural description' (1981: 169). The way Fodor lets metatheory rule over theory leads him to assimilate or amalgamate different entities and different levels. This may lead to conservative research because Fodor tends to present it as an analytical fact that there is structural isomorphy between content ascribing sentences of English, mental representations, and the syntactical properties of mental representations. One may wonder whether a modularist theory needs to be committed to the notion that English linguistics, the psychology of language understanding, and the study of its underlying processes, all carve the cognitive system up the same way and all postulate the same modules.

So it turns out that for Fodor, as for Carnap, philosophy of science and psychology of the scientist are intimately linked. Yet Fodor adds an extra dimension to the Carnapian panorama and that way he makes the serpent eat its tail. Like Carnap, Fodor is interested in a philosophical explanation of psychology's successes and in the epistemology of cognitive psychology. He adopts a Carnapian solution to the issue of individual knowledge by assuming that a Carnapian metalanguage is actually installed in the cognitive system of the knower. On this account, the task of cognitive psychology reduces to the study of the internal language. Yet this is not as cryptic a definition as it sounds. Fodor closes the logical-cognitivist circle when he adds that English sentences spoken by the scientist have structural descriptions. The scientist's statements are reliable to the extent that they are products of cognitive architecture or have corresponding translations in the language of thought.

MODULARITY: AN ANCHOR FOR THE OBSERVATION–THEORY DISTINCTION?

We noted at the beginning that the observation–theory distinction passes for the hallmark of logical empiricism. Many critics of positivism have focused their attacks on this distinction and it is this distinction which, presumably, is the dogma overthrown by the cognitive revolution. Yet, the distinction between observation and theory is not the easy or straightforward one its critics take it to be. This section should bring out that the observation–theory distinction belongs to more than just one level of scientific discourse. The consequence of this fact is that it is difficult to see just which observation–theory distinction has been overthrown by the cognitive revolution and which one has been reinstated by modular cognitive psychology.

We have assembled some elements for decoding Fodor's claims about the relation between modularity and observation–theory distinction. We see that these claims have their origin in his logical cognitivism, his reconstruction of cognitive psychology in the style of Carnap. Some implications particularly important for our topic follow from this: the distinction between observation and theory is not clear or operational outside the idea of an epistemological reconstruction of science. It is a distinction between two kinds of terms in the language of science as logical empiricism reconstructs scientific discourse. It is not a distinction between kinds of psychological processes. In other words, the distinction is itself theory-dependent. If so, the observation–theory distinction is not one of a kind for which the second cognitive revolution being the modularity perspective, can marshal support. I review each of these points in turn.

In Carnap's perspective there is no way of telling what belongs to observation and what belongs to theory until the logical reconstruction of science is well on its way. In other words, in no sense is the distinction given or does the observation part correspond to what is presumably given in observation preceding the interpretations and constructions of the theorist. There is no other way of reading the modularity thesis than along these same lines. For example, Fodor is not claiming that the first half of the cognitive processes consists of making observations of the external world which are then passed on to the second half of the cognitive process concerned with inference, interpretation, and theory. If this were his view, it would be much clearer to talk about the contrast between perception and cognition. This picture disregards the fact that Fodorean modules have their origin in a cognitive theory of the mind and that Fodor defends a thoroughly cognitive concept of modules. The description of modular-processing requires a cognitive vocabulary and not the vocabulary of physical reality and sensory parameters. Modules typically compute a description of the environment that is couched in a non-physical vocabulary. And the central part in the description of modular processes consists in formulating what specific knowledge is embodied in the module, or against what domain specific background knowledge modular computations are performed.

However, when one reads the modularity thesis this way, one wonders what becomes of its link with claims about the observation–theory distinction. Modules are not in the business of providing the observation basis, at least not on a common-sense understanding of observation. The paradox only resolves in the light of the project of logical cognitivism. It is only when the project of logical reconstruction of psychology is underway and the contours of the language of thought are in sight, that the theorist of psychology will be able to assign propositions to either central or modular levels. If we push this theme a bit further we are forced to conclude that only in the case of modules or theories about them will the enterprise of logical reconstruction be successful. Central processing is by definition recalcitrant in the sense that it escapes the efforts of the logical reconstructivist. If the feasibility of logical reconstruction sets the boundaries of empirical inquiry in cognitive psychology, one should expect that the study of central processes falls outside the boundaries laid down for sensible empirical questions. This is exactly what Fodor concludes. But he presents his thesis on the boundaries of the scientific study of cognition as the inevitable conclusion of the failure of thirty years of research on central cognitive processes. Whatever else is at stake, this thesis must also be viewed as the logical consequence of the style of epistemological reconstruction of cognitive psychology he has adopted.

I now come to the point of the theory-dependency of the observation–theory distinction. We noted how, in Fodor's view, what psychology can achieve, its chances of empirical success depends on its logical and epistemological foundations. But at the same time he argues that reflection on the epistemological framework marks the beginning of empirical research which will show where to locate the border between modular and non-modular processes. Does this mean that in the end, empirical research may just show that the distinction is itself untenable? In that case modularism would no longer vindicate the observation–theory distinction, but the logical empiricist enterprise would be superseded by cognitive psychology.

Given our earlier presentation of logical cognitivism, some puzzling questions arise here. If, as we claim is the case, logical cognitivism is the true locus of the distinction between modular and non-modular processes, how can it ever be the case that such a metatheoretical distinction is either supported or refuted by the progress of science? As a matter of principle, scientific theories underdetermine the logical reconstruction offered for them. If one ignores this principle, there is *ipso facto* no room for quoting novel scientific developments in support of a metatheory or vice versa.

Will logical cognitivism or the logical reconstruction of cognitive psychology be successful or must it, like logical empiricism, remain a blueprint for a project that is doomed to fail? How do the observation terms get their meaning? Where do non-observation terms get their semantics and how does their meaning connect with observations? How do we learn to use non-observation terms and how does their meaning change over time? Fodor's answer to the first question is, predictably, that the meaning of the primitive terms are given. They are given with the mental faculties of the organism in the sense that they have an objective psychological basis in the organism (Fodor, 1987). As we noted, it is the job of the modularist psychologist to find out which observation terms there are. Having said so much, Fodor is tempted to continue the story by providing an account of our non-observation terms which stays within the boundaries of modularism and respects the arguments that have laid to it. The resulting picture is a computational model of the scientist. What about the concepts for whom we are unlikely to find a psychophysical base in the organism, like, for example 'proton'? For the post-empiricist Fodor claims himself to be, definition of theoretical terms in observation terms is excluded. Also is excluded the appeal to higher cognitive processes embodying theoretical knowledge. The link between the scientist's observation and his propositions about protons cannot rest on observation combined with theory based inferences. If so, the theory would be the source of the concept's meaning and we would be back with meaning holism, the major enemy for Fodor's semantic naturalization project. Non-observation terms are causally connected to the world not because of their role in a theory about the world nor because of the scientist's belief in such a theory. Those aspects are important in their own right, but they do not matter when we try to understand the relation of concepts to the world. All that is needed to understand that relation is a non-intentional or a naturalized perspective on the denotation of non-observation concepts. The story must run along the same lines as the story of the semantics of observation terms. The required causal connection follows from the fact that (scientific) theories about the world are calculating devices or formalisms.

> The picture is that there's, as it were, a computer between the sensorium and the belief box, and that the tokening of certain psychological concepts eventuates in the computer's running through certain calculations that in turn lead to tokenings of 'proton' (or of 'horse', or whatever) on the appropriate occasions . . . all *that* requires is that the computer output 'proton' when its inputs are tokenings of psychophysical concepts for which 'protons' are in fact causally responsible. (Fodor, 1987: 123)

Fodor is no exception to the dominant way philosophers in this century have thought about knowledge. The philosophical problem of representing knowledge focuses on axiomatizing knowledge in a formalized language. Fodor has evidently taken this approach a step further by combining it with the project of naturalized epistemology.

Logical empiricism was never an empiricist philosophy, even if it accidentally was made into one by philosophers of science typically confusing observation statements with perceptual reports. As approached here, Fodorian or logical cognitivist observation is not to be confused with the empirical activity of perception. That Fodor's terminology itself seems to hesitate between perception as the empirical psychological notion and observation as the theoretical notion may be taken as a symptom of the double edgedness mechanics of the whole logical-cognitivist enterprise whereby ideally epistemology is naturalized through an appeal to cognitive psychology which in the process is itself rationally reconstructed.

REFERENCES

Carnap, R. (1928), *Die logische Aufbau der Welt*, Hamburg: Felix Meiner Verlag.

—— (1932/3), *Erkenntnis Vol. II & III*.

—— (1934), *The Unity of Science*, London: Kegan Paul.

—— (1959), 'Psychology in Physical Language', in A. J. Ayer (ed.), *Logical Positivism*. Glencoe, Il.: Free Press, 165–98.

Churchland, P. M. (1981), 'Eliminative Materialism and the Propositional Attitudes', *Journal of Philosophy*, 78: 67–90.

—— (1986), *Neurophilosophy*, Cambridge, Mass.: MIT Press.

Cicourel, A. (1973), *Cognitive Psychology: New Directions*, London: Routledge & Kegan Paul.

De Gelder, B. (1985), 'The Cognitivist Conjuring Trick or How Development Vanished', in R. Harris and C. J. Bailey (eds.), *Developmental Mechanisms of Language*, Oxford: Pergamon Press.

—— (1992), 'Why Does Consciousness Matter to Cognitive Psychology?' in J. Alegria, D. Holender, J. Morais, and M. Radeau (eds.), *Analytic Approches to Human Cognition*, Amsterdam: Elsevier Science Publishers, 379–93.

Dennett, D. C. (1978), 'Intentional Systems', repr. in *Brainstorms, Philosophical Essays on Mind and Psychology*, Montgomery, Vt.: Bradford Books, 3–22.

—— (1988), Précis of *The Intentional Stance, Behavioral and Brain Sciences*, 11: 495–505.

Goodwin, B. C. (1978), 'A Cognitive View of Biological Processes', *Journal of Social and Biological Structures*, 1: 117–125.

Goldman, A. I. (1986), *Epistemology and Cognition*', Cambridge, Mass.: Harvard University Press.

Feigl, H. (1967), *The 'Mental' and the 'Physical': The Essay and a Postscript*, Minneapolis, Minn.: University of Minneapolis Press.

Fodor, J. A. (1968), *Psychological Explanation*, New York: Random House.

—— (1975), *The Language of Thought*, New York: Thomas Y. Crowell.

—— (1980), 'Methodological Solipsism Considered as a Research Strategy in Cognitive Psychology', *Behavioral and Brain Sciences*, 3: 63–73.

—— (1981), *Representations. Philosophical Essays on the Foundations of Cognitive Science*, Brighton, Harvester Press.

—— (1983), *The Modularity of Mind: An Essay on Faculty Psychology*, Cambridge, Mass.: MIT Press.

—— (1984), 'Observation reconsidered', *Philosophy of Science*, 51: 23–43.

—— (1987), *Psychosemantics*, Cambridge, Mass.: MIT Press.

—— (1991), 'The Dogma that Didn't Bark (A Fragment of a Naturalized Epistemology)', *Mind*, 100: 201–20.

Hacking, I. (1975), *Why Does Language Matter to Philosophy?* Cambridge: Cambridge University Press.

Harman, G. (1973), *Thought*, Princeton, NJ: Princeton University Press.

Haugeland, J. (1981), *Mind Design*, Cambridge, Mass.: MIT Press.

Hempel, C. G. (1980), 'The Logical Analysis of Psychology', in N. Block (ed.), *Readings in Philosophy of Psychology*, i, Cambridge, Mass.: Harvard University Press, 14–23.

Jackendoff, R. (1986), *Language and Cognition*, Cambridge, Mass.: MIT Press.

Kuhn, T. S. (1962), *The Structure of Scientific Revolutions*, Chicago: University of Chicago Press.

Langacker, R. W. (1987), *Foundations of Cognitive Grammar*, i, Stanford, Calif.: Stanford University Press.

Marr, D. (1982), *Vision*, San Francisco: Freeman.

Palermo, D. S. (1971), 'Is a Scientific Revolution Taking Place in Psychology?' *Science Studies*, 1: 135–155.

Proust, J. (1986), *Questions de forme*, Paris: Fayard.

Pylyshyn, Z. W. (1984), *Computation and Cognition. Toward a Foundation for Cognitive Science*, Cambridge, Mass.: MIT Press.

Quine, W. V. O. (1966), *The Ways of Paradox, and Other Essays*, New York: Random House.

Shallice, T. (1984), 'More Functionally Isolable Subsystems but Fewer "modules"'? *Cognition*, 17, 243–52.

Stich, S. (1983), *From Folk Psychology to Cognitive Science*, Cambridge: Mass.: MIT Press.

Suppe, F. (1974), *The Structure of Scientific Theories*, Urbana, Il.: University of Illinois Press.

Weiner, W. B., and Palermo, D. S. (eds.) (1974), *Cognition and the Symbolic Processes*, i, New York: Wiley & Sons.

9

Folk Psychology and Naïve Physics

MURRAY SHANAHAN

———•———

INTRODUCTION

The subject of this essay is a particular sort of activity, namely
everyday problem-solving, an aptitude for which is displayed by
each human being in his ability to attain simple goals, such as
navigating an unfamiliar city, or making a cup of tea, or driving
a car. Even cats and dogs display such an aptitude, to a lesser
degree than human beings but to a greater degree than house flies,
in their capacity to find food and shelter and sexual solace.

Folk psychology is the day-to-day 'theory' used to explain and
predict such activity. As a folk psychologist, I have a degree of understanding of everyday problem-solving, but I seek a deeper understanding, an understanding to which folk psychology, as it stands,
is inadequate, an understanding sufficient for the fulfilment of the
vision of artificial intelligence (AI) research. Beginning with a
portrait of contemporary folk psychology, I will proceed to a discussion of the goals of AI research, and will go on to explore the
relationship between the two, emphasizing the importance of the
capacity to translate between the language of the folk psychologist
and the language of the AI scientist.

1. FOLK PSYCHOLOGY

Folk psychology is the day-to-day theory we use to explain and
predict everyday problem-solving behaviour. We can imagine a
languageless folk psychologist, who could not explain but who
could predict, and whose capacity to do so would be reflected in
an ability to influence the actions of her subject according to her

own desires, and to adapt her own actions to what she expects her subject to do. This is what is meant by the *practices* of folk psychology. Such practices are not linguistic, although it is hard to imagine someone acquiring them without the aid of language. In contrast, the *customs* of folk psychology are reflected in folk-psychological talk, in the verbal *attitude* ascriptions involved in everyday explanations of action. With the prevailing folk psychology, the nature of predictive practice is revealed in explanatory custom. By investigating the language of the folk psychologist we discover the state of the art in the folk understanding of everyday problem-solving.

Suppose that the folk psychologist is sitting in a pub and is asked to explain the behaviour of someone who goes to the bar and buys a drink. She might say something like this: 'He saw that the bar was open, he knew that the bar sold drinks and he was thirsty so he approached the bar and bought a drink.' A folk-psychological explanation involves the ascription of various propositional attitudes to a subject—beliefs, desires, hopes, fears, intentions, suspicions, etc. (in this essay I shall concentrate on belief and desire), which are characterized by their use of *embedded sentences*. It also involves the assumption that certain 'causal' relationships obtain between a subject's perceptions, propositional attitudes, and actions—perceptions give rise to attitudes, attitudes interact to form further attitudes, and attitudes give rise to actions. The folk psychologist is able to make (reasonably) accurate predictions and to give (fairly) satisfactory explanations of a subject's behaviour. So folk psychology is a sort of theory, albeit an unwritten one, manifest only in practices and customs.[1]

It is sometimes useful to categorize the beliefs ascribed by the folk psychologist—they can be about particular states of affairs, such as this room at this instant, or they can be part of the subject's grasp of some concept, such as water or London or the number five. If the folk psychologist says of someone: 'He believes that the sink is full of water', then she is crediting him with possessing the concept of water, the concept of a sink and with an understanding of what it is for something to be full of a liquid. Let us consider

---

[1] See P. M. Churchland, 'Eliminative Materialism and the Propositional Attitudes', *Journal of Philosophy*, 78/2 (1981), 67–90, 67 and A. Clark, 'From Folk Psychology to Naïve Psychology', *Cognitive Science*, 11 (1987), 139–54 for opposing views on the status of folk psychology as a theory.

what it is to possess the concept of water. The subject is able to recognize water—he knows what it looks like, that it is clear and sparkles and shines, he knows what it sounds like, gushing, trickling, or splashing, he knows what it feels like and tastes like. He knows how it behaves, how it falls and splashes, how it spreads across surfaces or soaks into them, how it runs downhill, how it fills containers, and how they overflow. He knows the many uses of water, for drinking, for swimming in, for washing with.[2] The concept of water (in some form or other) is common to (almost) all human beings, whilst other concepts are less common, such as the concept of my pet budgie or of transcendental idealism.

The folk psychologist displays an understanding of her subject's perceptual apparatus when she says: 'He saw that the sink was full of water.' She knows the circumstances in which he can see such a thing; he must be looking in the right direction, his eyes must be open, there must be enough light to see by, etc. When she describes what her subject perceives, the folk psychologist employs the terms of the web of conceptual beliefs she has attributed to him.

The folk psychologist attributes to her subject certain dispositions to form and revise beliefs about particular states of affairs according to what he perceives, and to reason from one such belief to another. Suppose it is close to last orders in the pub and that someone goes to the bar to buy a drink. When he arrives he sees that there is no one to serve him, so he concludes that the bar is closed, and walks away. But then the barman (who has been changing the barrel) comes rushing in to take last orders, and the customer returns. The folk psychologist says: 'He saw that the barman had gone, so he thought that the bar was closed. But then he realized that the barman was only changing the barrel. So he went back and bought a drink.'

The folk psychologist only ascribes *dispositions* to reason from one belief to another. If someone asked her whether the barman knew that 'Tigers don't have pink stripes', she would consider it a most peculiar question. She might say something like this: 'In a sense he knew it, because everyone knows that tigers have only

---

[2] I am not, of course, claiming that all of the beliefs mentioned are necessary for a grasp of the concept of water. I am simply suggesting some beliefs which seem to us to be characteristic of such a grasp.

black stripes. But he surely didn't need to know it to change the barrel.'

If the subject does not possess a particular concept, then the folk psychologist's predictions and explanations can cope, although the more exotic the subject seems to her, the less intelligible she finds his behaviour and the more work is involved in understanding it. Suppose the folk psychologist is dealing with a particularly peculiar subject, who doesn't know that water is drinkable. Then she might still say of him: 'He believes the sink is full of water', and she might also add 'But he doesn't know that water is drinkable (poor chap).' His lack of grasp of the concept will be manifest in his behaviour—he refuses to drink water, even when he is thirsty and has access to it. Of course, a subject's lack of grasp of a concept admits of degree, depending on what beliefs are missing and how important they are.

It may happen that the subject will learn that water is drinkable. He may observe somebody drinking it, or he may accidentally ingest some himself and find it agreeable. The folk psychologist can cope with such changes in conceptual belief. She says of her subject: 'He saw someone drinking water and realized that it was drinkable.' Similarly, the folk psychologist has an understanding of concept acquisition. Consider a young child who has not yet learnt how to use a knife and fork. The folk psychologist sees him playing with them and says: 'He is learning about knives and forks.' She can tell when he makes progress, when he begins to display an ability to wield his cutlery properly. She even knows how to speed up the child's progress, through suitable instruction and demonstration.

So the folk psychologist conceives her subject's web of conceptual beliefs to be in a continuous state of flux. New beliefs can be acquired and old ones revised and, as Quine points out,[3] the revision of one belief may in turn bring about the revision of other beliefs which are logically related. There are some *important* conceptual beliefs whose revision would cause major disruption to a subject's web of conceptual beliefs, such as the belief that nothing can be in two places at once. There are others, less important, whose revision would cause only minor disruption, such as the belief that

---

[3] W. V. O. Quine, 'Two Dogmas of Empiricism', in *From a Logical Point of View*, Cambridge, Mass.: Harvard University Press.

the pub is always busy on Fridays. And there are, of course, beliefs of every intermediate shade of doxastic importance. The folk psychologist tends to project her own important conceptual beliefs, her own *conceptual framework*, onto her subject.

Characterizations like that above barely scratch the surface of our folk-psychological understanding. They are necessarily imprecise —the customs and practices in question do not admit of precise characterization, they manifest themselves differently in different individuals, they vary from culture to culture, and are subject to evolution. These customs and practices are embedded in a linguistic culture which encourages the habit of philosophical enquiry. In particular, it allows the Socratic question: 'What is belief?', and it admits discourse on the nature of belief even though this discourse consistently fails to produce satisfactory answers and generates the illusion of a puzzle. The field of AI hopes to foster a very different sort of understanding.

2. ARTIFICIAL INTELLIGENCE

The term 'artificial intelligence' is applied to many kinds of research, ranging from the study of search algorithms, through the construction of theorem-provers and the design of certain programming languages, to the study of computational models of cognition. Whilst much of this research produces tools with immediate application outside the sphere of AI itself, there is a clearly discernible vision motivating AI research, and each of these tools is a prospective contribution towards its realization.

There is no reason to think that artificial intelligence, unlike other disciplines, has a unique goal. It is inspired, however, by a unique vision—of fully autonomous, flexibly intelligent, rational (though artificial) agents.[4]

But it is not enough merely to be able to build such machines. What is sought is a thorough understanding of everyday problem-solving. What does it mean to have such an understanding? In some sense, a spider understands webs. This understanding is manifest in an ability to spin them and repair them in a variety of differently

---

[4] D. Israel, 'A Short Companion to the Naïve Physics Manifesto', in J. R. Hobbs and R. C. Moore (eds.), *Formal Theories of the Commonsense World*, Ablex, 1985: 427–47.

shaped niches. But a spider has a very meagre understanding of tension and stress and structures. It could not apply its understanding to the construction of bridges, nor could it communicate its understanding to other spiders. There are different degrees and different kinds of understanding.

Central to the realization of the AI vision is a formal study of methods for problem-solving in the everyday world, because a great deal of intelligent behaviour just is problem-solving in the everyday world, and the development of a proper understanding of everyday problem-solving demands a rigorous, mathematically founded investigation of its underlying principles. So, both folk psychology and AI are concerned, amongst other things, with everyday problem-solving, but their approaches are very different in style. By restricting her domain of enquiry to everyday problem-solving, the AI scientist avoids serious philosophical issues, like subjectivity and privacy and first-personal perspective, but through the rigour and precision of her language helps to dispel illusory ones, like the nature of belief.

Let us be quite clear about the scope of this enquiry. Quine remarks that,

Different persons growing up in the same language are like different bushes trimmed and trained to take the shape of identical elephants. The anatomical details of twigs and branches will fulfil the elephantine form differently from bush to bush, but the overall outward results are alike.[5]

A certain sort of enquiry would be interested in the shape of the bush, another sort might be interested in particular anatomical structures which realize this shape. Note that a description of the shape of the bush captures the space of possible anatomical structures which could realize that shape. Everyday problem-solvers are also like appropriately trimmed and trained bushes. The kind of AI research which is the subject of this essay is interested in the shape of the bushes—the nature of the activity not the mechanisms underlying that activity.[6]

It may turn out that in order to usefully describe this activity, we require certain constructions of language—such as the propositional attitudes of folk psychology. But in using this sort of language we

---

[5] W. V. O. Quine, *Word and Object*, Cambridge, Mass.: MIT Press, 1960: 8.
[6] This kind of AI is sometimes identified with the 'McCarthy school', as opposed to the 'Minsky school'. See D. Israel, 'A Short Companion to the Naïve Physics Manifesto', 427.

are not saying anything about mechanism. The domain of folk psychology is not restricted to humans. We tend also to use it to explain and predict the activity of certain animals and machines, and would probably use it for Martians if we ever happened to meet any. Even the actions of a wooden golem which worked by magic would be within the domain of folk psychology. As Dennett points out, the behaviour of a chess computer could be explained in terms of the algorithms it employs or even in terms of its physical construction. But it is easier to adopt the 'intentional stance' and employ the language of folk psychology, invoking the machine's beliefs and desires (such as a desire to 'get its queen out early').[7] If somebody *forced* us to employ attitude talk only with respect to humans, then it would be necessary to invent new linguistic constructions which performed the same function but which had wider scope.

Furthermore, the products of AI research are insensitive to the *particular* world (or simulated world) to which they happen to be connected. It is a matter of indifference to the AI scientist whether her system is attached to a simulated environment (the programmer taking the role of a Cartesian demon), to our Earth, or to Twin Earth. The AI scientist, then, is a kind of 'methodological solipsist'.[8] Suppose the AI scientist is asked to consider the beliefs of a system connected to our Earth and those of a system connected to a simulated environment. She might say of both that they believe the sink is full of water. If we then pointed out to her that the beliefs are, in a sense, different, she might say: 'Of course they are different. The system connected to the simulated environment doesn't have a belief about a real sink, whilst the other system does. However, this doesn't affect my research programme.'[9]

3. NAÏVE PHYSICS

One approach to the realization of the AI vision involves an attempt at a deep analysis of basic folk-theoretical concepts in the

[7] D. C. Dennett, 'Intentional Systems', in *Brainstorms*, Hassocks, Sussex: Harvester Press, 1978: 3–22.

[8] See H. Putnam, 'The Meaning of Meaning', in *Essays on Mind, Language and Reality*, Cambridge: Cambridge University Press, 1975: 215.

[9] The so-called wide/narrow debate is explored in P. Pettit and J. McDowell (eds.), *Subject, Thought, and Context*, Oxford: Oxford University Press, 1986.

hope that this will yield a sufficiently formal theory—a theory which will illuminate the concept's role in the production of behaviour. The analysis of folk-theoretical concepts involves making public a number of sentences about those concepts, instituting a convention which will more firmly fix their meaning. But every sentence made public employs more folk-theoretical terms, which may require further conceptual analysis. According to the *logicist* thesis, this process will converge on a body of sentences whose interpretation is universally agreed, and which are written in a formal language. This body of sentences will capture the common-sense knowledge which is brought to bear in everyday problem-solving. I shall not rehearse the arguments for the logicist position, which can be consulted elsewhere.[10] My concern here is with the philosophical status of prospective products of the logicist research programme.

Someone whose everyday world is, say, present-day London, has a grasp of a great many culturally specific concepts—things like buses, tube trains, shops, and restaurants. Even the shallowest conceptual analysis of such things soon exposes a collection of underlying naïve physical and metaphysical concepts—of objects, arrangements of objects, the stuff that objects can be made from, the ways objects behave, when they are lifted, pushed, dropped, hit, or simply left alone—of spatial and temporal location, of up and down, far away and near, in front and behind, before and after. Naïve physical and metaphysical concepts are the components out of which complex conceptual frameworks are built, and their analysis is the first step towards an understanding of such frameworks. The project of performing such an analysis deeply enough to yield a formal theory is described by Hayes.[11]

I propose the construction of a formalization of a sizable portion of common-sense knowledge about the everyday physical world: about objects, shape, space, movement, substances (solids and liquids), time, etc.[12]

[10] P. J. Hayes, 'In Defence of Logic', *Proceedings IJCAI*, 77: 559. R. C. Moore, 'The Role of Logic in Knowledge Representation and Commonsense Reasoning', *Proceedings AAAI*, 82: 428. See also D. McDermott, 'A Critique of Pure Reason', *Computational Intelligence*, 3/3: 151, and the many commentaries in the same volume.

[11] P. J. Hayes, 'The Second Naïve Physics Manifesto', in *Formal Theories of the Commonsense World*, 1–36.

[12] Ibid. 2.

Hayes's motivation for this project is partly to get away from the 'toy domains' which have been the traditional concern of AI research, such as the Blocks World, and to provide a richer domain for the study of problem-solving. He suggests that the project should not initially be concerned with the inference mechanisms that will be used on the resulting formalization, and he recommends the first-order predicate calculus as its 'reference language'.[13] The resulting theory is expected to be very large, comprising perhaps a hundred thousand axioms, and it seems unlikely that it will contain any isolated sub-theories. It may, however, be structured into *clusters*. A cluster is a densely connected (though not isolated) collection of axioms, which fix the meanings of a number of closely related concepts. For instance, there seems to be a family of concepts associated with places and positions, whose analysis will yield a cluster.

Consider the following collection of words: inside, outside, door, portal, window, gate, way in, way out, wall, boundary, container, obstacle, barrier, way past, way through, at, in.
  I think these words hint at a cluster of related concepts which are of fundamental importance to naïve physics. This cluster concerns the dividing up of three-dimensional space in pieces which have physical boundaries, and the ways in which these pieces of space can be connected to one another, and how objects, people, events, and liquids can get from one such place to another.[14]

Besides places and positions, Hayes discusses our everyday concepts of spaces and objects, qualities, quantities and measurement, change, time and histories, energy, effort, and motion. Writing about the composition of objects, Hayes says,

As far as I can judge, all naïve-physical objects are either a single piece of homogenous stuff, or are made up as a composite out of parts which are themselves objects. The essence of a composite is that its component parts *are* themselves objects, and that it can (conceptually if not in practice) be taken apart and reassembled, being then the same object. Examples of composites include a car, a cup of coffee, a house, four bricks making a platform. Examples of homogenous objects are a bronze statue, a plank of wood, the Mississippi, a brick. Homogenous objects have no

---

[13] By 'reference language', Hayes means a single language into which more exotic representation languages can be translated. He does not object to the use of such exotic languages if it is convenient.
[14] Ibid. 19.

parts, and can only be taken apart by being broken or divided in some way, resulting in *pieces*.[15]

Hayes goes on to attempt a formalization of our everyday concept of liquids—the containment of liquid, its behaviour, and the individuation of liquid objects.[16] The seventy-four axioms he provides are powerful enough to permit the prediction of the behaviour of liquids in various circumstances. For instance, they can be used to predict the behaviour of a glass of milk as it is poured onto a flat table, spreads out to the sides, and spills over the edges. Work has also been done on formalizing other everyday concepts, such as shape[17] and substance.[18] Alongside naïve physics, which is a theory of everyday middle-sized objects, the logicist requires other theories, of naïve topography[19] and naïve psychology, for example.[20]

As Hayes comments,[21] (human) naïve physics is pre-Galilean.[22] But the falsity of a theory in naïve physics, human or machine, is no cause for concern. So long as the cases which would falsify the theory do not arise given the precision of the naïve physicists' measurements, then the theory continues to be useful. More precisely, a naïve theory can be said to be adequate with respect to a given *granularity*.[23] For certain purposes, a coarse grain of representation is adequate—at a coarse grain, the human body can be represented simply as a cylinder, and this would suffice for tackling the problem of moving about in a crowd (so long as the crowd was not too dense). For some purposes, a finer grain is required—the human body could be represented as a collection of variously sized, connected cylinders (arms, legs, torso, and so on),

[15] Ibid. 27.

[16] P. J. Hayes, 'Naïve Physics 1: Ontology for Liquids', in *Formal Theories of the Commonsense World*, 71–107.

[17] Y. Shoham, 'Naïve Kinematics: Two Aspects of Shape', in J. Hobbs (ed.), *Commonsense Summer*: Final Report, SRI International, AI Center, 1984.

[18] G. Hager, Naïve Physics of Materials: A Recon Mission, in J. Hobbs (ed.), *Commonsense Summer*: Final Report, SRI International, AI Center, 1984.

[19] See E. Davies, *Representing and Acquiring Geographical Knowledge*, London: Pitman.

[20] Although they have similar domains, it is important to distinguish the AI scientist's formal theory of naïve psychology from the unwritten 'theory' of the folk psychologist.

[21] P. J. Hayes, 'The Naïve Physics Manifesto', in D. Michie (ed.), *Expert Systems in the Micro-electronic Age*, Edinburgh: Edinburgh University Press, 1979: 242–70.

[22] I emphasize *human* naïve physics here because the AI scientist is not necessarily concerned to model human mistakes in reasoning about everyday objects.

[23] See J. R. Hobbs, 'Granularity', *Proceedings AAAI*, 85: 432.

and this would be suitable for problems involving more intimate forms of interaction. Similarly, if a naïve theory displays ontological promiscuity or betrays contentious metaphysical presuppositions, there is no problem so long as the theory serves its purpose.

Whilst a *weak* logicist believes that logic can be used to describe the knowledge required for everyday problem-solving, a *strong* logicist believes that logic can also be used to *represent* it in a computer. The fulfilment of the strong logicist research programme demands the development of a whole battery of techniques for the construction and use of naïve theories, corresponding to the various capacities familiar to the folk psychologist: mechanisms for theory formation, mechanisms for default reasoning, reason-maintenance systems, and planners.[24] But whether she has taken the strong or weak logicist approach, the AI scientist can explain her creation's behaviour as if it were the product of an ever-changing set of logical formulae, expressed in naïve-theoretical terms, which mediates between perception and action.

The AI scientist, who is familiar with the construction of naïve theories, is adept at translation between the formal language in which a naïve theory is expressed and the language of folk psychology. Translation is possible because of the close correspondence between the sentences of folk psychology and predicate calculus formulae. Knowing the role of a given set of such formulae in the production of behaviour, she can ascribe folk-psychological attitudes to her creations. Conversely, she can generate a set of formulae which correspond (roughly, since folk-psychological language is imprecise) with any given folk-psychological description of a set of attitudes. As well as facilitating communication between AI scientists, the capacity to translate between formal and folk-psychological language affords relief to the sense of puzzlement about the nature of belief, and thus serves an important philosophical purpose.

CONCLUDING REMARKS

In sum then, the AI scientist is interested in describing a particular causal surface—the interface between an inner and an outer to

---

[24] For a detailed inventory of the logicist's toolbox see N. J. Nilsson and M. R. Genesereth, *Logical Foundations of Artificial Intelligence*, Morgan Kaufmann, 1987.

whose structure she is indifferent, though, in a sense, the causal surface in question defines the space of possible such structures. The causal surface in question is picked out by the prevailing folk-psychological customs and practices. What the AI scientist seeks is an improved set of customs and practices—one which displays a deeper understanding, manifest first in a language which admits of less ambiguity and leaves fewer unanswered (unanswerable) questions, and second in the construction of machines which exhibit a capacity for everyday problem-solving. Rather than displacing the old folk-psychological customs and practices, the new language supplements them, and neutralizes some of their apparent puzzles via their translation into a purer idiom.

10

Why Concept Learning is a Good Idea

CHRISTOPHER J. THORNTON

---

1. INTRODUCTION

In general, an *implementation* of a concept c is any mechanism which partitions some set of possible data elements into two subsets: the subset covered by the concept and the subset not covered. Any mechanism which produces such black boxes can be construed as a concept learner. The class of all such mechanisms is large. It encompasses concept learners proper, e.g. symbolist methods such as Candidate–Elimination [1, 2], Focusing [3, 4], Classification [5], and Conceptual Clustering [6, Fisher, Learning from 7, 8, 9]. It also encompasses mechanisms which do not have concept learning as an explicit goal but which nevertheless produce the requisite black boxes, e.g. connectionist mechanisms such as Back-Propagation, Competitive Learning [10], and numerical taxonomy methods such as hierarchical clustering [11, 12].

In connectionist learning, the candidates for concept implementations are 'feature detectors'. These produce high levels of output for certain classes of input so can be thought of as *probabilistic* concepts covering the classes in question. Clustering mechanisms produce dendrograms which can be thought of as disjunctive concepts in the manner of the decision trees produced by symbolist mechanisms such as ID3 [5, 13].

The fact that so many computational mechanisms do (or can be seen as doing) concept learning seems to suggest that the process must be rather significant cognitively speaking. But what is its significance? Putting the question another way: What is the *point* of concept learning? Why is it a good idea? Some authors argue that concept learning is useful because it helps to make the world simpler and more easily comprehended. For example, Smith and Medin begin their book on 'Categories and Concepts' as follows.

Without concepts, mental life would be chaotic. If we perceived each entity as unique, we would be overwhelmed by the sheer diversity of what we experience and unable to remember more than a minute fraction of what we encounter. And if each individual entity needed a distinct name, our language would be staggeringly complex and communication virtually impossible. Fortunately, though, we do not perceive, remember, and talk about each object and event as unique, but rather as an instance of a class or concept that we already know something about [14, p. 1].

This sort of argument makes a compelling appeal to intuition but it does not provide an answer in terms of any existing theories. In contrast, the present paper provides an *information-theoretic* account of the processes of and effects achieved by concept learning. The account shows that concept learning can usually be viewed[1] in terms of a cognitive agent's attempt to minimize both the information content and equivocation of messages (inputs) from the environment. Moreover, different outcomes in a learning process can usually be understood in terms of the discovery of locally optimal positions in a trade-off between information-reduction and equivocation-increase.

1.1. *Motivation*

There are three main arguments which justify this work. They are as follows.

- Computational mechanisms for empirical concept learning are known to be quite limited in power. No existing mechanism will continue to acquire new concepts indefinitely. There will come a point after which it will cease to produce any worthwhile results. A clear information-theoretic account for the process may shed new light on this limitation.
- Interest in concept learning extends across a number of different paradigms (e.g. symbolism, connectionism, statistics, psychology). Typically the results, ideas, and methods associated with one paradigm are difficult to assimilate into the framework

---

[1] The model developed is applicable only in the case where the computational abilities of the learner are subject to certain constraints.

of another. The development of an information-theoretic account might provide a framework via which to make cross-paradigm links.

- Many researchers in both the symbolist paradigm and the connectionist paradigm argue that there is a need to identify the information-theoretic foundations for the computational methods developed in the cognitive sciences [15, 16]. This work is precisely an attempt to bring out one such foundation.

2. SIMILARITY-BASED CONCEPT LEARNING

A substantial proportion of mechanisms which generate (or can be seen as generating) concepts do so in a particular way. In machine learning the method is called *similarity-based learning* (SBL) [17]. Its central aim is to identify and define groupings of similar data elements. (These are normally called 'descriptions' in symbolist learning, 'input vectors' in connectionist learning, and 'data points' in numerical taxonomy.)

Let us take as an example the symbolist-learning mechanism called Focusing. This is an algorithm which effectively manipulates the boundaries of two regions in the data-space: an outer region enclosing all elements which are not known to be excluded from the concept and an inner region enclosing all elements which are known to be included in the concept.[2]

The algorithm attempts to expand the inner region and shrink the outer region until they are identical. The definition of the region forms the target concept, i.e. it forms a rule which generalizes all positive instances but no negative instances [18]. The point to note is that the method is effectively a way of exploiting the fact that the positive instances of a concept will tend to be more *similar* to (and therefore closer in data-space to) each other than to negative instances.

Connectionist mechanisms frequently employ the delta learning rule [10, ch. 2]. This is a way of manipulating a weight-vector so as to ensure that the inner product of some input vector with the weight vector is maximized for some particular subset of inputs. If vectors are normalized then this operation effectively involves

---

[2] The algorithm actually manipulates marks in generalization trees.

'defining' groups of similar data elements in terms of their centroid point, [cf. 10, ch. 5]. In Competitive learning for example, the potential centroids (weight-vectors) are moved around in data-space until they lie at the centre of groups of similar elements. Again, the point to note is that the method is a way of exploiting the notion that the instances covered by a concept will tend to be more similar to each other than to negative instances.

Many more examples could be provided here. Suffice it to say that there is a large class of mechanisms which produce, either as a main result or as a side-effect, computational components which can be classified as concepts—and that they do so using a technique which effectively seeks to capture groups of *similar* data elements. The effective goal of this sort of mechanism is to produce concepts which maximize intra-class similarity and minimize inter-class similarity, [cf. 19].

3. A GENERIC MODEL

The ultimate aim of the paper is to provide an *information-theoretic* explanation for similarity-based (concept) learning. To do this we need to solve various problems and answer a number of questions. An initial problem is the fact that the information theoretic (IT) paradigm is somewhat at odds with the similarity-based learning (SBL) paradigm in its view of the world. Information theory decomposes the world into entities such as 'source', 'receiver', 'channel' whereas most SBL models assume a decomposition in terms of 'learner', 'environment', etc. Our approach will be to set up a generic model which can be reconciled with both viewpoints. The model involves the following entities.

- K–a cognitive agent
- U–a universe
- D–a data or input language (a set of possible data elements)
- M–a total set of inputs generated by some universe
- f–a differentiation function.

In an instantiation of the model, K is a particular cognitive agent in a particular universe U. U is characterized purely in terms of D, M, and f, with M being a subset of D. Two elements of D may be more or less distinct: their differentiation is given explicitly by the function f (whose range is assumed to be some sequence of values). Note that U may be a continuous or discrete universe. Its continuous properties are captured in f. If U is discrete, f always returns one of two values—indicating 'same' or 'different'.

We can use the model to map the entities which are of significance in the information-theoretic view of the world into the entities which are of significance in similarity-based concept learning. In information-theoretic terms, K is the 'receiver' and U is the 'source'. A message passing from source to receiver corresponds to the appearance of a new input in K. In SBL terms, K is the learner or classifier, D is the description language, and M is the source of the training instances. In connectionist terms, K is a network, D is the data or input language, M is the set of potential training vectors.

4. PREDICTION AND INFORMATION

The framework allows us to pose a number of questions. For example, given some particular instantiation of the model (involving a given K and a given U), we might ask how much knowledge K has about U. In general we expect that the more knowledge an agent has about some universe the better the agent can predict that universe. In terms of the model, predicting U means being able to accurately identify M. But what does *this* mean?

In the case where U is perfectly discrete, it means enumerating M; or, in general, assigning high probabilities to all members of M and relatively low probabilities to all members of D–M. In the case where U is not necessarily discrete, it means that for every element m in M, K identifies a relatively high probability to an element of D which is very similar to m.

In information theory we find this relationship between knowledge and predictive ability turned on its head. The situation in which K assigns relatively high probabilities to real inputs (i.e. members of M) from U is viewed as a situation in which K receives relatively little information from U. This is a complementary rather than a contradictory view of the situation. Our assumption is that being able to predict U means being able to assign relatively high probabilities to members of M. But if every real input is assigned a relatively high probability then every real input contains little surprise for K and the information content of inputs is therefore low. Hence, being able to predict U means receiving little information from U, and vice versa.

5. OPTIMIZING PREDICTIVE ACCURACY MEANS MINIMIZING INFORMATION

Given the remarks above, we can see that there is a relationship between acquiring knowledge about U and reducing the information content of messages from U. In particular, it is clear that K can *reduce* input information by acquiring knowledge about U. But can K acquire knowledge of U by attempting to reduce input information?

Let us consider the special case where K is initially completely knowledgeless. The information content of each new input to K is

$$- \log_2 p,$$

where p is the probability assigned to the input by K. To minimize the average amount of information content of new inputs it is necessary to assign the highest possible probability to all members of M. This means assigning high probabilities to the members of the set M. But in the absence of any knowledge about U, there is no way to decide which members of D are in M. Therefore, all members must be assigned the same probability value. Moreover, this value must be related to the size of D. If n is K's estimate of the size of M, then K must assign a probability of

$$n \ / \ |D|$$

to each element of D in order to minimize the information content of new inputs [20, 21]. In this context, the information content of each new input is

$$- \log_2 (n \ / \ |D|)$$

6. FORWARDED MESSAGES

Does the situation change if we allow K to process the received inputs in some way? In particular, is there any way in which K can process new inputs so as to further reduce their information content? We can think of the situation in which K processes inputs in terms of the application of some function to the inputs received at any given point. But there are two quite different cases to be considered. K might be able to process inputs one at a time or K might be able to process n inputs all in one go. Putting it more precisely, K might be able to apply a 1-place ('context-free') function to input data. Alternatively, K might be able to apply a n-place ('context-sensitive') function to input data.[3]

The first case here—involving the 1-place function—is the simpler one; it can be given a fairly straightforward informational account. Our approach will be to think of the 1-place function as a kind of black box which accepts inputs direct from U and 'forwards' them to K. This allows us to work out what the information content of the *outputs* of f will be in given situations.

Let us denote the set of all possible outputs as D'. In the case where f implements a genuine many-to-1 mapping (where there is at least one group of inputs which are mapped onto the same output), the size of D' is less than the size of D. But if $|D'| < |D|$ then K is justified in assigning higher probabilities to members of D' than to members of D. K therefore potentially receives less information from forwarded inputs than from direct inputs.

But this seems a little absurd. If K can reduce the amount of information received from U simply by mapping unique inputs onto non-unique outputs then surely all that has to be done to minimize the information received (and therefore maximize predictive ability) is to map all inputs onto *one* output. This would mean that $|D'| = 1$; the probability of the single output would be 1 and the amount of information received would always be zero (implying that K has perfect knowledge of U). Well, obviously, there is a catch. And it is called *noise*.

7. NOISE AND EQUIVOCATION

If K maps all inputs onto one output, that output tells K absolutely nothing about what the input was: it is completely ambiguous. On the other hand, if K maps almost all inputs onto unique outputs, then a given output can give a completely accurate indication of

---

[3] We assume that in either case the function is deterministic, i.e. that it always produces the same output for the same input. It may, of course, produce a unique output for unique inputs; alternatively, some inputs may evoke the same output.

what the input was. In reducing the absolute number of outputs K reduces their information content but also, inevitably, increases their ambiguity. In information-theoretic terms, this introduction of ambiguity is understood in terms of the introduction of noise, or more precisely, *equivocation* [22].

In the case where inputs are perfectly discrete entities, information theory states that the ambiguity can be quantified in terms of the conditional entropy of the outputs. This is just the entropy of the set of probability values derived when we work out what is the probability—given a particular input—of the output taking on each of the entire range of possible values.

In the continuous case, equivocation is a more complex beast. However, we can think of it as working just like discrete equivocation provided we imagine that the space of possible outputs is divided up into cells such that the conditional probability of getting any output in the cell for some given input is the same. Intuitively, we can think of the equivocation in the continuous case as the average perturbation or inaccuracy of messages (inputs) from U [22, ch. 4].

8. MINIMIZING EQUIVOCATION

Clearly, by mapping unique inputs onto non-unique outputs K reduces their information content but pays a price in terms of increased equivocation. Ideally, K must find some way of minimizing both the information content of inputs *and* their equivocation. To minimize input information it is necessary to make D' as small as possible, i.e. to map as many inputs as possible onto the same output. To minimize the equivocation of outputs, K must minimize their ambiguity, i.e. must minimize the degree to which messages are perturbed as they are forwarded (via the 1-place function).

To achieve this minimization it is only necessary to ensure that any set of unique inputs which are mapped onto the same output are as similar (according to the differentiation function f) as possible and that the output is as similar to all of the inputs as possible. Provided the similarity of any set of inputs evoking a unique output is maximized (for any given level of information-reduction), the average perturbation (inaccuracy) of inputs from U is minimized too.

9. THE INFORMATION/EQUIVOCATION TRADE-OFF

K, then, is confronted with a *trade-off* between information and equivocation. K can reduce the information content of inputs but only by allowing their equivocation (ambiguity) to increase. K can reduce equivocation but only by allowing the information content of inputs to increase. For some fixed reduction in input information, there is some *minimum* price that K must pay in terms of equivocation. The price is kept to a minimum only if maximally similar inputs are mapped onto unique outputs. For some fixed equivocation, there is some maximum reduction in input information which can be achieved. Again, this is only achieved if maximally similar inputs evoke unique outputs from f. Thus, there is a set of optimal ways of combining information-reduction and equivocation-increase.

We can visualize the situation in terms of a two-dimensional graph in which information content is plotted on the vertical axis and equivocation is plotted on the horizontal axis; see Figure 1. A given point corresponds to a particular information/equivocation combination. Points corresponding to feasible information/equivocation combinations form a region whose boundary represents the locus of optimal information/equivocation combinations, i.e. the set of points for which the ratio of information reduction to equivocation increase is maximized.

10. IS EQUIVOCATION SUCH A BAD THING?

Recall that our initial notion was that by minimizing the information content of inputs, K becomes better able to make accurate predictions about U and therefore, in some sense, acquires knowledge about U. We have seen that K can reduce input information by allowing equivocation to increase and also that the information-reduction/equivocation ratio is maximized in the case where the average pairwise similarity for input-groups (i.e. set of inputs mapped onto given outputs) is maximized. But what does all this mean for predictive accuracy?

As we might expect, maximizing the information-reduction/equivocation ratio effectively optimizes predictive accuracy. In the

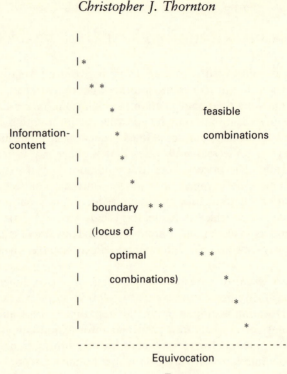

FIG. 1

case where inputs are forwarded via the many-to-1 mapping, being able to predict U implies assigning high probabilities to some subset of elements of D which are, collectively, relatively similar to M. Since we are assuming that K is knowledgeless, we know that assigned probabilities will always be the same. Therefore, predictive accuracy will be related only to the average similarity between inputs and their corresponding outputs.

Now, in minimizing equivocation at some fixed level of information-reduction, we minimize both input-group differences and the average difference between an arbitrary input-group member and the corresponding output. Thus we necessarily optimize predictive accuracy. We effectively ensure that for any arbitrary input, there is an element of D—to which K assigns an equal probability—which is as similar to the input as possible.

11. SBL = KNOWLEDGE MAXIMIZATION

We can summarize the points made above thus. In the special case where K has no prior knowledge of U and is only allowed to process inputs using a 1-place (context-free) function, K maximizes the accuracy of predictions about U (and therefore optimizes knowledge about U) by maximizing the information-reduction/equivocation ratio. This is done by identifying groups of maximally similar inputs and mapping them onto maximally representative outputs (i.e. outputs which are as similar to members of the input group as possible).

Now, as was noted above, similarity-based learning is a process which attempts to map groups of data elements onto concepts in such a way as to maximize intra-group similarity and minimize inter-group similarity. This is precisely the optimal course of action for any agent who is (i) subject to the constraints mentioned above who (ii) attempts to maximize predictive accuracy for an arbitrary universe. The identification of groups of different grain-size—a common property of SBL mechanisms [17]—corresponds to the identification of particular positions along the information-reduction/equivocation trade-off.

12. CONCLUDING COMMENTS

The paper has argued that the process known as similarity-based learning in symbolist work—which also plays a role in connectionist work and in numerical taxonomy—can be understood as an attempt on the part of a cognitive agent to maximize predictive accuracy in the training domain. More precisely, it has shown that similarity-based learning maximizes predictive accuracy (and an information-reduction/equivocation ratio) in any agent who can only process inputs using a context-free (i.e. 1-place) function.

The question of how predictive accuracy might be maximized in an agent who can process inputs using *arbitrary* context-sensitive (i.e. n-place) functions has not been addressed. Indeed, there are reasons for thinking that there will be no simple answer to this, much more general, question. If n-place functions can be applied to inputs then the agent is, in principle, able to detect arbitrary types of relationship between inputs and, therefore, abstract patterns in the data. In a worst-case scenario, agents would exploit each different type of abstract pattern (for the purposes of making predictions) in a different way. Thus there would be no single answer to the question of how an agent might exploit context-free input processing, just a myriad of special cases. How closely this worst-case scenario approximates to reality is an important issue for further research.

REFERENCES

[1] Mitchell, T. M. (1977), 'Version Spaces: A Candidate Elimination Approach to Rule Learning', *Proceedings of the Fifth International Joint Conference on Artificial Intelligence*, 305–10.

[2] Mitchell, T. M. (1982), 'Generalization as Search', *Artificial Intelligence*, 18: 203–26.

[3] Young, R., Plotkin, G., and Linz, R. (1977), 'Analysis of an Extended Concept-Learning Task', in R. Eddy (ed.), *Proceedings of the Fifth International Joint Conference on Artificial Intelligence*, 285.

[4] Bundy, A., Silver, B., and Plummer, D. (1985), 'An Analytical Comparison of Some Rule-Learning Programs', *Artificial Intelligence*, 27/2: 137–81.

[5] Quinlan, J. R. (1983), 'Learning Efficient Classification Procedures and Their Application to Chess End Games', in R. S. Michalski, J. G. Carbonell, and T. M. Mitchell (eds.), *Machine Learning: An Artificial Intelligence Approach*, Palo Alto: Tioga, 463–82.

[6] Fisher, D., and Langley, P. (1985), 'Approaches to Conceptual Clustering', *Proceedings of the Ninth International Joint Conference on Artificial Intelligence*: ii, Los Altos, Calif.: Morgan Kaufmann.

[7] Fisher, D. (1987), 'Conceptual Clustering, Learning from Examples and Inference', *Proceedings of the Fourth International Workshop on Machine Learning* (June 22–5 University of California, Irvine), Los Altos, Calif.: Morgan Kaufmann, 38–49.

[8] Michalski, R., and Stepp, R. (1983), 'Learning from Observation: Conceptual Clustering', in R. Michalski, J. Carbonell, and T. Mitchell (eds.), *Machine Learning: An Artificial Intelligence Approach*, Palo Alto: Tioga.

[9] Stepp, R. E., and Michalski, R. S. (1986), 'Conceptual Clustering: Inventing Goal-Oriented Classifications of Structured Objects', in R. S. Michalski, J. G. Carbonell, and T. M. Mitchell (eds.), *Machine Learning: An Artificial Intelligence Approach*: ii, Los Altos, Calif.: Morgan Kaufmann, 471–98.

[10] Rumelhart, D. E., McClelland, J. L., and the PDP Research Group (eds.) (1986), *Parallel Distributed Processing: Explorations in the Microstructure of Cognition*, i and ii, Cambridge, Mass.: MIT Press.

[11] Romesburg, H. (1984), *Cluster Analysis for Researchers*. Belmont, Calif.: Wadsworth.

[12] Anderberg, M. R. (1973), *Cluster Analysis for Applications,* New York: Academic Press.

[13] Quinlan, J. R. (1986), 'Induction of Decision Trees', *Machine Learning*, 1: 81–106.

[14] Smith, E. E., and Medin, D. L. (1981), *Categories and Concepts*, Cambridge, Mass.: Harvard University Press.

[15] Wolff, G. (1989), 'Information and Redundancy in Computing and Cognition', *AISB Quarterly*, 68: 14–17.

[16] Thornton, C. (1988), 'Links between Content and Information-Content', *Proceedings of the Eighth European Conference on Artificial Intelligence*, Munich, 1–5 August, London: Pitman; also available as CSRP 109, School of Cognitive Sciences, University of Sussex, 1988.

[17] Kodratoff, Y. (1988), *Introduction to Machine Learning*, London: Pitman.

[18] Thornton, C. (1987), 'Hypercuboid-Formation Behaviour of Two Learning Algorithms', CSRP 067, University of Sussex (extended version of paper in IJCAI-87).

[19] Gluck, M., and Corter, J. (1985), 'Information, Uncertainty, and the Utility of Categories', *Proceedings of the Seventh Annual Conference of the Cognitive Science Society*, Irvine, Calif.: Lawrence Erlbaum Associates, 283–7.

[20] Brillouin, L. (1962), *Science and Information Theory*, New York: Academic Press.

[21] Baierlien, R. (1971), *Atoms and Information Theory*, San Francisco: Freeman.

[22] Shannon, C. E., and Weaver, W. (1949), *The Mathematical Theory of Communication*, Urbana, Il.: University of Illinois Press.

11

Analogy-Making, Fluid Concepts, and Brain Mechanisms

DOUGLAS R. HOFSTADTER

—————◆—————

INTRODUCTION

How can one best study human cognition? The assumption under-lying this paper is that it is *by creating a computer model*. Accord-ingly, this paper is about such a computer model. And what is the crux of human cognition? The assumption underlying this paper is that it is *human concepts*. Accordingly, a rudimentary model of human concepts is found at the core of the model presented herein. And what is the crucial property of human concepts that makes them so subtle and hard to model on a computer? The assumption underlying this paper is that it is that they are *fluid*. What, then, is conceptual fluidity—or, more generally, *mental fluidity* (the collective result of the fluidity of all the concepts in a mind)? The phenomenon is complex and elusive, and therefore more easily demonstrated by example than by definition. Accordingly, the paper opens with a presentation of various examples of mental fluidity, and then explains the reasons underlying the domain selected for the model. The bulk of the paper is devoted to describing the model at a high level of abstraction, in an attempt to get across the fundamental imagery underlying it. At the end of the pre-sentation of the model, an attempt is made to convey a sense of its

Special thanks to Melanie Mitchell for her many years of collaboration on the Copycat project and her detailed help with this paper. Thanks also to Robert French and David Moser for numerous spirited discussions on all the topics in this paper. Research on Copycat has been supported by grants from the National Science Foundation (grant DCR 8410409); Mitchell Kapor, Ellen Poss, and the Lotus Development Corporation; Apple Computer, Inc.; the University of Michi-gan; and Indiana University.

generality. The paper concludes with a discussion of how models and microworlds such as those described herein relate to brain mechanisms and the Turing Test.

1. COPYCAT AND MENTAL FLUIDITY

Analogy problems in the Copycat domain

Copycat is a computer program designed to be able to discover insightful analogies in a very small but surprisingly subtle domain. Not to beat around the bush for a moment, here is an example of a typical, rather simple analogy problem in the domain:

> *1.* Suppose the letter-string **abc** were changed to **abd**; how would you change the letter-string **ijk** in 'the same way'?

Almost everyone answers **ijl**. It is not hard to see why; most people feel that the natural way to describe what happened to **abc** is to say that *the rightmost letter was replaced by its alphabetic successor*; that operation can then be painlessly and naturally 'exported' from the **abc** framework to the other framework, namely **ijk**, to yield the answer **ijl**. Of course this is not the only possible answer. For instance, it is always possible to be a 'smart alec' and to answer **ijd** (rigidly choosing to replace the rightmost letter by **d**) or **ijk** (rigidly replacing all **c**'s by **d**'s) or even **abd** (replacing the whole structure blindly by **abd**), but such 'smart-alecy' answers are suggested rather infrequently, and when they are suggested, they seem less compelling to virtually everybody, even to the people who suggested them. Thus **ijl** is a fairly uncontroversial winner among the range of answers to this problem.

There is much more subtlety to the domain than that problem would suggest, however. Let us consider the following closely related but considerably more interesting analogy problem:

> *2.* Suppose the letter-string **aabc** were changed to **aabd**; how would you change the letter-string **ijkk** in 'the same way'?

Here as in Problem 1, most people look upon the change in the first framework as *the rightmost letter was replaced by its alphabetic successor*. Now comes the tricky part: should this rule simply be transported rigidly to the other framework, yielding **ijkl**? Although rigid exportation of the rule worked in Problem 1, here it seems rather crude to most people, because it ignores the obvious fact that the **k** is doubled. The two **k**'s together seem to form a natural unit, and so it is tempting to change *both* of them, yielding the answer **ijll**. Using the old rule literally will simply not give this answer; instead, under pressure, one 'flexes' the old rule into a very closely related one, namely *replace the rightmost group by its alphabetic successor*. Here, the concept *letter* has 'slipped', under pressure, into the related concept *group of letters*. Coming up with such a rule and corresponding answer is a good example of human mental 'fluidity' (as contrasted with the mental rigidity that gives rise to **ijkl**). There is more to the story of Problem 2, however.

Many people are perfectly satisfied with this way of exporting the rule (and the answer it furnishes), but some feel dissatisfied by the fact that the doubled **a** in **aabc** has been ignored. Once one focuses in on this consciously, it jumps to mind easily that the **aa** and the **kk** play similar roles in their respective frameworks. From there it is but a stone's throw to 'equating' them (as opposed to equating the **c** with the **kk**), which leads to the question, 'What then is the counterpart of the **c**?' Given the already-established mapping of *leftmost* object (**aa**) onto *rightmost* object (**kk**), it is but a small leap to map *rightmost* object (**c**) onto *leftmost* object (**i**). At this point, we could simply take the successor of the **i**, yielding the answer **jjkk**.

However, few people who arrive at this point actually do this; given that the two crosswise mappings (**aa** ⇔ **kk**; **c** ⇔ **i**) are an invitation to read **ijkk** in reverse, which reverses the alphabetical flow in that string, most people tend to feel that the conceptual role of alphabetical *successorship* in **aabc** is now being played by that of *predecessorship* in **ijkk**. In that case, the proper modification of the **i** would not be to replace it by its successor, but by its alphabetical *predecessor*, yielding the answer **hjkk**. And indeed, this is the answer most often reached by those people who consciously try to take into account *both* of the doubled letters. Such people, under pressure, have flexed the original rule into this variant of itself: *replace the leftmost letter by its alphabetic predecessor*. Another way of saying this is that a very fluid transport of the original rule from its home framework to the new one has taken place; during this transport, two concepts 'slipped', under pressure, into neighbouring concepts: *rightmost* into *leftmost*, and *successor* into *predecessor*.

Mental fluidity: Slippages induced by pressures

Hopefully, the pathways leading to these two answers to Problem 2—**ijll** and **hjkk**—convey a good feeling for the term 'mental fluidity'. There is, however, a related notion used above that still needs some clarification, and that is the phrase 'under pressure'. What does it mean to say 'concept A *slips* into concept B *under pressure*'? It might help to spell out the intended imagery behind these terms. An earthquake takes place when subterranean structures are under sufficient pressure that something suddenly slips. Without the pressure, obviously, there would be no slippage. An analogous statement holds for pressures bringing about conceptual slippage: only under specific pressures will concepts slip into related ones. For instance, in Problem 2, pressure results from the doubling of the **a** and the **k**; one could look upon the doubling as an 'emphasis' device, making the left end of the first string and the right end of the second one stand out and in some sense 'attract' each other. In Problem 1, on the other hand, there is nothing to suggest mapping the **a** onto the **k**—no pressure. In the absence of such pressure, it would make no sense at all to slip *leftmost* into *rightmost* and then to read **ijk** in reverse, which would in turn suggest a slippage of *successor* into *predecessor*, all of which would finally lead to the downright bizarre answer **hjk**. That would be *unmotivated* fluidity, which is not characteristic of human thought.

Two other problems help flesh out the abstract space of problems that the Copycat architecture is designed to handle. Here is one:

> 3. Suppose the letter-string **abc** were changed to **abd**; how would you change the letter-string **mrrjjj** in 'the same way'?

For most people, the following answer comes to mind quite quickly: **mrrkkk**. It is very similar to the answer **ijll** to Problem 2, in that a *group* rather than a letter is seen as playing the role of 'rightmost letter' in the target string. There is still a somewhat disconcerting mismatch between the strings **abc** and **mrrjjj**, because the former is clearly woven together by a successorship fabric, whereas the latter has no such fabric. In Problem 2, when a spatial reversal was made as a consequence of 'equating' **aa** with **kk**, a mismatch of fabrics ensued. Fortunately, that mismatch was readily remediable by a conceptual slippage—*successor* slipped to *predecessor* to yield the answer **hjkk**. However, **mrrjjj** is no more a predecessor group than it is a successor group, so that avenue is completely blocked. What to do? Some people may simply accept the somewhat flawed 'feel' of the answer **mrrkkk**, but others may be led to re-examining the basis of their initial answer.

If one focuses on the two obvious *sameness groups* in **mrrjjj**—namely **rr** and **jjj**—one may start to feel, in some inchoate way, a slight subterranean mental pressure to bring the concept *sameness group* to bear uniformly throughout the string. In other words, a slight top-down pressure will arise, trying to 'force' that concept into the picture even where it would seem, a priori, somewhat unnatural. In particular, there may be some pressure to reperceive or redescribe the single letter **m** as a *group*, despite its anomalous length. The mind rebels: 'Group of length one!? But that's weird!' None the less, under the pressures exerted by this context, it may yield and form the 'weird' group, at least tentatively.

At that moment, the concept of *group length* suddenly jumps into prominence; after all, it is the group's anomalous length that makes it weird. Once this unanticipated concept has thus arisen from dormancy, the mind cannot help but play with it a bit; and before it knows it, the other group lengths, namely '2' and '3', are also explicitly 'on stage', to be used if reasonable. And indeed, the formerly unseen but now highly visible sequence of group lengths '1–2–3' *does* turn out to be of interest, due to its own totally unexpected successorship fabric.

All of a sudden, there is seen to be a much more fruitful way to relate **abc** with **mrrjjj**—namely through their shared successorship fabrics, one alphabetic, the other numerical. This new way of perceiving things involves an unanticipated conceptual slippage: *letter* slips to *group length*. (Of course, all slippages are unanticipated, but in some sense, this one is *very* unanticipated!) The rule *replace the rightmost letter by its successor* thus flexes, under these very special contextual pressures, into *replace the rightmost group length by its successor*, which yields the answer **mrrjjjj**. This answer seems distinctly more satisfying to most people than **mrrkkk**, despite the initial appeal of that answer.

The subtlety of Problem 3 is that a totally unanticipated concept—*group length*—has to be brought out from dormancy. How does dissatisfaction with a fairly reasonable-seeming answer become manifested in pressures for further exploration? What subtle cue tips the mind off that a new concept might be relevant? How does the mind follow up that cue? How resistant is the mind, and how resistant *should* it be, to the new concept? How inevitable is the succession of stages that ensue, leading to the completed insight? These are central questions about fluid and creative thinking.

The final sample problem is once again about insight under pressure. The problem is as follows:

> 4. Suppose the letter-string **abc** were changed to **abd**; how would you change the letter-string **xyz** in 'the same way'?

Naturally, the focus is on the letter **z**, and one immediately feels challenged by its lack of successor. Many people, eager to *construct* a successor of **z**, invoke the common notion of circularity, thus conceiving of **a** as the successor of **z**. This is a type of creative leap, and not to be looked down upon. However, for important reasons, this move is disallowed in the Copycat domain; it is rigidly stated that **z** has no successor. This 'ups the ante', so to speak, making one look harder for a way out of the seeming impasse.

Several possible thoughts come to mind: replace the **z** by nothing at all, thus yielding the answer **xy**. Or replace the **z** by the literal letter **d**, yielding answer **xyd**. This is a case where an ordinarily rigid-seeming manœuvre suddenly appears rather fluid and insightful. Other answers, too, are possible, such as **xyz** itself (since the **z** cannot move farther along, just leave it alone); **xyy** (since you can't take the *successor* of the **z**, why not take its *predecessor*, which seems like second best?); **xzz** (since you can't take the successor of the **z** itself, why not take the successor of the letter sitting next to it?); and many others.

However, this is a case where one small key insight can bring about a true conceptual breakthrough. If one focuses on the lack of successorship of **z**, what may come to mind is the fact that **z** is the *last* letter of the alphabet. This may in turn bring to mind what was in principle always available but stayed subterranean— namely the fact that **a** is the *first* letter of the alphabet. Normally, there is simply no reason to pay attention to that property of **a**, and so the concept *first* remains—and *should* remain—dormant (as it did in Problems 1–3). After all, one does not want to clutter up the mind with all sorts of extraneous interfering notions.

Here, however, through the indirect pressure of **z**'s *successorlessness* and hence *lastness*, **a**'s *firstness* emerges as possibly relevant.

Indeed, once *both* these facts are out on the table, the basis for a new connection is opened up. Specifically, the **a** and the **z**, formerly totally unrelated, are suddenly seen as reasonable counterparts of each other. A pair of conceptual slippages are entailed in this act of 'equating' the **a** with the **z**: *first* into *last*, and *leftmost* into *rightmost*.

Once this connection has been seen, a radical perceptual reversal takes place in a flash: instead of reading **xyz** from left to right, one reverses it and sees it from right to left. And along with this reversal of *spatial* direction, one also reverses the *alphabetical* direction. In other words, two further mental slippages are implicated in this perceptual reversal: *leftwards* and *rightwards* reverse roles, and simultaneously, *successor* and *predecessor* reverse roles. Under this complete conceptual reversal, the original rule flexes exactly as it did in Problem 2—namely into *replace the leftmost letter by its alphabetic predecessor*. This yields the answer **wyz**, which most people consider elegant and superior to all the other answers proposed above.

Note how similar and yet how different Problems 2 and 4 are. The key idea in both is to effect a double slippage (i.e. to reverse one's perception of the target string both spatially and alphabetically). However, it seems considerably easier for people to come up with this insight in Problem 2, even though in that problem there is no 'snag', as there is in Problem 4, serving to *force* a search for radical ideas. The very same insight is harder to come by in Problem 4 because the cues are subtler; the resemblance between **a** and **z** lurks quite far beneath the surface, whereas the resemblance between **aa** and **kk** is quite immediate. Any model of mental fluidity and creativity must faithfully reflect this notion of distinct 'levels of subtlety'.

Copycat is a thoroughgoing exploration of the nature of mental pressures, the nature of concepts, and their deep interrelationships, focusing particularly on how pressures can engender slippages of concepts into 'neighbouring' concepts. When one ponders these issues deeply, many questions arise, such as the following ones: What is meant by 'neighbouring concepts'? How much pressure is required to make a given conceptual slippage likely? Just how big a slippage can be made—that is, how far apart can two concepts be and still be potentially able to slip into each other? How can one conceptual slippage create a new pressure leading to another conceptual slippage, and then another, and so on, in a cascade? Do some concepts resist slippage more than others? Can particular pressures none the less bring about a slippage of such a concept while another concept, usually more 'willing' to slip, remains untouched? Such are the questions at the very heart of the Copycat project. (Readers who wish to see Copycat 'in action' are recommended to consult Mitchell and Hofstadter (1990), a short paper that discusses Problem 4 in detail; Hofstadter and Mitchell (1994), a longer paper that discusses Problem 3 in great detail and the other problems presented above in less detail; and finally, Mitchell (1993), a book that discusses all the problems presented above in great detail.)

The intended universality of Copycat's microdomain

The Copycat project, which sprang out of two predecessors, Seek-Whence (Meredith, 1986 and 1991) and Jumbo (Hofstadter, 1983), has been under development since 1983. A casual glance at the project might give the impression that since it was specifically designed to handle analogies in a particular tiny domain, its mechanisms are not general. However, this would be a serious misconception. All the features of the Copycat architecture were in fact designed with an eye to great generality. A major purpose of this article is to demonstrate this generality by describing the features of Copycat in very broad terms, and to show how they transcend not just the specific micro-domain, but even the very task of analogy-making itself. That is, the Copycat project is not about simulating analogy-making *per se*, but about simulating the very crux of human cognition: fluid concepts. The reason the project focuses upon analogy-making is that analogy-making is perhaps the quintessential mental activity where fluidity of concepts is called for, and the reason the project restricts its modelling of analogy-making to a specific and very small domain is that doing so allows the general issues to be brought out in a very clear way—far more clearly than in an alleged 'real-world' domain.

Copycat's microdomain was designed to bring out very general issues—issues that transcend any specific conceptual domain. In that sense, the microdomain was designed to 'stand for' other domains. Thus one is intended to conceive of, say, the *successor* (or *predecessor*) relation as an idealized version of *any* non-identity relationship in a real-world domain, such as 'parent of', 'neighbour of', 'friend of', 'employed by', 'close to', etc. A successor group (e.g. **abc**) then plays the role of any conceptual chunk based on such a relationship, such as 'family', 'neighbourhood', 'community', 'workplace', 'region', etc. Of course, inclusion of the notion of *sameness* needs no defence; sameness is obviously a universal concept, much as is *opposite*. Although any real-world domain clearly contains many more than two basic types of relationship, two already suffice to make an inexhaustible variety of structures of arbitrary complexity.

Aside from the idealized repertoire of *concepts* in the domain, there are also the *structures* used to create problems. In particular, allowed structures are linear strings made from any number— usually a small number—of instances of letters of the alphabet. Thus one immediately runs into the *type–token distinction*, a key issue in understanding cognition. The alphabet can be thought of as a very simple 'Platonic heaven' in which exactly twenty-six letter *types* permanently float in a fixed order; in contrast to this, there is a very rudimentary 'physical world' in which any number of letter *tokens* can temporarily coexist in an arbitrary one-dimensional juxtaposition. In this extremely simple model of physical space, there are such physical relationships and entities as *left-neighbour, leftmost edge, group of adjacent letters*, and so on (as contrasted with such relationships and entities in the Platonic alphabet as *predecessor, alphabetic starting-point, alphabetic segment*, etc.). Both the Platonic heaven and the physical world of Copycat are very simple on their own; however, the psychological processes of perception and abstraction bring them into complex interaction, and can cause extremely complex and subtle mental representations of situations to come about.

Copycat's alphabetic microworld is meant to be a tool for exploring general issues of cognition rather than issues specific to the domain of letters and strings. Thus certain aspects specific to people's knowledge of letter strings—such as shapes, sounds or connotations, or words that strings of letters might happen to form—have not been included in this microworld. Moreover, problems should not depend on arithmetical facts about letters, such as the fact that **t** comes exactly eleven letters after **i**, or that **m** and **n** flank the midpoint of the alphabet. This may seem to eliminate almost everything about the alphabet, but as Problems 1 through

4 show, there is still plenty left to play with. Reference to the alphabet's *local* structure is fine; for example, it is perfectly legitimate to exploit the fact that **u** comes immediately after **t**. It is also legitimate to exploit the fact that the Platonic alphabet has two distinguished members—namely **a** and **z**, its starting- and ending-points. Likewise, inside a string such as **hagizk**, local relationships, such as 'the **g** is the right-neighbour of the **a**', can be noticed, but long-distance observations, such as 'The **a** is four letters to the left of the **k**', are considered out of bounds.

Finally, while humans tend to scan strings of roman letters from left to right, are much better at recognizing forwards alphabetical order than backwards alphabetical order, and have somewhat greater familiarity with the beginning of the alphabet than its middle or end, the Copycat program is completely free of these biases. This should not be regarded as a defect of the program, but a strength, because it keeps the project's focus away from domain-specific and non-generalizable details.

A perception-based, emergent architecture for mental fluidity

When one describes the Copycat architecture in very abstract terms, the focus is not only on how it discovers mappings between situations, but also on how it perceives and makes sense of the miniature and idealized situations it is presented with. The present characterization will therefore read very much like a description of a computer model of *perception*. This is not a coincidence; one of the main ideas of the project is that even the most abstract and sophisticated mental acts deeply resemble perception. In this view, the essence of understanding a situation is the awakening from dormancy of a relatively small number of prior concepts—precisely the relevant ones—and applying them judiciously so as to identify the key entities, roles, and relationships in the situation. Creative human thinkers manifest an exquisite selectivity of this sort—when they are faced with a novel situation, what bubbles up from their unconscious and pops to mind is typically a small set of concepts that 'fit like a glove', without a host of extraneous and irrelevant concepts being consciously activated or considered. To get a computer model of thought to exhibit this kind of behaviour is a great challenge.

Aside from being inspired by perception, the Copycat architecture has another interesting property: it is neither symbolic nor connectionist, but rather, is situated somewhere in between these extremes. It is an *emergent* architecture, in the sense that its top-level behaviour emerges as a statistical consequence of myriad small computational actions. The concepts that Copycat uses in creating analogies can thus be considered to be a realization of 'statistically emergent active symbols' (Hofstadter, 1985). The inspiration for the architecture comes in part from the Hearsay II speech-understanding project (Erman, Hayes-Roth, Lesser, and Raj Reddy, 1980) and in part from the metabolism in a biological cell (these inspirations are discussed in more detail in Hofstadter, 1984*a* and in Mitchell, 1993).

The remainder of the presentation of Copycat's architecture is structured as follows. Section 2 is a description of the three main components of the architecture and their interactions. Section 3 deals with the notion of conceptual fluidity and shows how this architecture implements a model, albeit rudimentary, thereof. Section 4 tackles the seeming paradox of randomness as an essential ingredient of fluid mentality and intelligence. Section 5 discusses the generality of Copycat's mechanisms.

2. THE MAJOR COMPONENTS OF THE COPYCAT ARCHITECTURE

There are three major components to the architecture: the Slipnet, the Workspace, and the Coderack. In very quick strokes, they can be described as follows. (i) The Slipnet is the site of all *permanent Platonic concepts*. It can be thought of, roughly, as Copycat's long-term memory. As such, it contains only concept *types*, and no *instances* of them. The strengths of relationships among concepts in the Slipnet can change over the course of a run, and at any given moment they determine what slippages are likely and unlikely. (ii) The Workspace is the locus of *perceptual activity*. As such, it contains *instances* of various concepts from the Slipnet, combined into *temporary perceptual structures*. It can be thought of, roughly, as Copycat's short-term memory or working memory, or, to borrow a term from Hearsay II, its 'blackboard'. (iii) Finally, the Coderack can be thought of as a 'stochastic waiting room', in which small agents who wish to carry out tasks in the

Workspace wait to be called. It has no close counterpart in other architectures, but one can liken it somewhat to an *agenda* (a queue containing tasks to be executed in a specific order). The critical difference is that agents are selected *stochastically* from the Coderack, rather than in a determinate order. The reasons for this initially puzzling feature will be spelled out and analysed in detail below. They turn out to be at the crux of fluid mentality.

We now shall go through each of the three components once again, this time in more detail.

The Slipnet—Copycat's network of Platonic concepts

The basic image for the Slipnet is that of a network of interrelated concepts, each concept being represented by a *node* (caveat: what a concept is, in this model, is actually a bit subtler than just a pointlike node, as will be explained shortly), and each conceptual relationship by a *link* having a numerical length, representing the 'conceptual distance' between the two nodes involved. The shorter the distance between two concepts is, the more easily pressures can induce a slippage between them.

The Slipnet is not static; it dynamically responds to the situation at hand as follows: Nodes *acquire* varying levels of activation (which can be thought of as a measure of relevance to the situation at hand), *spread* varying amounts of activation to neighbours, and over time *lose* activation by decay. In sum, the perceived relevance of each concept is a sensitive, time-varying function of the way the program currently understands the situation it is facing.

In addition, conceptual links in the Slipnet adjust their lengths dynamically. Thus, conceptual distances gradually change under the influence of the evolving perception (or conception) of the situation at hand, which of course means that the current perception of the situation enhances the chance of certain slippages taking place, while rendering that of others more remote.

Each node in the Slipnet has one very important static feature called its *conceptual depth*. This is a number intended to capture the generality and abstractness of the concept. For example, the concept *opposite* is deeper than the concept *successor*, which is in turn deeper than the concept **a**. It could be said roughly that the depth of a concept is how far that concept is from being directly perceptible in situations. For example, in Problem 2, the presence of instances of a is trivially perceived; recognizing the presence of *successorship* takes a little bit of work; and recognition of the presence of the notion *opposite* is a subtle act of abstract perception. The further away a given aspect of a situation is from direct perception, the more likely it is to be involved in the situation's *essence*. Therefore, once aspects of greater depth are perceived, they should have more influence on the ongoing perception of the situation than aspects of lesser depth.

Assignment of conceptual depths amounts to an a priori ranking of 'best-bet' concepts. There is of course no guarantee that deep concepts will be relevant in any particular situation, but history has demonstrated that such concepts crop up over and over again across many different types of situations, and that the best insights come when deep concepts 'fit' naturally. There is thus built into the architecture a strong drive, if a deep aspect of a situation is perceived, to try to use this aspect in constructing an overall understanding of the situation.

Note that the hierarchy defined by different conceptual-depth values is quite distinct from abstraction hierarchies such as

$$poodle \Rightarrow dog \Rightarrow mammal \Rightarrow animal \Rightarrow living\ thing \Rightarrow thing.$$

These terms are all potential descriptions of a particular object at different levels of abstraction. By contrast, the terms a, *successor*, and *opposite* are not descriptions of one particular object in Problem 2, but of different aspects of that situation, at different levels of abstraction.

Conceptual depth has a second important aspect—namely the deeper a concept is, the more resistant it is (all other things being equal) to slipping into another concept. In other words, there is a built-in propensity in the program to prefer slipping shallow concepts rather than deep concepts when slippages have to be made. The idea of course is that insightful analogies tend to link situations that share a deep *essence*, allowing shallower features to slip if necessary. This basic idea can be summarized in a motto: 'Deep stuff doesn't slip in good analogies.' There are, however, interesting situations in which specific constellations of pressures arise that cause this basic tendency to be overridden.

Some details about the flow of activation: (i) each node spreads activation to its neighbours according to their distance from it, with near neighbours getting more, distant neighbours less; (ii) each node's conceptual-depth value sets its *decay rate*, in such a way that deep concepts always decay slowly and shallow concepts decay quickly. This means that, once a concept has been perceived as relevant, then, the deeper it is, the longer it will remain relevant, and thus the more profound an influence it will exert on the system's developing view of the situation—as indeed befits an abstract and general concept likely to be close to the essence of the situation.

Some details about the Slipnet's dynamical properties: (i) there are a variety of *link types*, and for each given type, all links of that type share the same *label*; (ii) each label is itself a concept in the network; and (iii) every link constantly adjusts its length according to the activation level of its label, with high activation giving rise to short links, low activation to long ones. Stated another way: If concepts A and B have a link of type L between them, then as concept L's relevance goes up (or down), concepts A and B become conceptually closer (or further apart). Since this is happening all the time all throughout the network, the Slipnet is constantly altering its 'shape' in attempting to mold itself increasingly accurately to fit the situation at hand. An example of a label is the node *opposite*, which labels the link between nodes *right* and *left*, the link between nodes *successor* and *predecessor*, and several other links. If the node *opposite* gets activated, these links will all shrink in concert, rendering the potential slippages they represent more probable.

The length of a link between two nodes represents the conceptual proximity or degree of association between the nodes: the shorter the link, the greater the degree of association, and thus the easier it is to effect a slippage between them. There is a probabilistic 'cloud' surrounding any node representing the likelihood of slippage to other nodes; the cloud's density is highest for near-neighbour nodes and rapidly tapers off for distant nodes. Neighbouring nodes can be seen as being included in a given concept probabilistically, as a function of their proximity to the central node of the concept.

This brings us back to the caveat mentioned above. Although it is tempting to equate a concept with a pointlike node, a concept is better identified with this probabilistic 'cloud' or halo *centred* on a node and extending outwards from it with increasing diffuseness. As links shrink and grow, nodes move into and out of each other's halos (to the extent that one can speak of a node as being 'inside' or 'outside' a halo). This image suggests conceiving of the Slipnet not so much as a hard-edged network of points and lines, but rather as a space in which many diffuse clouds overlap each other in an intricate, time-varying way.

Conceptual proximity in the Slipnet is thus context-dependent. For example, in Problem 1, no pressures arise that bring the nodes *successor* and *predecessor* into close proximity, so that a slippage from one to the other is highly unlikely; by contrast, in Problem 2, there is a good chance that pressures will activate the concept *opposite*, which will then cause the link between *successor* and *predecessor* to shrink, thus bringing each more into the other's halo, and enhancing the probability of a slippage between them. Because of this type of context-dependence, concepts in the Slipnet are emergent rather than explicitly defined.

Although the Slipnet responds sensitively to events in the Workspace (described in a moment) by constantly changing both its 'shape' and the activations of its nodes, its fundamental topology remains invariant. That is, no new structure is ever built, or old structure destroyed, in the Slipnet. The next subsection discusses a component of the architecture that provides a strong contrast to this type of topological invariance.

The Workspace—Copycat's locus of perceptual activity

The basic image for the Workspace is that of a busy construction site in which structures of many sizes and at many locations are being worked on simultaneously by independent crews, some occasionally being torn down to make way for new, hopefully better ones. (This image comes essentially from the biological cell; the Workspace corresponds roughly to the cytoplasm of a cell, in which enzymes carrying out diverse tasks all throughout the cell's cytoplasm are the construction crews, and the structures built up are all sorts of hierarchically structured biomolecules.)

At the start of a run, the Workspace is a collection of unconnected raw data representing the situation with which the program is faced. Each item in the Workspace initially carries only bare-bones information—that is, for each letter token, just its alphabetic type is provided, as well as—for those letters at the very edges of their strings—the descriptor *leftmost* or *rightmost*. Other than that, all objects are absolutely barren. Over time, through the actions of many small agents 'scouting' for features of various sorts (these agents, called 'codelets', are described in the next sub-section), items in the Workspace gradually acquire various *descriptions*, and are linked together by various *perceptual structures*, all of which are built entirely from concepts in the Slipnet.

Objects in the Workspace do not by any means all receive equal amounts of attention from codelets—the probability that an object will attract a prospective codelet's attention is determined by the object's *salience*, which is a function of the set of descriptions it currently has. There are two factors that contribute to salience. An object is *important* to the extent that its descriptions are built out of highly activated concepts in the Slipnet. The more descriptions an object has and the more activated the nodes involved, the more attention that object would seem to deserve. However, there is a second factor, *unhappiness*, that modulates this tendency. Unhappiness is a measure of how integrated the object is with other objects. An unhappy object is one that has few or no connections to the rest of the objects in the Workspace, and thus seems to cry out for more attention. Salience is a dynamic quantity that takes into account both an object's importance and its unhappiness, and it determines how attractive that object will appear to codelets. Note that salience depends intimately on both the state of the Workspace and the state of the Slipnet.

A constant feature of the processing is that pairs of *neighbouring objects* (inside a single framework, i.e. letter-string) are probabilistically selected (with a bias favouring pairs that include salient objects) and scanned for similarities or relationships, of which the most promising are likely to get 'reified' (i.e. realized in the Workspace) as inter-object *bonds*. For instance, the two **k**'s in **ijkk** in Problem 2 are likely to get bonded to each other rather quickly by a *sameness* bond. Similarly, the **i** and the **j** are likely to get bonded to each other, although not as fast, by a *successorship bond* or a *predecessorship bond*. Each bond has a dynamically varying *strength*, reflecting not only the activation and conceptual depth of the concept representing it in the Slipnet (in the case of **kk**, the concept *sameness*, and in the case of **ij**, either *successor* or *predecessor*) but also the prevalence of similar bonds in its immediate neighbourhood. The idea of bonds is of course to start weaving unattached objects together into a coherent mental structure.

A set of objects in the Workspace bonded together by a uniform 'fabric' (i.e. bond type) is a candidate to be 'chunked' into a higher-level kind of object called a *group*. A simple example of a *sameness group* is **kk**, as in Problem 2. Another simple group is **abc**, as in Problem 1. This one, however, is a little ambiguous; depending on which direction its bonds are considered to go in; it is either a *successor group* (left to right) or a *predecessor group* (right to left). (It cannot be seen as both at once, although the program can switch from one vision to the other relatively easily.) The more salient a potential group's component objects and the stronger its fabric, the more likely it is to be reified.

Groups, just like more basic types of objects, acquire their own descriptions and salience values, and are themselves candidates for similarity-scanning, bonding to other objects, and possibly becoming parts of yet higher-level groups. As a consequence, hierarchical perceptual structures get built up over time, under the guidance of biases emanating from the Slipnet. A simple example would be the successor (or predecessor) group **ijkk** in Problem 2, made up of three elements: the **i**, the **j**, and the short sameness group **kk**.

Another constant feature of the processing is that pairs of objects in *different* frameworks (i.e. strings) are probabilistically selected (again with a bias favouring salient objects) and scanned for similarities, of which the most promising are likely to get reified as *bridges* (or *correspondences*) in the Workspace. Effectively, a bridge establishes that its two end-objects are considered each other's counterparts—meaning either that they are intrinsically similar objects or that they play similar roles in their respective frameworks (or hopefully both).

Consider, for instance, the **aa** and **kk** in Problem 2. What makes one tempted to equate them? One factor is their intrinsic similarity —both are doubled letters (sameness groups of length 2). Another factor is that they fill similar roles, one sitting at the left end of its string, the other at the right end of its string. If and when a bridge gets built between them, concretely reifying this mental correspondence, it will be explicitly based on both these facts. The fact that **a** and **k** are unrelated letters of the alphabet is simply ignored by most people. Copycat is constructed to behave similarly. Thus, the fact that **aa** and **kk** are both sameness groups will be embodied in an *identity mapping* (here, *sameness* ⇔ *sameness*); the fact that one is leftmost while the other is rightmost will be embodied in a *conceptual slippage* (here, *leftmost* ⇔ *rightmost*); the fact that nodes **a** and **k** are far apart in the Slipnet is simply ignored.

Whereas identity mappings are always welcome in a bridge, conceptual slippages always have to overcome a certain degree of resistance, the precise amount of which depends on the proposed slippage itself and on the circumstances. The most favoured slippages are those whose component concepts not only are shallow but also have a high degree of overlap (i.e. are very close in the Slipnet). Slippages between highly overlapping *deep* concepts are more difficult to build, but pressures can certainly bring them about.

Once any bridge is built, it has a *strength*, reflecting the ease of the slippages it entailed, the number of identity mappings helping to underpin it, and its resemblance to other bridges already built. The idea of bridges is of course to build up a coherent mapping between the two frameworks.

As the Workspace evolves in complexity, there is increasing pressure on new structures to be *consistent*, in a certain sense, with pre-existent structures, especially with close-by ones. For two structures to be consistent sometimes means that they are instances of the very same Slipnet concept, sometimes that they are instances of very close Slipnet concepts, and sometimes it is a little more complex. In any case, the Workspace is not just a hodgepodge of diverse structures that happen to have been built up by totally independent codelets; rather, it represents a coherent vision built up piece by piece by many agents all indirectly influencing each other. Such a vision will henceforth be called a *viewpoint*. A useful image is that of highly coherent macroscopic structures (e.g. physical bridges) built by a colony of thousands of myopic ants or termites working semi-independently but none the less co-operatively. (The 'ants' of Copycat—namely codelets—will be described in the next subsection.)

There is constant competition, both on a local and a global level, among structures vying to be built. A structure's likelihood of beating out its rivals is determined by its *strength*, which has two facets: a context-independent facet (a contributing factor would be, for instance, the depth of the concept of which it is an instance) and a context-dependent facet (how well it fits in with the rest of the structures in the Workspace, particularly the ones that would be its neighbours). Out of the rough-and-tumble of many,

many small decisions about which new structures to build, which to leave intact, and which to destroy comes a particular global viewpoint. Even viewpoints, however, are vulnerable; it takes a very powerful rival to topple an entire viewpoint, but this occasionally happens. Sometimes these 'revolutions' are, in fact, the most creative decisions that the system as a whole can carry out.

As was mentioned briefly above, the Slipnet responds to events in the Workspace by selectively activating certain nodes. The way activation comes about is that any discovery made in the Workspace—creation of a bond of some specific type, a group of some specific type, etc.—sends a substantial jolt of activation to the corresponding concept in the Slipnet; the amount of time the effect of such a jolt will last depends on the concept's decay rate, which depends in turn on its depth. Thus, a deep discovery in the Workspace will have long-lasting effects on the activation pattern and 'shape' of the Slipnet; a shallow discovery will have but transient effects. In Problem 2, for example, if a bridge is built between the groups **aa** and **kk**, it will very likely involve an *opposite* slippage (*leftmost* ⇔ *rightmost*). This discovery will reveal the hitherto unsuspected relevance of the very deep concept *opposite*, which is a key insight into the problem. Because *opposite* is a deep concept, once it is activated, it will remain active for a long time and therefore exert powerful effects on subsequent processing.

It is clear from all this that the Workspace affects the Slipnet no less than the Slipnet affects the Workspace; indeed, their influences are so reciprocal and tangled that it is hard to tell the chicken from the egg.

The Coderack—*source of emergent pressures in Copycat*

All acts of describing, scanning, bonding, grouping, bridge-building, destruction, and so forth in the Workspace are carried out by small, simple agents called *codelets*. (As was mentioned earlier, a codelet can be likened to an enzyme in a biological cell or an ant in an ant colony.) The action of a single codelet is always but a tiny part of a run, and whether any particular codelet runs or not is not of much consequence. What matters is the collective effect of many codelets.

There are two types of codelets: *scout codelets* and *effector codelets*. A scout merely looks at a potential action and tries to estimate its promise; the only kind of effect it can have is to create one or more codelets—either scouts or effectors—to follow up its findings. By contrast, an effector codelet actually creates (or destroys) some structure in the Workspace.

Each codelet, when created, is placed in the *Coderack*, which is a pool of codelets waiting to run, and is assigned an *urgency value*—a number that will determine its probability of being selected from that pool as the next codelet to run. The urgency is a function of the estimated importance of that codelet's potential action, which in turn reflects the biases embodied in the current state of the Slipnet and the Workspace. Thus, for example, a codelet whose purpose is to seek instances of some lightly activated Slipnet concept will be assigned a low urgency and will therefore most probably have to wait a long time, after being created, to get run. By contrast, a codelet likely to further a Workspace viewpoint that is currently strong will be assigned a high urgency and will therefore have a good chance of getting run soon after being created.

It is useful to draw a distinction between *bottom-up* and *top-down* codelets. Bottom-up codelets (or 'noticers') look around in an unfocused manner, open to what they find, whereas top-down codelets (or 'seekers') are on the look-out for a particular kind of phenomenon, such as successor relations or sameness groups. Codelets can be viewed as *proxies* for the pressures in a given problem. Bottom-up codelets represent pressures present in all situations (the desire to make descriptions, to find relationships, to find correspondences, and so on). Top-down codelets represent specific pressures evoked by the situation at hand (e.g. the desire, in Problems 1 and 2, to look for more successor relations, once some have already been discovered). Top-down codelets can infiltrate the Coderack only when triggered from 'on high'—i.e. from the Slipnet. In particular, activated nodes are given the chance to 'spawn' top-down scout codelets, with a node's degree of activation determining the codelet's urgency. The mission of such a codelet is to scan the Workspace in search of instances of its spawning concept.

It is very important to note that the calculation of a codelet's urgency takes into account (directly or indirectly) numerous factors, which may include the activations of several Slipnet nodes as well as the strength or salience of one or more objects in the Workspace; it would thus be an oversimplification to picture a top-down codelet as simply a proxy for the particular concept that spawned it. More precisely, a top-down codelet is a proxy for one or more *pressures* evoked by the situation. These include *workspace pressures*, which attempt to maintain and extend a coherent viewpoint in the Workspace, and *conceptual pressures*, which attempt to realize instances of activated concepts. It is critical to understand that pressures, while they are very *real*, are not represented *explicitly* anywhere in the architecture; each pressure is spread out among urgencies of codelets, activations, and link-lengths in the Slipnet, and strengths and saliences of objects in the Workspace. Pressures, in short, are implicit, emergent consequences of the deeply intertwined events in the Slipnet, Workspace, and Coderack.

Any run starts with a standard initial population of bottom-up codelets (with preset urgencies) on the Coderack. At each time step, one codelet is chosen to run and is removed from the current population on the Coderack. As was said before, the choice is probabilistic, biased by relative urgencies in the current population. Copycat thus differs from an 'agenda' system such as Hearsay II, which, at each step, executes the waiting action with the highest estimated priority. The urgency of a codelet should not be conceived of as representing an estimated *priority*; rather, it represents the estimated relative *speed* at which the pressures represented by this codelet should be attended to. If the highest-urgency codelet were always chosen to run, then lower-urgency codelets would never be allowed to run, even though the pressures they represent have been judged to deserve *some* amount of attention. Since any single codelet plays but a small role in helping to further a given pressure, it never makes a crucial difference that a particular codelet be selected; what really matters is that each *pressure* move ahead at roughly the proper speed over time. Stochastic selection of codelets allows this to happen, even when judgements about the intensity of various pressures change over time. Thus allocation of resources is an emergent statistical result rather than a preprogrammed deterministic one. The proper allocation of resources could not be programmed ahead of time, since it depends on what pressures emerge as a given situation is perceived.

The Coderack would obviously dwindle rapidly to zero if

codelets, once run and removed from it, were not replaced. However, replenishment of the Coderack takes place constantly, and this happens in three ways. First, *bottom-up* codelets are continuously being added to the Coderack. Secondly, codelets that run can, among other things, add one or more *follow-up* codelets to the Coderack before being removed. Thirdly, active nodes in the Slipnet can add *top-down* codelets. Each new codelet's urgency is assigned by its creator as a function of the estimated promise of the task it is to carry out. Thus the urgency of a follow-up codelet is a function of the result of the evaluation done by the codelet that posted it, while the urgency of of a top-down codelet is a function of the activation of the node that posted it. (The urgency of bottom-up codelets is context-independent.) Thus as the run proceeds, the population of the Coderack adjusts itself dynamically in response to the system's needs as judged by previously run codelets and by activation patterns in the Slipnet, which themselves depend on the current structures in the Workspace.

The shifting population of the Coderack bears a close resemblance to the shifting enzyme population of a cell, which evolves in a sensitive way in response to the ever-changing make-up of the cell's cytoplasm. Just as the cytoplasmic products of certain enzymatic processes trigger the production of new types of enzymes to act further on them, structures built in the Workspace by a given set of codelets cause new types of codelets to be brought in to work on them. And just as, at any moment, certain genes in the cell's DNA are allowed to be expressed (at varying rates) through enzyme proxies, while other genes remain essentially repressed (dormant), certain Slipnet nodes get 'expressed' (at varying rates) through top-down codelet proxies, while other nodes remain essentially repressed. In a cell, the total effect is a highly coherent metabolism that emerges without any explicit top-down control; in Copycat, the effect is similar.

Note that though Copycat runs on a serial computer and thus only one codelet runs at a time, the system is roughly equivalent to one in which many independent activities are taking place in parallel and at different speeds, since codelets, like enzymes, work locally and to a large degree independently. The speed at which an avenue is pursued is an a priori unpredictable statistical consequence of the urgencies of the many diverse codelets pursuing that avenue.

3. THE EMERGENCE OF FLUIDITY IN THE COPYCAT ARCHITECTURE

Commingling pressures—the crux of fluidity

One of the central goals of the Copycat architecture is to allow many pressures to simultaneously coexist, competing and co-operating with one another to drive the system in certain directions. The way this is done is by converting pressures into flocks of very small agents (i.e. codelets), each having some small probability of getting run. As was stated above, a codelet acts as a proxy for several pressures, all to differing degrees. All these little proxies for pressures are thrown into the Coderack, where they wait to be chosen. Whenever a codelet is given the chance to run, the various pressures for which it is a proxy make themselves slightly felt. Over time, the various pressures thus 'push' the overall pattern of exploration different amounts, depending on the urgencies assigned to their codelets. In other words, the causes being pushed for by the different pressures get advanced in parallel, but at different speeds.

There is a definite resemblance to classical time-sharing on a serial machine, in which any number of independent processes can be run concurrently by letting each one run a little bit (i.e. giving it a 'time slice'), then suspending it and passing control to another process, and so forth, so that bit by bit, each process eventually runs to completion. Classical time-sharing, incidentally, allows one to assign to each process a different speed, either by controlling the *durations* of its time slices or by controlling the *frequency* with which its time slices are allowed to run. The latter way of regulating speed is similar to the method used in Copycat; however, Copycat's method is probabilistic rather than deterministic (comments on why this is so follow in brief order).

This analogy with classical time-sharing is helpful but can also mislead. The principal danger is that one might get the impression that there are pre-laid-out *processes* to which time slices are probabilistically granted—more specifically, that any codelet is essentially a time slice of some preordained process. This is utterly wrong. In the Copycat architecture, the closest analogue to a classical process is a pressure—but the analogy is certainly not close. A pressure is nothing like a determinate sequence of actions; in very broad brushstrokes, a *conceptual* pressure can be portrayed as a concept (or cluster of closely related concepts) trying to impose itself on a situation, and a *workspace* pressure as an established viewpoint trying to entrench itself further while keeping rival viewpoints out of the picture. Whereas classical processes are cleanly distinguishable, this is not at all the case for pressures. A given codelet, by running, can advance (or hinder) any number of pressures.

There is thus no way of conceptually breaking up a run into a set of distinct foreordained processes each of which advances piecemeal by being given time slices. The closest one comes to this is when a series of effector codelets' actions *happen* to dovetail so well that the codelets *appear* to have been parts of some predetermined high-level construction process. However, what is deceptive here is that scattered amongst the actions constituting the visible 'process', a lot of other codelets—certainly many scouts, and probably other effectors—have played crucial but less visible roles. In any case, there was some degree of luck because randomness played a critical role in bringing about this particular sequence of events. In short, although some large-scale actions tend to look planned in advance, that appearance is illusory; patterns in the processing are all *emergent*.

A useful image here is that of the course of play in a basketball game. Each player runs down the court, zigzagging back and forth, darting in and out of the enemy team as well as their own team, manœuvring for position. Any such move is simultaneously *responding* to a complex constellation of pressures on the floor as well as slightly *altering* the constellation of pressures on the floor. A move is thus fundamentally deeply ambiguous. Although the crowd is mostly concerned with the sequence of players who have the ball, and thus tends to see a localized, serial process unfolding, the players who seldom or never have the ball none the less play pivotal roles in that they mould the globally felt pressures that control both teams' actions at all moments. A tiny feint of the head or lunge to one side alters the probabilities of all sorts of events happening on the court, both near and far. After a basket has been scored, even though sports announcers and fans always try to account for the structure of the event in clean, spatially local, temporally serial terms (thus trying to impose a *process* on the event), in fact the event was in an essential way distributed all over space and time, amongst all the players. The event consisted of distributed, swiftly shifting pressures pushing *for* certain types of plays and *against* others, and impositions of locality and seriality, though they contain some truth, are merely ways of simplifying what happened for the sake of human consumption. The critical point to hold onto here is the *ambiguity* of any particular action *en route* to a basket; each action contributes to many potential continuations and cannot be thought of as a piece of some unique 'process' coexisting with various other independent 'processes' supposedly taking place on the court.

Much the same could be said for Copycat: an outside observer is free, after a run is over, to 'parse' the run in terms of specific, discrete processes, and to attempt to impose such a vocabulary on the system's behaviour; however, that parsing and labelling is not intrinsic to the system, and such interpretations are in no way unique or absolute, any more than in a basketball game. In other words, a long sequence of codelet actions can add up to what could be perceived, a posteriori and by an outsider, as a single coherent drive towards a particular goal, but that is the outsider's subjective interpretation.

The parallel terraced scan

One of the most important consequences of the commingling of conceptual pressures is the *parallel terraced scan*. The basic image is that of many 'fingers of exploration' simultaneously feeling out various potential pathways at different speeds, thanks to the co-existence of pressures of different strengths. These 'fingers of exploration' are tentative probes made by scout codelets, rather than actual events realized by effector codelets. In the Workspace, there is only one *actual* viewpoint at any given time. However, in the background, a host of nearby variants on the actual viewpoint—*virtual* viewpoints—are constantly flickering probabilistically. If any virtual viewpoint is found sufficiently promising by scouts, then they create effector codelets that, when run, will attempt to realize that alternative viewpoint in the Workspace. This entails a 'fight' between the incumbent structure and the upstart; the outcome is decided probabilistically, with the weights being determined by the strength of the current structure as opposed to the promise of the rival. This is how the system's actual viewpoint develops with time. There is always a probabilistic 'halo' of many *potential* directions being explored, and the more attractive of these tend to be the *actual* directions chosen. Incidentally, this aspect of the Copycat architecture reflects a psychologically important fact, which is that conscious (macroscopic) experience is essentially unitary, although to be sure it is a consequence of many parallel unconscious (microscopic) processes.

A metaphor for the parallel terraced scan is provided by the image of a vast column of ants marching through a forest, with hordes of small scouts at the head of the column making small random forays in all directions (although exploring some directions more eagerly and deeply than others) and then returning to report; the collective effect of these many 'feelers' will then determine the direction to be followed by the column as a whole. This is going on at all moments, of course, so that the column is constantly adjusting its pathway in slight ways.

The term 'parallel terraced scan' comes from the fact that scouting expeditions are structured in a *terraced* way; that is, they are carried out in stages, each stage contingent upon the success of the preceding one, and probing a little more deeply than the preceding one. Since the first stage is computationally very cheap, the system can afford to have many first-stage scouts probing in all sorts of directions, including quite unlikely directions. Succeeding stages are less and less cheap; consequently the system can afford fewer and fewer of them, which means that it has to be increasingly selective about the directions it devotes resources to looking in. Only after a pathway has been explored quite deeply by scouts and found to be very promising are effector codelets created, which then will try to actually swerve the whole system down that pathway.

The constellation of conceptual (i.e. top-down) pressures at any given time controls the biases in the system's exploratory behaviour, and also plays a major role in determining the actual direction the system will move in; ultimately, however, top-down pressures, no matter how strong, must bow to the reality of the situation itself, in the sense that prejudices alone cannot force inappropriate concepts to fit to reality. Conceptual pressures must adapt when the pathways they have urged turn out to fail. The model is made explicitly to allow this kind of intermingling of top-down and bottom-up processing.

Time-evolving biases

At the very start of a run, the Coderack contains exclusively bottom-up similarity-scanners, which represent no situation-specific pressures. In fact, it is their job to make small discoveries that will then start generating such pressures. As these early codelets run, the Workspace starts to fill up with bonds and small groups and, in response to these discoveries, certain nodes in the Slipnet are activated. In this way, situation-specific pressures are generated and cause top-down codelets to be spawned by concepts in the Slipnet. In this way, gradually, top-down codelets come to dominate the Coderack.

At the outset of a run, the Slipnet is 'neutral' (i.e. in a standard configuration with a fixed set of concepts of low depth activated), meaning that there are no situation-specific pressures. At this early stage, all observations made in the Workspace are very local and superficial. Over the course of a run, the Slipnet moves away from its initial neutrality and becomes more and more biased toward certain organizing concepts—*themes* (highly activated deep concepts, or constellations of several such concepts). Themes then guide processing in many pervasive ways, such as determining the saliences of objects, the strengths of bonds, the likelihood of various types of groups to be made, and in general, the urgencies of all types of codelets.

It should not be imagined, incidentally, that a 'neutral' Slipnet embodies no biases whatsoever; it certainly does (think of the permanent inequality of various nodes' conceptual depths, for instance). The fact that at the outset, a sameness group is likely to be spotted and reified faster than a successor group of the same length, for instance, represents an initial bias favouring sameness over successorship. The important thing is that at the outset of a run, the system is more open than at any other time to *any* possible organizing theme (or set of themes); as processing takes place and perceptual discoveries of all sorts are made, the system loses this naïve, open-minded quality, as indeed it ought to, and usually ends up being 'closed-minded'—that is, strongly biased towards the pursuit of some initially unsuspected avenue.

In the early stages of a run, almost all discoveries are on a very small, local scale: a primitive object acquires a description, a bond is built, and so on. Gradually, the scale of actions increases: small groups begin to appear, acquire their own descriptions, and so on. In the later stages of a run, actions take place on an even larger scale, often involving complex, hierarchically structured objects. Thus, over time there is a clear progression, in processing, from locality to globality.

Temperature as a regulator of open-mindedness

At the start of a run, the system is open-minded, and for good reason: it knows nothing about the situation it is facing. It doesn't matter all that much *which* codelets run, since one wants many different directions to be explored; hence decision-making can be fairly capricious. However, as swarms of scout codelets and local effector codelets carry out their jobs, that status gradually changes; in particular, as the system acquires more and more information, it starts creating a coherent viewpoint and focusing in on organizing themes. The more informed the system is, the more important it is that top-level decisions not be capriciously made. For this reason, there is a variable that monitors the stage of processing, and helps to convert the system from its initial largely bottom-up, open-minded mode to a largely top-down, closed-minded one. This variable is given the name *temperature*.

What controls the temperature is the *degree of perceived order* in the Workspace. If, as at the beginning of every run, no structures have been built, then the system sees essentially no order, which translates into a need for broad, open-minded exploration; if, on the other hand, there is a highly coherent viewpoint in the Workspace, then the last thing one wants is a lot of voices clamouring for irrelevant actions in the Workspace. Thus, temperature is essentially an inverse measure of the *quality of structure* in the Workspace: the more structures there are, and the stronger (and thus more coherent) they are, the lower the temperature. Note that although the overall trend is for temperature to wind up low at the end of a run, a *monotonic* drop in temperature is not typical; often, the system's temperature goes up and down several times during a run, reflecting the system's uncertain advances and retreats as it builds and destroys structures in its attempts to home in on the best way to look at a situation.

What the temperature itself controls is the *degree of randomness used in decision-making*. Decisions of all sorts are affected by the temperature. Consider a codelet, for instance, trying to decide where to devote its attention. Suppose that Workspace object A is exactly twice as salient as object B. The codelet will thus tend to be more attracted to A than to B. However, the precise discrepancy in attractive power between A and B will depend on the temperature. At some mid-range temperature, the codelet will indeed be twice as likely to go for A as for B. However, at very *high* temperatures, A will be hardly any more attractive than B to the codelet. By contrast, at very *low* temperatures, the probability of choosing A over B will be much greater than two to one. For another example, consider a codelet trying to build a structure that is incompatible with a currently existing strong structure. Under low-temperature conditions, the strong structure will tend to be very stable (i.e. hard to dislodge), but if the temperature should happen to rise, it will become increasingly susceptible to being swept away. In 'desperate times', even the most huge and powerful structures and worldviews can topple.

The upshot of all this is that at the start of a run, the system explores possibilities in a wild, scattershot way; however, as it builds up order in the Workspace and simultaneously homes in on organizing themes in the Slipnet, it becomes an increasingly conservative decision-maker, ever more deterministic and serial in its style. Of course, there is no magic crossover point at which parallel processing turns into serial processing; there is simply a gradual tendency in that direction, controlled by the system's temperature.

Note that the notion of temperature in Copycat differs from that in simulated annealing, an optimization technique sometimes used in connectionist networks (Kirkpatrick *et al.*, 1983; Hinton and Sejnowski, 1986; Smolensky, 1986). In simulated annealing, temperature is used exclusively as a top-down randomness-controlling factor, its value falling monotonically according to a predetermined, rigid annealing schedule. By contrast, in Copycat, the value of the temperature reflects the current quality of the system's understanding, so that temperature acts as a feedback mechanism that determines the degree of randomness used by the system.

Overall trends during a run

In most runs, despite local fluctuations here and there, there is a set of overall tendencies characterizing how the system evolves in the course of time. These tendencies, although they are all tightly linked together, can be roughly associated with different parts of the architecture, as follows.

- In the Slipnet, there is a general tendency for the initially activated concepts to be *conceptually shallow*, and for concepts that get activated later to be increasingly *deep*. There is also a tendency to move from *no themes* to *themes* (i.e. clusters of highly activated, closely related, high-conceptual depth concepts).
- In the Workspace, there is a general tendency to move from a state of *no structure* to a state with *much structure*, and from a state having *many local, unrelated objects* to a state characterized by *few global, coherent structures*.
- As far as the processing is concerned, it generally exhibits, over time, a gradual transition from *parallel* style toward *serial* style, from *bottom-up* mode to *top-down* mode, and from an initially *non-deterministic* style toward a *deterministic* style.

4. THE INTIMATE RELATION BETWEEN RANDOMNESS AND FLUIDITY

It may seem deeply counterintuitive that randomness should play a central role in a computational model of intelligence. However, careful analysis shows that it is inevitable if one believes in any sort of parallel, emergent approach to mind.

Randomness as lack of bias

A good starting-point for such analysis is to consider the random choice of codelets (biased according to their urgencies) from the Coderack. The key notion, stressed in earlier sections, is that the urgency attached to any codelet represents the estimated proper *speed* at which to advance the pressures for which it is a proxy. Thus it would make no sense at all to treat higher urgencies as higher *priorities*—that is, always to pick the highest-urgency codelets first. If one were to do that, then lower-urgency codelets would never get run at all, so the effective speeds of the pressures they represent would all be zero, which would totally defeat the notion of commingling pressures, the parallel terraced scan, and temperature.

A more detailed analysis is the following. Suppose we define a 'grass-roots' pressure as a pressure represented by a swarm of low-urgency codelets, and an 'élite' pressure as one represented by a small number of high-urgency codelets. Then a policy to select high-urgency codelets most of the time would arbitrarily favour 'élite' pressures. In fact, it would allow situations wherein any number of 'grass-roots' pressures, which could easily constitute the vast majority of the *total* urgency—that is, the sum of the urgencies of all the codelets in the Coderack at the time—could be entirely squelched by just one 'élite' pressure. Such a policy would result in a very distorted image of the overall makeup—i.e. the distribution of urgencies among various pressures—in the Coderack. In summary, it is imperative that during a run, low-urgency codelets get mixed in with higher-urgency codelets, and in the right proportion—namely in the proportions dictated by urgencies, no more and no less. As was said earlier, only by using probabilities to choose codelets can the system achieve (via statistics) a *fair* allocation of resources to each pressure, even when the strengths of various pressures change as processing proceeds.

Randomness and aynchronous parallelism

One might well imagine that the need for such randomness (or biased non-determinism) is simply an artefact of this architecture's having been designed to run on a sequential machine; were it redesigned to run on parallel hardware, then all randomness could be done away with. This turns out to be not at all the case, however. To see why, we have to think carefully about what it would mean for this architecture to run on parallel hardware. Suppose that there were some large number of parallel processors to which tasks could be assigned, and that each processor's speech could be continuously varied. It is certainly not the case that one could assign *processes* to *processors* in a one-to-one manner, since, as has been stressed, there is no clear notion of 'process' in this architecture. Nor could one assign one *pressure* to each processor, since codelets are not univalent as to the pressures that they represent. The only possibility would be to assign a processor to every single codelet, letting it run at a speed defined by that codelet's urgency. (Note that this requires a very large number of co-processors—hundreds, if not thousands. Moreover, since the codelet population varies greatly over time, the number of processors in use at different times will vary enormously. However, on a conceptual level, neither of those poses a problem in principle.)

Now notice a crucial consequence of this style: since all the processors are running at speeds that are completely independent of one another, they are effectively carrying out *asynchronous* computing, which means that relative to one another, the instants at which they carry out actions in the (shared) Workspace are totally decoupled—in short, entirely random relative to one another. This is a general fact: asynchronous parallelism is inseparable from processors' actions being random relative to one another (as pointed out in Hewitt, 1985). Thus parallelism provides no escape from the inherent randomness of this architecture. When it runs on serial hardware, some *explicit* randomizing device is utilized; when it runs on parallel hardware, the randomness is *implicit*, but no less random for that.

The earlier image of the swiftly changing panorama of a basketball game may help to make this necessary connection between asynchronous parallelism and randomness more intuitive. Each player might well feel that the snap decisions being made constantly inside their own head are anything but random—that, in fact, their decisions are rational responses to the situation. However, from the point of view of *other* players, what any one player does is not predictable—a player's mind is far too complex to be modelled, especially in real time. Thus, because all the players on the court are complex, independent, asynchronously acting systems, each player's actions *necessarily* have a random (i.e. unpredictable) quality from the point of view of all the other players. And obviously, the more unpredictable a team seems to its opponents, the better.

A *seeming paradox: Randomness in the service of intelligence*

Even after absorbing all these arguments, one may still feel uneasy with the proposition that greater intelligence will come from making *random* decisions than from making *systematic* ones. Indeed, when the architecture is described this way, it sounds nonsensical. Isn't it always wiser to choose the *better* action than to choose at *random*? However, as is the case in so many discussions about mind and its mechanisms, this appearance of nonsense is an illusion caused by a confusion of levels.

Certainly it would seem extremely counter-intuitive—in fact, down-right nonsensical—if one suggested that a melody-composition program (say) should choose its next note by throwing dice, even weighted dice. How could any global coherence come from such a process? This objection is of course totally valid—good melodies cannot be produced in that way (except in the absurd sense of millions of monkeys plunking away on piano keyboards for trillions of years and coming up with 'Blue Moon' once in a blue moon). But the Copycat architecture in no way advocates such a coarse type of decision-making procedure!

The choice of next note in a melody is a *top-level* macro-decision, as opposed to a low-level act of 'micro-exploration'. The purpose of micro-exploration is to efficiently explore the vast, foggy world of possibilities lying ahead without getting bogged down in a combinatorial explosion; for this purpose, randomness, being equivalent to non-biasedness, is the *most efficient* method. Once the terrain has been scouted out, then a lot of information has been gained, and in most cases some macroscopic pathways have been found to be much more promising than others. Moreover—and this is critical—the more information that has been uncovered, the more the temperature will have dropped—and the lower the temperature is, the less randomness is used. In other words, the more confidently the system believes, thanks to lots of efficient and fair micro-scouting in the fog, that it has identified a particular promising pathway ahead, the more certain it is to make the macro-decision of picking that pathway. Only when there is a very close competition is there much chance that the favourite will not win, and in such a case, it hardly matters since even after careful exploration, the system is not persuaded that there is a clear best route to follow.

In short, in the Copycat architecture, hordes of random forays are employed on a microscopic level when there is a lot of fog ahead, and their purpose is precisely to get an evenly distributed sense of what lies out there in the fog rather than simply plunging ahead blindly, at random. The foggier things are, the more un-biased should be the scouting mission, hence the more randomness is called for. To the extent that the scouting mission succeeds, the temperature will fall, which in turn means that the well-informed macroscopic decision about to be taken will be made *non*-randomly. Thus, randomness is used *in the service of*, and not in opposition to, intelligent non-random choice.

A subtle aspect of this architecture is that there are all shades between complete randomness (much fog, high temperature) and complete determinism (no fog, low temperature). This reflects the fact that one cannot draw a clean, sharp line between micro-exploratory scouting forays and confident, macroscopic decisions. For instance, a smallish, very local building or destruction operation carried out in the Workspace by an effector codelet working in a mid-range temperature can be thought of as lying somewhere in between a micro-exploratory foray and a well-informed macroscopic decision.

As a final point, it is interesting to note that non-metaphorical fluidity—that is, the physical fluidity of liquids like water—is inextricably tied to random microscopic actions. A liquid could not flow in the soft, gentle, *fluid* way that it does, were it not composed of tiny components whose micro-actions are completely random relative to one another. This does not, of course, imply that the top-level action of the fluid *as a whole* takes on any appearance of randomness; quite the contrary! The flow of a liquid is one of the most non-random phenomena of nature that we are familiar with. This does not mean that it is by any means *simple*; it is simply familiar and natural-seeming. Fluidity is an emergent quality, and to simulate it accurately requires an underlying randomness.

5. THE GENERALITY OF COPYCAT'S MECHANISMS

The crucial question of scaling up

As was stated at the outset, the Copycat project was never conceived of as being dependent in any essential way on specific aspects of its small domain, nor even on specific aspects of analogy-making *per se*. Rather, the central aim was to model the emergence of insightful cognition from fluid concepts, focusing on how slippages can be engendered by pressures.

One of the key questions about the architecture, therefore, is whether it truly is independent of the small domain and the small problems on which it now works. It would certainly be invalidated if it could be shown to depend on the relative smallness of its repertoire of Platonic concepts and the relatively few instances of those concepts that appear in a typical problem. However, from the very conception of the project, every attempt has been made to ensure that Copycat would not succumb to a combinatorial explosion if the domain were enlarged or the problems became bigger. In some sense, Copycat is a caricature of genuine analogy-making. The question is, what makes a caricature faithful? What is the proper way to construct a cognitive model that will scale up?

There's more than one way to copy a cat

With the exception of Copycat, virtually all present-day computer models of analogy-making are claimed by their designers (and the claim goes surprisingly unquestioned by most cognitive scientists) to operate in 'real-world' domains, with full-fledged concepts. When one looks behind those claims, however, one sees that the only 'real-world' aspect of the concepts is the *words* that are used as their names. For instance, consider a computer program that manipulates data structures that contain the English words 'nucleus' and 'electron', 'sun' and 'planet', and that are intended to encode a few basic propositions about the hydrogen atom and the solar system. Now suppose that the program comes up with a mapping in which 'nucleus' turns out to correspond with 'sun', and 'electron' with 'planet'. This gives the appearance of operating with considerable insight in the real world—in fact, not merely in the mundane everyday world, but in the highly abstruse scientific world—as opposed to Copycat, which merely operates with uninterpreted letters. However, the apparent success of a program that seems to map the solar system onto the hydrogen atom does not in the least mean that the computer has the same imagery as a human who makes the analogy—or indeed, that it has any imagery at all. The computer would have done just as good a job if *letters* rather than English words had been used: 'n' corresponds to 's', and 'e' to 'p'. Nobody would then have any reason to suspect that 'n' might stand for 'nucleus' and 's' for 'sun'. This hollowness of the alleged concepts in 'real-world' programs is surprisingly seldom mentioned.

One might try to level the same criticism at Copycat, by saying that when *successor* slips to *predecessor*, for instance, it might as well simply be *S* slipping to *P*—the machine wouldn't care. That of course is true, but there is a profound difference. A human watching the performance of Copycat and seeing the letter 'S' evoked by the presence of successor relationships and successorship groups in problem after problem after problem might after a while come to say, 'Oh, I guess that the letter "*S*" must mean "successor".' In other words, whether or not an English façade is used, the symbols in Copycat have at least some degree of genuine meaning, thanks to their correlation with actual phenomena, even if those phenomena take place in a tiny and artificial world. By contrast, in other analogy-making programs, there is no tiny and artificial world (let alone a big and real one) that could imbue the symbols they so deftly manipulate with any meanings.

Although the following analogy is doubtless somewhat biased, it gives the flavour of the difference between Copycat and its rivals. Suppose one wanted to create an exhibit explaining the nature of feline life to an intelligent alien creature made of, say, interstellar plasma or some substrate radically different from that of terrestrial life. The Copycat approach might be likened to the strategy of sending a live ant along with some commentary aimed at relating this rather simple creature to its far larger, far more complex feline cousins. The rival approach might be likened to the strategy of sending along a battery-operated stuffed animal—a cute and furry life-size toy kitty that could miaow and purr and walk. This strategy preserves the surface-level size and appearance of cats, as well as some rudimentary actions, while sacrificing faithfulness to the deep processes of life itself, whereas the previous strategy, sacrificing nearly all surface appearances, concentrates instead on conveying the abstract processes of life in a tiny example and attempts to remedy that example's defects by explicitly describing some of what changes when you scale up the model.

The price that one must pay, if one wishes to have a computer give the appearance of reproducing real-world analogies in their full glory, is that one must be willing to have people play a crucial filtering role, that of drastically reducing real-world situations into tiny artificial structures built from empty labels—clean, carefully tailored data structures that no longer pose the vast challenges of perceptual and conceptual focusing and filtering, challenges that are inseparable from real-life analogy-making. One must also accept the necessity of substituting brute-force search techniques for the truly fluid human mental mechanisms that can handle enormous, ill-defined situations with ease.

On the other hand, the price that one must pay, if one wishes to have a computer model the genuine processes of analogy-making, is that one must be willing to drastically reduce the repertoire and richness of the concepts and problems involved, while taking great care not to throw the baby out with the bath-water—that is, while keeping the model concepts just rich enough that the essential qualities of 'concepthood' seem preserved, and while making the model problems just complex enough that, for their solution, the essential aspects of fluidity, pressures, slippages, and perception are indispensable. Furthermore, one must vigilantly guard against even the slightest trace of brute-force search techniques creeping into one's model, because that would destroy its psychological plausibility.

Shades of grey and the mind's eye

Real cognition of course occurs in the essentially boundless real world, not in a tiny artificial world. This fact seems to offer the following choice to would-be 'cognition architects': either have humans scale down all situations by hand in advance into a small set of sharp-edged formal data structures, so that a brute-force architecture can work, or else let the computer effectively do it instead—that is, use a heuristic-based architecture that at the outset of every run makes a sharp and irreversible cut between concepts, pathways, and methods of attack that might eventually be brought to bear during that run, and ones that might not. There seems to be no middle ground between these two types of strategy, because either you must be willing to give *every* approach a chance (the brute-force approach), or you must choose some approaches while a priori filtering others out (what might be called the 'heuristic-chop' approach).

The only way out would seem to involve a notion of 'shadedness', in which concepts, facts, methods of attack, objects, and so on, rather than being ruled 'out' or 'in' in a black-and-white way, would be present in shades of grey—in fact, shades of grey that change over time. At first glance, this seems impossible. How can a concept be invoked only *partially*? How can a fact be neither fully ignored nor fully paid attention to? How can a method of attack be merely 'sort of' used? How can an object fall somewhere in between being considered 'in the situation' and being considered 'not in the situation'?

It is a premiss of the Copycat architecture that these 'shades of grey' questions lie at the crux of the modelling of mind. For this reason, they merit further discussion. A special fluid quality of human cognition is that often, solutions to a problem—especially the most ingenious ones, but even many ordinary ones—seem to come from far outside the problem as conceived of originally. This is because problems in the real world do not have sharp definitions; when one is in, or hears about, a complex situation, one typically pays no conscious attention to the question of what counts as 'in' the situation and what counts as 'out' of it. Such matters are almost always vague, implicit, and intuitive.

Using the metaphor of the 'mind's eye', we can liken the process of considering an abstract situation to the process of visually perceiving a physical scene. Like a real eye, the mind's eye has a limited field of vision, and cannot focus on several things simultaneously, let alone large numbers of them. Thus one has to choose where to have the mind's eye 'look'. When one directs one's gaze at what one feels is the situation's core, only a few centrally located things will come into clear focus, with more tangential things being less and less clear, and then at the peripheries there will be lots of things of which one is only dimly aware. Finally, whatever lies beyond the field of vision seems by definition to be outside of the situation altogether. Thus 'things' in the mind's eye are definitely shaded, both in terms of how clear they are, and in terms of how aware one is of them.

The very vague term 'thing' was used deliberately above; the intent was to include both *abstract Platonic concepts* and *concrete specific individuals*—in fact, to blur the two notions, since there is no hard-and-fast distinction between them. To make this clearer, think for a moment of the very complex situation that the Watergate affair was. As you do this, you will notice (if you followed Watergate at all) that all sorts of different events, people, and themes float into your mind with different degrees of clarity and intensity. To make this even more concrete, turn your mind's eye's gaze to the Senate Select Committee, and try to imagine each different Senator on that committee. Certainly, if you watched the hearings on television, some will emerge vividly while others will remain murky. Not just *Platonic abstractions* like 'senator' are involved, but many *individual* senators have different degrees of mental presence as you attempt to 'replay' those hearings in your mind. Needless to say, the memory of anyone who watched the Watergate hearings on television is filled to the brim both with Platonic concepts of various degrees of abstractness (ranging from 'impeachment' to 'cover up' to 'counsel' to 'testimony' to 'paper shredder') and with specific events, people, and objects at many levels of complexity (ranging from the 'Saturday night massacre' to the Supreme Court, from Maureen Dean to the infamous 18½-minute gap, and all the way down to the phrase 'expletive deleted' and even Sam Ervin's gavel, with which sessions were rapped to order). When one conjures up one's memories of Watergate, all of these 'things' have differential degrees of mental presence, which change as one's mind's eye scans the 'scene'.

Note that in the preceding paragraph, all the 'things' mentioned were carefully chosen so that readers—at least readers who remember Watergate reasonably well—would give them unthinking acceptance as 'parts' of Watergate. However, now consider the following 'things': England, France, communism, socialism, the Vietnam War, the Six-Day War, the Washington Monument, the *New York Times*, Spiro Agnew, Edward Kennedy, Howard Cosell, Jimmy Hoffa, Frank Sinatra, Ronald Reagan, the AFL–CIO, General Electric, the electoral college, college degrees, Harvard University, helicopters, keys, guns, flypaper, Scotch tape, television, pianos, secrecy, accountancy, and so on. Which of these things are properly thought of as being 'in' Watergate, and which ones as 'out' of it? It would obviously be ludicrous to try to draw a sharp line. One is forced to accept the fact that for a model of a mind to be at all realistic, it must be capable of imbuing all concrete objects and individuals, as well as all abstract Platonic concepts, with shaded degrees of mental presence—and of course, those degrees of presence must be capable of changing over time.

Like a real eye, the mind's eye can be attracted by something glinting in the peripheries, and shift its gaze. When it does so, things that were formerly out of sight altogether now enter the visual field. By a series of such shifts, 'things' that were totally out of the situation's initial representation can wind up at the very centre of attention. This brings us back, finally, to that special fluid quality of human thought whereby initially unsuspected notions occasionally wind up being central to one's resolution of a problem, and reveals how intimately such fluidity is linked with the various 'shades-of-grey' questions given above.

Copycat's shaded exploration strategy

Let us return to the list of 'shades-of-grey' questions given above: How can a concept be invoked only *partially*? How can a fact be neither fully ignored nor fully paid attention to? How can a method of attack be merely 'sort of' used? How can an object fall somewhere in between being considered 'in the situation' and being considered 'not in the situation'? These questions were not asked merely rhetorically; in fact, it was precisely to answer the challenges that they raise that the probabilistic architecture of Copycat was designed. Copycat's architecture has in common with brute-force architectures the fact that every possible concept, fact, method, object, and so on is *in principle* available at all times; it has in common with heuristic-chop architectures the fact that out of all available concepts, facts, methods, objects, and so on, only a few will get very intensely drawn in at any given moment, with most being essentially dormant and an intermediate number having a status somewhere in between. In other words, virtually all aspects of the Copycat architecture are riddled by shades of grey instead of by hard-edged, black-and-white cut-offs. In particular, *activation* (with continuous values rather than a binary on/off distinction) is a mechanism that gives rise to shadedness in the Slipnet, while *salience* and *urgency* serve similar purposes in the Workspace and Coderack, respectively. These are just three of a whole family of related 'shades-of-grey mechanisms' whose entire *raison d'être* is to defeat the scaling-up problem.

An architecture thus pervaded by shades of grey has the very attractive property that although no concept or object (etc.) is ever *strictly* or *fully* ruled out, only a handful of them are at any time *seriously* involved. Thus at any moment the system is focusing its attention on just a small set of concepts, objects, etc. However, this 'searchlight of attention' can easily shift under the influence of new information and pressures, allowing a priori very unlikely concepts, objects, or methods of attack to enter the picture as serious contenders.

The list below summarizes the various mechanisms in the Copycat architecture that incorporate shades of grey in different ways. In this list, the term 'shaded' should be understood as representing the opposite of a binary, black/white distinction; it often means that one or more *real numbers* are attached to each entity of the sort mentioned, as opposed to there being an on/off distinction. The term 'dynamic' means that the degree of presence—the 'shade', so to speak—can change with time.

Shades of grey in the Slipnet

- shaded, dynamic presence of Platonic concepts (via dynamic activation levels)
- shaded, dynamic conceptual proximities (via dynamic link-lengths)
- shaded, dynamic spreading of activation to neighbour concepts (giving rise to 'conceptual halos')
- shaded conceptual depths of nodes
- shaded decay rates of concepts (determined by conceptual depths)
- shaded, dynamic emergence of abstract themes (stable activation patterns of interrelated conceptually deep nodes)

Shades of grey in the Workspace

- shaded, dynamic number of descriptions for any object
- shaded, dynamic importance of each object (via activation levels of descriptors in Slipnet)
- shaded, dynamic unhappiness of each object (determined by degree of integration into larger structures)
- shaded, dynamic presence of objects (via dynamic salience levels)
- shaded, dynamic tentativity of structures (via dynamic strengths)

Shades of grey associated with the Coderack

- shaded, dynamic degrees of 'promise' of pathways
- shaded, dynamic emergence of pressures (via urgencies of codelets and shifting population of Coderack)
- shaded, dynamic degree of willingness to take risks (via temperature)
- shaded, dynamic mixture of deterministic and non-deterministic modes of exploration

- shaded, dynamic mixture of parallel and serial modes of exploration
- shaded, dynamic mixture of bottom-up and top-down processing

There is one further aspect of shadedness in Copycat that is not localized in a single component of the architecture, and is somewhat subtler. This has to do with the fact that higher-level structures emerge over time, each of which brings in new and unanticipated concepts, and also opens up new and unanticipated avenues of approach. In other words, as a run proceeds, the field of vision broadens out to incorporate new possibilities, and this feeds on itself: each new object or structure is subject to the same perceptual processes and chunking mechanisms that gave rise to it. Thus there is a spiral of rising complexity, which brings new items of ever-greater abstraction into the picture 'from nowhere', in a sense. This process imbues the Copycat architecture with a type of fundamental unpredictability or 'openness' (Hewitt, 1985) that is not possible in an architecture with frozen representations. The ingredients of this dynamic unpredictability form an important addendum to the list of shades of grey given above.

Dynamic emergence of unpredictable objects and pathways

- creation of unanticipated higher-level perceptual objects and structures
- emergence of a priori unpredictable potential pathways of exploration (via creation of novel structures at increasing levels of abstraction)
- creation of large-scale viewpoints
- competition between rival high-level structures

By design, none of the mechanisms in the lists presented above has anything in the least to do with the size of the situations that Copycat is currently able to deal with, or with the current size of Copycat's Platonic conceptual repertoire. Note, moreover, that none of them has anything whatsoever to do with the subject-matter of the Copycat domain, or even with the task of analogy-making *per se*. Yet these mechanisms and their emergent consequences—especially commingling pressures and the parallel terraced scan—are what Copycat is *truly* about. This is the underpinning of the claim of the Copycat architecture's cognitive generality.

PHILOSOPHICAL EPILOGUE

Brain structures versus cognitive mechanisms

When one asserts 'Copycat is a model of thinking', what is really meant? Is Copycat in any sense a model of the human brain? Most people—even most cognitive scientists—would be inclined to answer 'no'. However, before discarding the idea, one should carefully consider what is meant by 'model of the brain'.

When one asks 'Is Copycat a model of *the brain?*' or says '*The human brain* can think', one is using a singular noun to refer to billions of distinct physical instantiations. Needless to say, it is those physical instances (specific human brains), not the non-physical Platonic category ('the human brain'), that carry out thinking. Moreover, it is common knowledge that each individual brain has its own unique wiring patterns, and in that sense is a unique physical substrate for thought. The unquestioned use of the singular term 'the brain' in spite of all this variability reveals our tacit assumption that there must be some abstract (but unspecified) level of description shared by all human brains. Therefore, when decoded, the sentence 'The human brain can think' really means the following rather subtle idea: 'There are abstract universal mechanisms, diversely instantiated over and over again in specific brains, that allow thinking to take place.' In short, the brain mechanisms responsible for thinking are not *literally* hardware; rather, they are located somewhere along the spectrum between hardware and software.

Today's excitement over neural networks has led many people to suppose that these mechanisms lie more toward the hardware end of the spectrum than people tended to suppose in the 1960s and 1970s. For that reason, there may well be a greater tendency today than a decade or two ago to describe cognitive science as a search for *brain structures* as opposed to a search for *mental mechanisms*. Trying to draw such a distinction is a tricky matter, though.

Being a very complex system, the brain (to use that questionable singular once again) contains many types of structures at many distinct hierarchical levels, including the following (just to list a few examples):

- atomic nuclei;
- water molecules;

- amino acids;
- neurotransmitters;
- synapses;
- dendrites;
- neurons;
- clusters of neurons;
- columns in the visual cortex;
- larger regions (such as area 19) in the visual cortex;
- the entire visual cortex;
- the entire left hemisphere.

Among these (and many other) diverse 'brain structures', which are the most likely to figure critically in an explanation of thinking? No one knows for sure. It is interesting, however, that in the last few years, the popular press has latched onto certain neurological experiments on synaptic-weight modification in various creatures large and small, often breathlessly describing them as 'unravelling the secrets of memory'. This dramatization amounts to the (quite literally *mindless*) presumption that there is nothing on an *organizational* level to human memory—that to fathom human memory in its full richness, one can simply be a chemist and concern oneself exclusively with the mechanisms behind local microscopic chemical changes. Psychological notions are thrown to the wind in this view.

The fact that there are so many levels and types of well-established *physical* structures reveals one type of blurriness inherent in the term 'brain structure', but to compound the complexity, there is another plausible type of 'brain structure', exemplified by such notions as:

- the concept *dog*;
- the associative link between the concepts *cow* and *milk*;
- an object file for a perceived object (as discussed by perceptual psychologist Anne Treisman in Treisman, 1988);
- 'geons' and '2½-D sketches' (as discussed in various models of vision);
- frames, scripts, and schemas;
- 'memory organization packets' (as in Roger Schank's models of memory);
- short-term memory;
- long-term memory;

- the various 'agents', 'K-lines', 'nemes', and 'nomes' posited in Marvin Minsky's 'society of mind' model (Minsky, 1986);
- codelets, urgencies, slippages, conceptual distances, conceptual depths, bonds, descriptions, bridges, groups, strengths, and temperature (as in Copycat).

This list is just a small sampling of plausible ingredients, at various levels, of various theories of thinking. Although, on first glance, each one seems to belong to a realm far removed from the brain, if the item in question is a valid aspect of cognition, then it must be somehow implemented in the physical substrate of the brain. Each of these entities stands at least *some* chance of becoming physically grounded in the next several decades, in much the same way as the once-theoretical notion of *genes* became physically grounded with the understanding of DNA. Therefore the elements of this list are reasonable candidates for being called 'brain structures', albeit in a somewhat different sense from those in the previous list.

As of yet, there is absolutely no certainty about the optimal level at which the hopefully universal brain structures (or cognitive mechanisms) ought to be characterized. Other branches of science have faced similar level-specification problems, some of which have been fairly satisfactorily resolved. If one thinks about the behaviour of gases, for instance, they are best described, for many purposes, by the macroscopic-level laws of thermodynamics, even though gases are well known to be composed of astronomical numbers of molecules, and can thus also be described at the lower level of statistical mechanics. Similarly, if one is interested in describing how DNA is the carrier of heredity, one does best by referring only to the high level of information-carrying codons and skipping most if not all references to the low-level details of the chemical makeup of DNA. Interestingly, there are distinct terms used to describe DNA at these distinct levels: DNA *qua* physical structure is called the 'double helix', while DNA *qua* information carrier is referred to as an organism's 'genome'.

What one hopes to achieve in cognitive science is a similar sophistication in talking about the functioning of 'the brain' at different levels. Specifically, one wants to know what level and type of brain structures are the most suitable for describing thought. Perhaps, in analogy with the two labels for DNA, we could refer to the brain *qua* physical structure as the 'double hemisphere', and the brain *qua* memory carrier and site of concepts as an organism's 'memome'.

Although it is not as common as it used to be, it is still respectable in cognitive science today to believe that some type of deductive formalism (such as the predicate calculus or some more recent representation language, e.g. KLONE) is somehow implemented in neurons, and that what really makes the behaviour thinking is the formalism, not the fact that this formalism is somehow implemented in neural hardware. Such a belief is no different from the truism that what makes a given program be a word processor (as opposed to, say, a weather predictor or a video game) is its source code, not the machine it is running on. Thus the 'brain structures' responsible for thought might, at least in principle, turn out to be very abstract (e.g. something like the features of a representation language such as KLONE) rather than relatively concrete (e.g. details of neural interconnectivity). Today, many cognitive scientists may find this once-bright hope implausible, but it cannot be absolutely ruled out, because no one yet knows for certain what level or type of 'brain structures' will turn out to support the essential features of thought.

In any case, almost all cognitive scientists, whatever they think of KLONE and related formalisms, *do* accept the premiss that the question 'At which level of description of the brain is thinking really going on?' is a meaningful question and has a meaningful answer. Presumably, then, the details *below* that critical level do not matter. (This is why cognitive scientists are almost certain that it is not worth while for their purposes to study molecular biology, quantum mechanics, or quarks.) It would be extremely revealing if one succeeded in making a thinking object that had a substrate very different from neurons. This may or may not come to pass, but if it did, such a success would reveal much to us about what level of machinery is necessary to support thought. We would learn that thinking critically depends on levels X and above, whereas below level X, various different substrates will do.

If we admit even the *conceivability* of the notion that a non-brain might be able to think, then we certainly need to have some set of criteria by which to recognize that such a system is thinking—otherwise, we will be unable to tell a thinking system from another type of system. Luckily, we have some hints about such criteria. We recognize human kindness by observing kind acts, not by verifying that a person has an underlying 'kindness gene' or doing a brain operation to see if some kind of 'empathy centre' has actually been engaged. We recognize a word processor by what it does on a screen in response to keyboard input, not by what hardware it runs on. We have behavioural criteria for kindness in humans. It would not be too hard to set up some behavioural criteria for recognizing word-processing programs. Turing, in his famous article, attempted to suggest a similar set of criteria for recognizing thinking entities.

In analogy to such criteria for recognizing kind acts or word processors, Turing's idea is to employ a set of high-level behavioural criteria as opposed to low-level implementational criteria. Turing did not make the dogmatic presumption that, simply because brains are made out of neurons, the only possible level of description of any system that could think is the level of neurons. Instead, he built on what people intuitively mean when they refer to thinking—namely the *fluid manipulation of ideas*. Turing does not a priori tie such manipulation to any kind of hardware; he remains open as to what the proper level of description of the mechanisms responsible will turn out to be.

When all the results of mind/brain research are finally in, will the best way to talk about 'the human brain' wind up being in terms of standard types of neural wiring patterns? Or standard types of neural clusters? Or standard types of interrelationships of neural clusters? Perhaps the details of neurons themselves will not matter. Conceivably, in fact, even the internal structure of neural clusters will not matter any more than do organic chemistry and quantum mechanics. In such a case, the underpinnings of thinking would be revealed to lie pretty distant from biology and much closer to abstract organizational principles—which is to say, software. Who knows—it might even turn out that the proper 'brain structures' required for the fluid manipulation of ideas are roughly at the level of the mechanisms of Copycat, or a little bit lower.

Scattering experiments versus 'direct' observation of phenomena

On first being exposed to the Turing Test, one might well think it would allow probing only at a very high level, and that it certainly would be incapable of getting at subcognitive or subsymbolic mechanisms, let alone neural-level mechanisms. Many people feel that the Turing Test, being concerned merely with 'behaviour', can barely scratch the surface of mechanisms. This issue—namely, the relationship between 'mere behaviour' and hidden mechanisms, and the depth to which the Turing Test can be used as a probe for hidden mechanisms—leads one to the question, 'Where is the boundary line between "direct" and "indirect" observation?'

Early this century, the physicist Ernest Rutherford sent a beam of alpha-particles through thin pieces of gold foil and collected statistics on the angles of scattering they underwent. From these (macroscopic) observations, he deduced that gold atoms must have a central nucleus surrounded by electrons, a finding that led eventually to the modern picture of 'the atom' (another of those questionable singulars). His conclusion depended, of course, on a mathematical theory of electromagnetic scattering, which predicts that such-and-such a microscopic internal structure will cause such-and-such a macroscopic distribution of scattered particles.

Rutherford's scattering experiments were so important and so reproducible that his basic technique became a standard element of the repertoire of experimental physics. What at first seemed to be an abstruse and *indirect* connection between macroscopic patterns and their underlying microscopic causes came eventually to be seen as an obvious and *direct* connection in physicists' minds. Of course, the end results of scattering experiments were never quite as direct as *pictures* of the observed structures would have been—they were mathematical or verbal descriptions. However, this was good enough for physicists.

Recently, though, with the phenomenal surges in computing power, the results of scattering experiments done with electron microscopes and X-ray microscopes can be processed to yield what are essentially *photographs* of objects the size of molecules, or even atoms. In principle, the calculations are no different from those in Rutherford's experiments, but so many more of them can be done, and done so much faster, that the results seem qualitatively different—certainly to the intuition.

Today, for instance, ultrasound allows us to see a foetus moving about inside a mother's womb in real time. Note that we feel no need to put quotes around the word 'see'—no more than around the word 'talk' in the sentence 'My wife and I talk every day over the phone.' A hundred years ago, perhaps people using telephones had a slight sense of doubt about whether they were really talking to, or being talked to by, a genuine person—but not so today. We don't picture the person as being inside the phone, but inside their home. If, fifty years ago, high-frequency sounds had been scattered off a foetus, there would have been no technology to convert the scattered waves into a television image, and any conclusions derived from measurements on the scattered waves would have been considered abstruse mathematical inferences; today, however, simply because fast computer hardware can reconstruct the scatterer from the scattered waves in real time, we feel we are *directly* observing the foetus. Examples like this—and they are legion in our technological era—show why any boundary between 'direct observation' and 'inference' is a subjective matter.

In fact, much of science consists of progress in blurring this seemingly sharp distinction. What at one point is considered very subtle inference becomes established, standardized, and computerized; then it is considered direct observation and taken for granted. This trend runs from optical telescopy to radio telescopy, from optical microscopy to electron microscopy to particle scattering, and so on. As with ultrasound, whether one intuitively feels a process to be 'direct observation' or not is simply determined by whether a sufficiently clear and vivid visual picture is produced by some computer. Today's abstruse inference is tomorrow's direct window!

The Turing Test and the visibility of deep mechanisms

All of this carries over to the Turing Test. Indeed, one can liken the Turing Test to a scattering experiment, in which the thinking device unwittingly reveals its (microscopic) internal mechanisms through its responses to questions (which in the scattering analogy play the role of the impinging waves or particles). The level of detail that can be probed in this manner is unlimited, although to carry out ever-finer levels of probing requires ever more and ever subtler types of questioning, as well as ever subtler ways of scrutinizing the responses.

Examining linguistic responses in novel ways is quite similar to examining the spectra of stars in novel ways (e.g. using new regions of the electromagnetic spectrum, higher degrees of resolution, using time-correlation data from widely separated receivers, etc.), and thereby inferring detailed stellar mechanisms of ever-subtler sorts, despite being hundreds of light-years from the star itself. In the Turing Test, some of the possible ways to scrutinize linguistic output include the following:

- looking at *word frequencies* (e.g. is 'the' the most common word? is 'time' the most common noun? are some low-frequency words used unnaturally often? is suspicion aroused if low-frequency words are used with a high frequency in the input questions?);
- observing sensitivity to *tone* (e.g. are formal and slang expressions understood? is humour based on improper mixtures of tone understood? is suspicion aroused by a strange mixture of tones in the input questions? in the generated text, are formal and informal levels kept suitably apart, or mixed in strange ways?);
- examining *types of errors* (e.g. misspellings, transposition errors, improperly used words or phrases, blends of all sorts, grammatical errors, and so on, which—as ought to be well known to any cognitive scientist—reveal a great deal about the mechanisms of thought);
- examining *word flavours* as a function of subtle details of the context (e.g. what contextual pressures lead to choosing 'jock' over 'athlete', or vice versa? to saying 'lady' as opposed to 'woman'? to saying 'endeavour' instead of 'try' or 'attempt' or 'strive'?);
- examining *level of abstraction of word choices* (e.g. what pressures lead to choosing between 'Fido', 'the dog', and 'some mammal'? to choosing between 'that pedestrian', 'that man', and 'that person'? to choosing between 'recliner', 'armchair', 'chair', 'piece of furniture', and 'thing'?);
- looking at *default assumptions regarding gender* (e.g. what kinds of circumstances lead to generation of agent nouns with feminine endings? when are 'generic' terms like 'man' and 'he' generated? what gender is assumed when neutral terms like 'pedestrian' and 'surgeon' appear in the input?);
- observing how *throwaway analogies* are understood and generated (e.g. is the abstraction hidden in remarks such as 'I've done that, too!' and 'Has that ever happened to you?' interpreted correctly and instantly? are such remarks produced in the standard contexts that would call for them?);

- observing how *throwaway counterfactuals* are understood and generated (e.g. is the subtle blend implicit in remarks such as 'I wouldn't do that if I were you' or 'What would *you* have done in my place?' interpreted correctly and instantly? are such remarks produced in the standard contexts that would call for them?);
- paying attention to *timing data* (the output stream might come character by character, line by line, or speech by speech, but in all cases the speed taken to generate the output can be used to make some inferences about the mechanisms behind the scenes);

and so on and so forth. This list could be extended and elaborated in enormous detail, but this is not the place to give a long list of such windows onto covert machinery, or to try to defend the validity and power of using such approaches (see French, 1990). The point is simply that there are many of them, and some of them are already well-established techniques in cognitive science (particularly cognitive psychology).

Anyone who seriously believes in the validity of the Turing Test does so precisely because they appreciate the subtlety of the probes it offers. As astronomers and physicists know, external behaviour far removed in location and scale from its sources, if scrutinized sufficiently carefully, can be phenomenally revelatory of mechanisms; likewise, cognitive scientists should appreciate the analogous fact about the behaviour of the mind. In short, the Turing Test, if exploited properly, can be used to probe mental mechanisms at arbitrary levels of depth and subtlety.

In the spirit of much of the best science of our century, the Turing Test blurs the line between external and internal probing, 'direct' and 'indirect' observation, and thus reminds us of the artificiality of such distinctions. Any model of mind that passes the Turing Test will agree with 'brain structures' all the way down to the level where the essence of thinking really takes place.

The Turing Test and basic research

Recently, a monetary prize was established for the first program to pass a restricted version of the Turing Test. Unfortunately, although the idea is amusing and even exciting in a strange way, such a competition is very premature today. Unless the people who play the interrogator role do so in a very sophisticated manner, they will wind up probing at a relatively coarse level, and this will turn the competition into nothing but a race for flashier and flashier natural-language 'front ends' with little substance behind them. This would be a shame, for when one looks carefully at models in the tiniest microdomains, such as Copycat, one sees that even they are still enormously far from achieving true mental fluidity. What is needed is a prize for advances in basic research, not a prize for window-dressing.

The Copycat project represents a conscious choice to work at a very basic, stripped-down level, far removed from the seductive glories of natural language. Whereas artificial-intelligence projects operating in allegedly real-world domains can do no more than implement the merest 'tips' of many iceberg-like real-world concepts, Copycat attempts to implement the *essence* of a very limited number of artificially simple concepts. While it is certain that no version of the Copycat program will ever come close to passing the Turing Test, one can hope that the development of Copycat may help lead, in the distant future, to architectures that go much further toward capturing the genuine fluid mentality that Alan Turing so clearly envisioned when he first proposed his deservedly celebrated Test.

REFERENCES

Erman, L. D., Hayes-Roth, F., Lesser, V. R., and Reddy, D. R. (1980), 'The Hearsay-II Speech-Understanding System: Integrating Knowledge to Resolve Uncertainty', *Computing Surveys*, 12/2: 213–53.

French, R. M. (1990), 'Subcognition and the Limits of the Turing Test', *Mind* 99/393: 53–65.

Hewitt, C. (1985), 'The Challenge of Open Systems', *Byte Magazine* 10/4: 223–42.

Hinton, G. E., and Sejnowski, T. J. (1986), 'Learning and Relearning in Boltzmann Machines', in D. E. Rumelhart and J. L. McClelland (eds.), *Parallel Distributed Processing*, i: 282–317, Cambridge, Mass.: Bradford/MIT Press.

Hofstadter, D. R. (1983), 'The Architecture of Jumbo', in Ryszard Michalski, Jaime, Carbonell, and Thomas Mitchell (eds.),

Proceedings of the International Machine Learning Workshop, Urbana, Il.: University of Illinois, 161–70.

—— (1984), *The Copycat Project: An Experiment in Nondeterminism and Creative Analogies*, AI Memo No. 755, AI Laboratory, Massachusetts Institute of Technology, Cambridge, Mass.

—— (1985), 'Waking Up from the Boolean Dream', *or*, 'Subcognition as Computation', in *Metamagical Themas*, New York: Basic Books, 631–65.

—— and Mitchell, M. (1994), 'The Copycat Project: A Model of Mental Fluidity and Analogy-Making', in Keith Holyoak and John Barnden (eds.), *Advances in Connectionist and Neural Computation Theory*, ii: *Analogical Connections*, Norwood, NJ: Ablex, 31–112.

Kirkpatrick, S., Gelatt Jr., C. D., and Vecchi, M. P. (1983), 'Optimization by Simulated Annealing', *Science*, 220: 671–80.

Meredith, M. J. (1986), 'Seek-Whence: A Model of Pattern Perception', unpublished doctoral dissertation, Dept. of Computer Science, Indiana University, Bloomington, Ind.

—— (1991), 'Data Modeling: A Process for Pattern Induction', *Journal for Experimental and Theoretical Artificial Intelligence*, 3: 43–68.

Minsky, M. (1986), *The Society of Mind*, New York: Simon & Schuster.

Mitchell, M. (1993), *Analogy-Making as Perception: A computer Model*, Cambridge, Mass.: MIT Press/Bradford.

—— and Hofstadter, D. R. (1990), 'The Emergence of Understanding in a Computer Model of Concepts and Analogy-Making', *Physica*, D 42: 322–34.

Smolensky, P. (1986), 'Information Processing in Dynamical Systems: Foundations of Harmony Theory', in D. E. Rumelhart and J. L. McClelland (eds.), *Parallel Distributed Processing*, i, Cambridge, Mass.: Bradford/MIT Press, 194–281.

Treisman, A. (1988), 'Features and Objects: The Fourteenth Bartlett Memorial Lecture', *Quarterly Journal of Experimental Psychology*, 40A: 201–37.

12

Encoding Psychological Knowledge

IAN PRATT

———— • ————

1. INTRODUCTION

The purpose of this paper is to challenge a widely accepted philosophical view concerning the nature of the *psychological concepts*. By 'psychological concepts', I mean, centrally, the concepts of *believing, desiring, intending, doubting, hoping, fearing*, and so on. According to the view I want to challenge, our grasp of these concepts is to be understood as our mastery of a *theory* governing their use—specifically, a theory consisting of that body of common-sense knowledge which David Lewis calls *folk psychology*. As Lewis puts it:

Think of common-sense psychology as a term-introducing scientific theory, though one invented long before there was any such institution as professional science. Collect all the platitudes you can think of regarding the causal relations of mental states, sensory stimuli, and motor responses ... Add also all the platitudes to the effect that one mental state falls under another—'toothache is a kind of pain', and the like. Perhaps there are platitudes of other forms as well. Include only platitudes which are common knowledge among us—everyone knows them, everyone knows that everyone else knows them, and so on. For the meanings of our words are common knowledge, and I am going to claim that the names of mental states derive their meaning from these platitudes.[1]

In the time this paper has been in press, my views have developed somewhat. See e.g. I. Pratt: 'Analysis and the Attitudes', in S. Wagner and S. Warner (eds.), *Naturalism: A Critical Appraisal*, Notre Dame, Ind.: University of Notre Dame Press, 1993: 273–94. However, the differences between that article and the present one are primarily matters of detail.

[1] David Lewis: 'Psychophysical and Theoretical Identifications', *Australasian Journal of Philosophy*, 50 (1972), 249–58.

Thus: psychological terms are to be defined in terms of a general theory of common-sense psychology governing their use; psychological concepts are to be analysed by outlining the general form of that theory; and our grasp of those concepts is to be understood as (implicit) knowledge of that theory.

In the sequel, I aim to show why, and in what sense, it is wrong to understand our grasp of psychological concepts—or our mastery of psychological vocabulary—as knowledge, however implicit, of any theory. My strategy will be to sketch a rival view of the cognitive mechanisms underlying our grasp of psychological concepts, and to show that the operation of those mechanisms cannot effectively be duplicated by our possessing any collection of beliefs, that is to say, by our knowing any theory. In doing so, I will pay particular attention to our knowledge of the typical environmental causes and behavioural effects of our psychological states, and I shall claim that such knowledge arises through processes of observation and simulation. The thrust of the paper will be to establish the fundamental differences between the account of our grasp of the psychological concepts as knowledge of folk psychology, and the rival account I present.

2. A THEORY OF PSYCHOLOGICAL INFERENCE

The purpose of this section is to present an account of psychological inference—an account, that is, of how we reason with the concepts of *believing, desiring, intending, doubting, hoping, fearing,* and so on. In subsequent sections, I shall argue that this account undermines the view which sees our grasp of psychological concepts as possession of a theory of folk psychology.

Perhaps a good place to start is with our knowledge of our own psychological states. Sometimes, it seems, we consciously monitor our thoughts through a process of introspection: not only do we believe *P, Q, R* and desire *X, Y, Z,* but we also believe that *we believe that P, Q, R,* and believe that *we desire that X, Y, Z.* But not all monitoring of our beliefs takes this conscious and deliberate form. Sometimes, it seems, we *un*consciously monitor the course of our thinking for later recall. For the fact that I can remember much of what I believed or desired yesterday (whether or not I still believe and desire these things) suggests that I monitored the occurrence of these thoughts at the time, even though I made no conscious effort to do so. So the first question we shall ask is: How might such monitoring processes be implemented? Or, more precisely: How might beliefs about one's own psychological states—beliefs of the form 'I believe *P*', 'I believed *P* yesterday', 'I desire *X*', 'I desired *X* yesterday', etc., be represented in our brains in order that these monitoring processes might be made to work?

We can simplify the answer by indulging in a little fictional psychology. Suppose that for you to believe that *P* is a matter of the tokening, in a suitable part of your brain—let us call it your *belief-box*—of a certain (physical) type of data-structure Δ_P. We shall say that, for you, Δ_P *encodes* the proposition *P*. Similarly, let us suppose that for you to desire that *X* is a matter of the tokening, in a suitable part of your brain—let us call it your *desire-box*—of a certain (physical) type of data-structure Δ_X, where Δ_X encodes, for you, the proposition *X*. And so on for all propositional belief-contents and all psychological modalities. Now we can suggest a way for you to encode propositions about your own current psychological states. To encode 'I believe *P*', take the data-structure Δ_P encoding the proposition *P*, and *tag* it with some special symbol denoting the modality of belief. By 'tagging', I mean literally altering the physical properties of Δ_P in some small way, so that it is easy to recover, if necessary, the original from the tagged version. To encode the propositions 'I believe *Q*', 'I believe *R*', just tag the corresponding data-structures Δ_Q, Δ_R, with the same symbol denoting belief. Similarly, to encode the proposition 'I desire *X*', take the data structure Δ_X, encoding the proposition *X*, and tag it with some special symbol denoting the modality of desire. To encode the propositions 'I desire *Y*', 'I desire *Z*', just tag the corresponding data-structures Δ_Y, Δ_Z with the same symbol denoting desire. Similarly for the other modalities: intending, doubting, fearing, etc. Let us denote above tagged data-structures by Δ_P^B, Δ_Q^B, Δ_R^B, Δ_X^D, Δ_Y^D, Δ_Z^D, etc.: believing 'I believe *P*' is then a matter of your having a token of Δ_P^B in your belief-box; believing 'I desire *X*' a matter of your having a token of Δ_X^D in your belief-box, and so on.

Given this rather simple-minded representation scheme, it is easy to see how the sort of monitoring mentioned above might work. The presence of the belief *P*, in the guise of the tokening of Δ_P in your belief-box, can give rise, via the tagging process just mentioned, to the presence of the belief 'I believe *P*' in the guise of the tokening of Δ_P^B in your belief-box. Similarly with beliefs about your other psychological states. And there is no reason why the tags thus attached to your mental data-structures cannot be time-stamped, and the resulting data-structures retained for an indefinite period in your belief-box. In this way, a tagged data-structure with a given time-stamp lying around in your belief-box encodes a proposition about one of your *previous* psychological states. Clearly, for you to be able to remember a previous belief P which you no longer hold, we must presume that the tag on the time-stamped data-structure Δ_P^B protects it from the ravages of whatever processes of belief-revision swept Δ_P away. And indeed, there seems no reason in principle why tagging data-structures should not thus alter the way in which belief-revision processes can latch onto them.

Now if you can monitor when you were in this or that psychological state—say, the belief that P—then you can, in principle, notice the conditions under which those psychological states arose in the past, whence you can induce generalizations about the typical aetiology of those psychological states. Since the mechanisms described above enable you to form beliefs about the correctness of your earlier beliefs, conclusions about the causes of the belief P, will not, in all cases, take the form: 'I believe P when and only when it is the case that P', but may contain information about the conditions under which you believed P even though (as you now know) it was false, or failed to believe P even though (as you now know) it was true. And there seems to be no limit, in principle, to the sophistication and detail of the knowledge you can garner in this way. Indeed, there is no reason, if the foregoing account of this sort of knowledge is correct, why your knowledge of the typical causes of the belief P need make reference to the proposition P at all: after all, most of my beliefs about hexagons were caused by books, or so I seem to remember.

I have spoken of the ability to form inductive generalizations concerning the causes of a *particular* belief P. But what of generalizations concerning the typical causes of, for example, beliefs *about cats*, or beliefs *about hexagons*, or beliefs *about sub-atomic particles*? In judging, if you did so judge, that most of your beliefs about hexagons were caused by reading books, you made a judgement concerning all beliefs whose contents belong to a certain class of propositions; yet all you could have observed by means of the introspective processes described above are, in the first in-stance, beliefs with *particular* contents: the belief 'Hexagons have six sides', 'The internal angles of a hexagon sum to 4π', and so on. How then might you induce generalizations about the causes of *classes* of beliefs identified by quantifying over belief-contents? Again, we see that the encoding scheme described above causes no particular problems. For since, by hypothesis, it is easy to recover the original data-structure Δ_P from the tagged version Δ_P^B, those inferential mechanisms by means of which you can determine that a given proposition—e.g. 'The internal angles of a hexagon sum to 4π'—is a proposition to do with *hexagons*, can also be de-ployed to determine that the proposition 'I believe that the inter-nal angles of a hexagon sum to 4π' is a proposition about a belief whose propositional content is to do with hexagons. That is: the fact that you can systematically transform Δ_P^B into the untagged data-structure Δ_P means that encoding propositions about your psychological states using such tagged data-structures renders the propositional contents of those beliefs available to the full range of your inferential machinery. In particular, the encoding scheme described above causes no problems in regard to determining logi-cal relationships between the propositional contents of psychologi-cal states thus represented.

Two final points concerning your knowledge of your own psy-chological states. First, just as the tagging and untagging mechan-isms postulated above give you access to arbitrarily sophisticated and detailed information concerning the environmental *causes* of your psychological states, those same mechanisms can yield infor-mation of similar quality about the behavioural *effects* of your psychological states. You might observe, for example, that an un-qualified intention to lift a small object, or to cross the road, or to utter a sentence, standardly issues in your actually performing the corresponding actions; you might observe, for example, that an intention to meet a paper deadline or solve a mathematical problem standardly does not. Second, although I have so far fo-cused on knowledge of the *environmental* causes and *behavioural* effects of psychological states, there is no reason why your intro-spective mechanisms should be limited to such extracranial condi-tions. There is no reason, that is, why you should not observe that whenever you have such-and-such (types of) beliefs and such-and-such (types of) intentions, then you invariably form such-and-such (types) of desires. Here, the conjunctions you notice are not between a thought and some external condition, but rather, between one constellation of thoughts and another.

So much then for encoding knowledge of your own psychological states. But how do you encode propositions about the psychological states of *others*? And how will that encoding allow you to acquire and reason with such information? The critical insight in understanding our knowledge of other people's minds, I believe, is stated by Hobbes thus:

> But there is another saying not of late understood, by which they might learn truly to read one another, if they would take the pains; and that is, *Nosce teipsum, Read thy self* . . . [which is meant] to teach us, that for the similitude of the thoughts, and Passions of one man, to the thoughts, and Passions of another, whosoever looketh into himself, and considereth what he doth, when he does *think, opine, reason, hope, feare*, &c, and upon what grounds; he shall thereby read and know, what are the thoughts, and Passions of all other men, upon the like occasions.[2]

That is, we assume that, when it comes to psychological states, the situation with other people will be much as it is with ourselves. If I have found, for example, that chancing on a cat strolling across my path in broad daylight usually causes me to believe that there is a cat in front of me, then I can assume that similar beliefs will be so caused in others. If I observe that my intention to stroke such an animal, or to attract its attention, usually results in my making such-and-such a sound or holding out my hand in such and such a way, then I might assume similar intentions to underlie such actions performed by others.

Nor is it hard to devise a natural method for encoding propositions about the psychological states of other persons. Just as the proposition 'I believe that P' is encoded by a tagged version Δ_P^B of the data-structure by Δ_P, so let the propostion 'S believes that P' be encoded by a differently tagged version $^S\Delta_P^B$ of the same data-structure, where this time, the tag incorporates a pointer to your concept of the person S in question. The point about such an encoding is that it facilitates the process of one's generalization about the causes (and effects) of one's own beliefs to the case of other people. For, under the suggested encoding, that process is

[2] Thomas Hobbes: *Leviathan* (ed. C. B. Macpherson), Harmondsworth: Penguin Books (1968), 82.

essentially one of systematically transforming data-structures of the form Δ_P^B to suitable data-structures of the form $^S\Delta_P^B$. In short: it is a process of tag rewriting. Similar remarks apply to the encoding of propositions about other psychological states—desires, intentions, hopes, fears, etc.—of other persons. Notice that, as with propositions about your own psychological states, the suggested encoding scheme makes the propositional contents of the represented psychological states readily available to the full range of your inferential mechanisms. So there is no problem, on that encoding scheme, about detecting logical relations between the propositional contents of others' psychological states.

I have so far been speaking of your ability to *observe* your own psychological states, as if your psychological knowledge relied on the constant vigilance of your mind's eye, always on the look-out (or should I say, *look-in*) for evidence for or against sundry generalizations concerning the interactions of your psychological states. But surely, it will be objected, to reason effectively about the thoughts of others (which will in general be different from your own thoughts), you will need to know about the interactions entered into by constellations of thoughts which you yourself have never had, and which you yourself could therefore not have observed by introspection. Thus it might be thought impossible that any amount of introspective vigilance could give you information about the likely evolution of the thoughts of others, and hence impossible that the mechanisms suggested above could give you the capacity to reason about the mental life of anyone whose thoughts are, in the relevant respects, different from your own.

Suppose, then, you have inferred that S believes P, Q, R and desires X, Y, Z, and that you wish now to know how that psychological state will develop. (I ignore other psychological modalities for brevity.) Here is one possibility, for some years now a familiar and hotly debated topic in the philosophy of mind. What if you *imagine* that P, Q, R were true and that X, Y, Z were desirable? For, in so doing, you would *simulate* the mind of one who really does have these thoughts. Extending our fictional psychological model we might suppose that such an act of imagination involves setting up a 'pretend' belief-box containing the data-structures Δ_P, Δ_Q, Δ_R and a 'pretend' desire-box containing the data-structures $\Delta_X, \Delta_Y, \Delta_Z$. (Recall that a tokening of Δ_P in your regular belief-box would amount to your believing P, and so on.) In addition, you must copy into these pretend belief- and desire-boxes the data-structures corresponding to those of your background beliefs and desires which you assume to be shared by S. Having cloned a suitable set of pretend beliefs and desires, you then let those data-structures interact with each other and with your standard infer-ential machinery to yield new data-structures (corresponding to new 'pretend' beliefs and desires) which you can then observe using your usual introspective powers as detailed above. Being data-structures whose occurrence in your normal belief- and de-sire-boxes would constitute your believing $P, Q, R, \ldots$ and desir-ing $X, Y, Z, \ldots$, the behaviour of these data-structures will provide a reliable guide to what you would have thought if you had be-lieved and desired those things. Therefore, if Hobbes is right, they will be a reliable guide to what any person *will* think who *does* believe and desire those things. Hence, the 'thoughts' you detect in your simulated cognitive predicament you may then presume to be the thoughts that are likely to come to S.

Thus the ability to imagine different situations, to simulate other people's presumed or putative cognitive predicaments, turns mere observation into experiment. For, in order to know how a given set of beliefs and desires will interact, you need never have observed the effects of such constellations of psychological states in yourself: the fact that you can imagine what it is like to be one who has these thoughts, that you can construct a model of such a person's psychological states, gives you access to all the data you require.

How does our suggested encoding scheme fare when it comes to such simulations? Again, very well. For suppose you encode the above propositions about S's beliefs and desires using the tagged data-structures $^S\Delta_P^B, {}^S\Delta_Q^B, {}^S\Delta_R^B$ (S's beliefs) and $^S\Delta_X^D, {}^S\Delta_Y^D, {}^S\Delta_Z^D$ (S's desires), as suggested. Then the task of constructing a model of S's beliefs and desires is merely one of inserting, into your auxiliary belief- and desire-boxes, the untagged versions of those data-structures: namely $\Delta_P, \Delta_Q, \Delta_R$ and $\Delta_X, \Delta_Y, \Delta_Z$. And, as we have said, systematically untagging data-structures is, by hypothesis, a simple operation. Similar remarks of course apply to encoding, as conclusions about S's likely thoughts, the results of the simulation: that is just a matter of tagging interesting data-structures produced in the simulacrum with labels indicating that they are the likely future beliefs of S, and of inserting the tagged data-structures into your own belief box.

Much has been written for and against the suggestion that psychological reasoning proceeds by simulation.[3] Yet it is clear that simulation, assuming it does have a part to play in psychological inference, can at best provide only a partial account of how such inferences proceed. For surely, much psychological inference is directed towards such questions as why someone acts in a certain way, what misconceptions he might be labouring under, whether and why he might be lying, what he must have known and how he could have come to know it. And it is hard to see how simulation, which provides no direct means to reason from effects to causes, can play anything more than an ancillary role in tackling such problems.[4] But my aim here is not to produce a workable piece of cognitive psychology. Rather, I merely want to illustrate what I believe to be the fundamental simplicity of the problem of encoding psychological knowledge in such a way that a wide range of psychological inferences become possible, at least in principle. For the existence of such encoding schemes has important consequences for the view according to which our grasp of the psychological concepts is to be seen as possession of a theory of common-sense psychology, as I shall now argue.

3. THE RELATIONSHIP BETWEEN THOUGHT AND OBJECT: COMPUTATIONAL HERMENEUTICS

The striking feature of the mechanisms for psychological inference sketched in the previous section is their lack of dependence on any specific features of the data-structures on which they are used. For it seems likely that the tagging and untagging operations which form the core of these mechanisms would work happily on an essentially unlimited variety of data-structures. Think of a computer implementation of these operations: tagging a data-structure might involve, perhaps, pairing it with some symbol in a list; and just about any data-structure can be paired with a symbol in a list. So,

---

[3] See e.g. R. M. Gordon: 'Folk Psychology as Simulation', *Mind and Language* 1 (1986), 158–171, and S. Stich and S. Nichols: 'Folk Psychology: Simulation or Tacit Theory?' *Mind and Language*, 7 (1992), 35–71.

[4] For a brief discussion of these issues, see I. Pratt, I. Leudar, and L. Xu: 'Understanding Detective Stories', *Proceedings of the Fourteenth Annual Conference of the Cognitive Science Society*, Hillsdale, NJ: Erlbaum, 1992: 1046–51.

if you augment your stock of concepts with a new type of data-structure which enters into all kinds of new interactions with the data-structures already in your head, your psychological inference mechanisms will cope effortlessly with your newly expanded conceptual repertoire. Whatever new propositions P this new data-structure enables you to encode, no sooner do you acquire the capability to entertain the proposition P (by tokening instances of some new data-structure in your brain), than you also acquire the capability to entertain the propositions 'S believes that P', 'S desires that P', and so on. Moreover, your ability to construct make-believe cognitive predicaments enables you to experiment with the behaviour of your new beliefs *vis-à-vis* collections of your other psychological states as and when required; so there is no need to wait for instances of these new beliefs fortuitously to present themselves before you acquire an extensive ability to reason about them. If your conceptual repertoire expands (by whatever processes people's conceptual repertoires expand) your mechanisms for psychological inference are well equipped to cope with their owner's new thoughts.

I explained early in the previous section how the suggested method for encoding propositions about what you *previously* believed enabled you to reach conclusions about the extracranial causes and effects of these beliefs. In particular, it enabled you to reach conclusions about the causal relationships, if any, between states of affairs in which P is the case and states of affairs in which you *believe P*. Thus, for example, you might have concluded that the belief 'This cat is black' is usually caused by the cat in question's being black, unless of course it is dark, or unless the cat is well camouflaged, or whatever. And, as we observed above, it is because you can *revise* your beliefs that the monitoring of those beliefs (and of their revision) can yield non-trivial conclusions about the relationship between those beliefs and the states of affairs they are about. Clearly also, the particular conclusions you reach concerning this relationship will depend on the way in which you are disposed to revise the beliefs in question. That is, it is *because* your beliefs about the colour of cats get revised in the way they do—*because*, that is, they interact with your perceptions and other of your psychological states in just the way they do—that you come to just the beliefs you do about the typical causal relationship between your belief 'This cat is black' and the colour of the relevant cat. So if, as a result of the enlargement of your conceptual repertoire, new types of beliefs arise, the generalizations you formulate about the conditions under which these new beliefs arise—and in particular, about the relationships between whatever states of affairs these new beliefs are about and the beliefs themselves—will depend on the way these new beliefs function, on the way they interact with your perceptions and with other of your psychological states. And, as we have already seen, the processes by which you arrive at these generalizations will work more or less whatever these new beliefs are, and however they function within your brain.

The following radical suggestion then presents itself. Perhaps we should allow more or less *any* new type of data-structure, having more or less *any* new patterns of interaction with your existing beliefs to count as a bona fide psychological state: as a belief, desire, intention, or what have you (depending on its broad functional characteristics). Perhaps we should say, that is, that any data-structure that can exist in your belief-box counts as a bona fide belief, and, *ipso facto*, as a bona fide belief *about something*. After all, it would appear that, on the encoding scheme suggested above, any new type of data-structure that can operate in our brains, happily interacting with other data-structures in sensible ways, can unproblematically be made the object of our psychological concepts. That is: if that new data-structure enables us to engage in certain new modes of thought, we can unproblematically think about our engaging in these modes of thought or about other persons' engaging in these modes of thought. So why not take *whatever* new data-structures can be incorporated into our regular cognitive systems to count as regular psychological states?

Suppose, then, that a new type of data-structure Δ is tokened in your belief-box. The question seems to arise: What will the belief you thereby have be *about*? That is: What proposition will Δ encode? The suggestion I wish to make—and here we see the radical nature of my proposal—is that, in general, the *only* way for someone to know what proposition a given type of data-structure in your head encodes is for him to *give himself* something like that data-structure, and to instantiate tokens thereof in his own brain. Then, of course, he will know what the belief is about, because he will be able to have it for himself. Moreover, once he can have this belief, once, that is, his conceptual repertoire has been suitably expanded, he should not experience any difficulty when it comes to expatiating on the connections between these new beliefs and what they are about. He can just apply his introspective and simulative mechanisms as outlined above.[5]

Looking at things in this way, the possible connections between beliefs and what those beliefs are about appear to be virtually open-ended, and appear moreover to be so without compromising your mastery of the notion of belief. To put the matter in somewhat Augustinian terms: if I ask you about the relationship between a *particular* state of affairs P and the state of affairs in which you believe that P, then, assuming of course that you can understand my question, you can tell me; but when I ask you what the relationship is *in general* between states of affairs and beliefs about those states of affairs, you cannot say. You cannot say, of course, because there is just nothing, at that level of generality, to be said.

To be sure, we may wish to impose certain minimal restrictions on the kind of behaviour which a mental data-structure can be allowed to get away with and still qualify as a belief or other psychological state. For example, we might insist that any new data-structure combine with existing data-structures by means of the standard logical operations, that it participate in all modes of thought—beliefs *and* desires *and* intentions, etc.—that it not vandalize one's psychological state by obliterating or scrambling data-structures with which it comes into contact, and so on. But these minimal restrictions imposed by the basic framework of psychological modalities may still leave vast latitude for novel kinds of cognitive function in general, yielding novel relationships between thought and object in particular.

The view we have arrived at might perhaps be called *computational hermeneutics*. According to that view, *any* data-structure in one's head obeying certain minimal restrictions counts *ipso facto* as a psychological state *about something*. And there is no general

---

[5] Here, complications intrude which, for the sake of clarity, I have suppressed in this paper. It is not correct to say that for me to know what proposition tokens of the physically-typed data-structure Δ encode for you is a matter of my somehow getting tokens of Δ into my own brain. What I should say is that it is a matter of my getting into my brain tokens of some type of data-structure Δ', whose *functional role* in my brain is the same as the functional role of Δ in yours. But such complications are not my main concern in this paper. I leave it to the reader to make corresponding adjustments throughout, where necessary.

way of saying what a given data-structure encodes other than to have that data-structure in one's own head.[6] But there is nothing mysterious about this view—at least, there shouldn't be. For I have been at pains to stress in this paper the fundamental simplicity of the computational mechanisms needed to manipulate the psychological concepts, when the relationship between thoughts and their objects is understood thus.

Let us return to the question of our grasp of the psychological concepts. I have argued that there is nothing in general to say about the relationship between the thought and its object, between the belief that P and P. It follows that that relationship cannot be captured by any set of principles, excepting, of course, an infinite listing containing on the order of one entry for each possible thought-content P. Therefore, there is no psychological 'theory', neither folk nor esoteric, knowledge of whose principles is equivalent to possession of the mechanisms for psychological inference outlined in the previous section. It is in this sense, then, and for foregoing reasons, that it is wrong to take our grasp of the psychological concepts to be a matter of our knowledge of folk psychology.[7]

4. ENCODING PSYCHOLOGICAL KNOWLEDGE

In *The Intentional Stance*, Dennett writes:

An interesting idea lurking in Stich's view is that when we interpret others we do so not so much by *theorizing* about them as by *using ourselves as*

---

[6] See n. 5.

[7] One important aspect of our grasp of psychological concepts which I have ignored in this paper concerns the allowed variation in how psychological states with the same content can function in different individuals and on different occasions. That some such variation exists is undeniable. Just because I have solved (or failed to solve) a mathematical problem that does not mean that you will reach the same result, even if you start with the same set of premises. Just because I am willing to generalize from a few data-points or accept a certain explanation as overwhelmingly plausible that does not mean that you will be so epistemically bold, even if you have the same evidence at your disposal. Peacocke (Christopher Peacocke, *A Study of Concepts*, Cambridge, Mass.: MIT Press, 1992: 168–71) uses this observation as an argument against a simulation-based account of the nature of the concept of belief. What, exactly, these allowable variations are, how they are recognized, and how they are taken into account in psychological inference, are intriguing problems about whose solutions I could only speculate here. Since such speculations would not affect the overall thrust of this paper, I shall refrain from them.

analog computers that produce a result. Wanting to know more about your frame of mind, I somehow put myself in it, or as close to being in it as I can muster, and see what I thereupon think (want, do . . .). There is much that is puzzling about such an idea. How can it work without being a kind of theorizing in the end? For the state I put myself in is not belief but make-believe belief. If I make believe I am a suspension bridge and wonder what I will do when the wind blows, what 'comes to me' in my make-believe state depends on how sophisticated my knowledge is of the physics and engineering of suspension bridges. Why should my making believe I have your beliefs be any different? In both cases, knowledge of the imitated object is needed to drive the make-believe 'simulation,' and the knowledge must be organized into something rather like a theory.[8]

As the recent flurry of interest in psychological simulation suggests, however, there is something more to the idea than Dennett here gives it credit for. Simulation does indeed loom large in the picture of psychological inference sketched in Section 2; but what is crucial about that picture is not the idea of simulation, but rather, of *observation*. It is because the cognitive mechanisms underpinning psychological inference are fundamentally mechanisms of *observation* that, as we argued in Section 3, those mechanisms are not equivalent to the possession of any psychological theory. Simulation, by contrast, is of secondary importance. What simulation does is to turn observation into experiment. It transports us, as it were, to any aspect of those data-structures we want to see. By allowing us to observe the behaviour of data-structures in mental situations in which we would not ordinarily encounter them, it removes the need to extract explicit generalizations about the behaviour of our psychological states in unexperienced situations.

Thus, Dennett's analogy, though understandable, proves misleading. Think of simulation and you think of models of bridges or weather systems or nuclear war or whatever: things which work because they have the programmer's knowledge of the relevant principles embodied in the computer code. But psychological inference—at least, the interesting parts of it—is not a matter of applying principles: it is a matter of making observations. The analogy with our knowledge of bridges, not that it is a particularly illuminating one, should run more as follows. If you want to know about all the different bridges in the world—how many

---

[8] D. C. Dennett, *The Intentional Stance*, Cambridge, Mass.: MIT/Bradford Books, 1987: 100–1.

struts they incorporate, what colour the pillars are, what company has its name stamped on the rivets—then you must go to the bridges and take a look. Since a bridge is, in general, a too big an object to be seen in detail all at once, those details are best seen by walking around and looking at the different parts of the bridge. But there is nothing general and true that can be said about the peculiarities of each and every possible bridge: there is no general *theory* which tells you about all the peculiarities of each and every possible bridge. Just so, if you want to know about the types of thoughts in your mind, then your cognitive mechanisms must tour those thoughts and inspect them one by one. Since the behaviour of thoughts cannot all be seen at once, you have in general, and if possible, to transport yourself, via the process of imagination, to different cognitive situations in which different aspects of your thoughts' behaviour can be observed. But there is nothing general and true that can be said about all the features of the behaviour of each and every possible thought: in particular, there is no general *theory* specifying the relationships between thoughts and their objects, between the belief that P and P.

But, surely, there are some general principles which apply to bridges; might the same then not be true of psychological states? Why, yes! I do not deny that there cannot be any general psychological principles; I only deny that knowing these principles could suffice on its own to endow us with the capacity to engage in psychological inference.

5. CONCLUSION

I began this paper by sketching a theory of psychological inference. True, the theory was greatly simplified, ignoring many important phenomena and finessing many difficult problems. But my aim was neither to develop a serious and detailed psychological proposal, nor to put forward an 'analysis' or 'definition' of psychological states or psychological concepts. Rather, it was to make a philosophical point about the way we should understand the relationship between thought and object, in the light of a plausible view concerning our grasp of psychological concepts. The point is this. It transpires that remarkably simple mechanisms, centred on the operations of tagging and untagging of data-structures, can form the basis of a wide range—perhaps the full range—of the functions required for psychological inference. It further transpires that these same mechanisms can gracefully accommodate an open-ended variety of data-structures, constituting, I suggested, beliefs and other psychological states standing in an open-ended variety of relationships to the states of affairs those psychological states are about. That is: the mechanisms underlying our mastery of psychological concepts impose only minimal restrictions on the relationships between thoughts and their objects. Thus our grasp of the psychological concepts—believing, desiring, intending, doubting, hoping, fearing, and so on—has the following property. However our conceptual repertoire may expand, whatever new kinds of thoughts we can entertain, we will always retain the ability to embed those concepts and thoughts within the scope of the psychological attitudes, and to gain knowledge of the causal (and other) relationships between those attitudes and what those attitudes are about. Yet we can do this even though there need be next to nothing that can be said in general about this relationship between thought and object. And if the relationship between thought and object really is open-ended in the way I suggest, then to encapsulate that relationship for every proposition we can entertain would require an infinite listing of cases containing on the order of one entry per possible thought-content. Therefore, our mechanisms for psychological inference—those mechanisms, that is, by which we can know, amongst other things, the relationship between thought and object in any case—cannot amount to knowledge of any set of principles (other than an infinite and unprincipled listing)—cannot, that is, amount to possession of any psychological theory.

Does Belief Exist?

L. JONATHAN COHEN

There are various ways in which professional philosophers can hope to assist the progress of cognitive science, and the analysis of familiar mental concepts is undoubtedly one of these. Whatever our views about the role or validity of our culture's folk psychology, we at least need to have available a sufficiently accurate account of its conceptual resources. Indeed, if such an account is not available, we lack an essential basis for evaluating that psychology. And the object of the present paper will be to illustrate this point by showing how philosophical analysis of the difference between belief and acceptance is relevant to Stich's claim that belief—in the folk-psychological sense of the term—is not a state or property of a person's mind. More specifically, I aim to show that Stich's experimentally based argument in support of that claim is undermined by the distinction that needs to be drawn between the concept of belief and the concept of acceptance. So the paper falls into two parts. The first outlines the distinction between belief and acceptance and demonstrates its importance by listing briefly some of the other issues to which it is relevant. The second summarizes Stich's relevant argument and establishes that it is invalidated by the distinction between belief and acceptance.

1. The difference between belief and acceptance has been largely ignored in recent philosophy. Yet when the two concepts are prised apart, and disentangled from the various confusions in which they have become embedded, new insights become available into a number of important issues that otherwise remain inadequately understood.

First then, and very briefly, belief that p is a disposition, when attending to issues raised, or items referred to, by the proposition that p, normally to feel it true that p and false that not-p, whether

or not one is willing to act or argue accordingly. But to accept that
p is to take it as given that *p*. It is to have or adopt a policy of
deeming, positing, or postulating that *p*, i.e. of going along with
that proposition in one's mind (either for the long term or for
immediate purposes only) as a premiss or inference-licence in some
or all contexts for one's own and others' deductions, proofs,
argumentations, inferences, deliberations, etc., whether or not one
feels it to be true that *p*. You answer the question whether you
believe that *p* by introspecting or reporting whether you are normally disposed to feel that *p* when you consider the issue. You
answer the question whether you accept that *p* by making or
reporting a decision, or by forming or reporting an intention,
about the foundations of your reasonings. Acceptance concerns
not what you feel to be true but what you premiss to be true.

There you have the heart of the matter. That is where the concepts of belief and acceptance need to be prised apart from one
another. That is how you can carve them at the joint. Belief is a
disposition to feel, acceptance a policy for inference. 'Belief' has
no implications about inference, 'acceptance' has no implications
about feelings.

But, as a second stage, some elucidatory glosses are certainly
needed.

Gloss no. 1. Belief is a disposition, not an occurrent state. Though
you can hear the relentless downpour through the curtains, you
may from time to time stop thinking about the rain, but you do
not then stop believing that it is raining—as presumably you would
do if belief were an occurrent state. Moreover, though many beliefs only commence at the time of their first manifestation, there
are many others that apparently antedate this, just as by being
dried in the sun a lump of clay may become brittle long before
pressure is applied and it breaks. Thus, if you have long believed
that London is larger than Oxford and that Oxford is larger than
St Andrews, then you will most probably have long believed that
London is larger than St Andrews, even if the belief has never
explicitly occurred to you until you were asked. People can say
about you without self-contradiction 'He almost certainly believes
it, even if he has never yet actually thought about it.' Why should
you have thought about it if there was no occasion for you to do
so? And, in any case, at any one time almost all a person's beliefs
have to be absent from his current consciousness, since no more
than a few such dispositions can be actualized at any one time.

On the other hand, some beliefs last only a very short while, and may perhaps be actualized throughout that period, as when one suddenly comes to believe that a gun has been fired, a moment later realizes that it was a car backfiring, and then forgets the matter altogether. The brevity of such an occurrence is not a reason for denying that a belief has come and gone (*pace* Kent Bach).[1] The sheet of glass that was smashed as soon as it was manufactured was certainly fragile even though not for long. Nor should the fact that some beliefs are concurrent with their actualizations tempt us to identify the one with the other. Such a concurrence, where it occurs, is a purely accidental feature.

Gloss no. 2. I have said that belief that p is a disposition *normally* to feel that p, and the point of this hedging needs to be clarified. What normally triggers the disposition is the mental state of thinking about whether it is the case that p, of thinking about something referred to by the proposition that p, or of thinking about some other such connected issue. But even when one or other of these conditions is satisfied feelings that would have actualized the belief that p sometimes do not occur. They may just fail to arise at the moment because you have difficulty in remembering that p or because you need to concentrate on other relevant matters. Or they may just be crowded out because you have too many relevant beliefs for them all to be actualized within the same span of consideration. Or occurrence of the feeling that p may be blocked at the outset by some accidental distraction or by some deliberate shift of attention. And not only are there thus various abnormal kinds of circumstances in which a belief fails to be actualized. It may also succeed in getting actualized even though none of the normal kinds of trigger is operative, as when a familiar thought suddenly, but quite irrelevantly, flashes before the mind.

Gloss no. 3. Belief is a disposition normally to feel that things are thus-or-so, not a disposition to say that they are. Of course, some people are so talkative that they try to tell you every belief they have, and perhaps every other feeling too, unless there is some special reason for keeping it to themselves or you manage to extricate yourself from their garrulousness. But others are reticent to the point of secrecy unless there is some special reason for disclosure, and they may have just as many beliefs and other feelings.

---

[1] K. Bach, 'An Analysis of Self-Deception', *Philosophy and Phenomenological Research*, 41 (1980–1), 354–57.

It may well be a psychological fact that most human belief-feelings emerge in the form of linguistic utterances, even if only subvocal ones. But this is not required a priori by the analysis of the concept of belief: otherwise infants and animals could not be credited with beliefs. Nor is belief at all like a disposition to bet that so-and-so is the case.[2] Some people are such gamblers that they will offer you odds on the truth of each belief that they have. But others are so averse to risk that they would never offer you odds on anything. And they too have beliefs.

Note, too, that the kinds of mental feelings to which believers are characteristically disposed belong in the same overall category as hopes-that, fears-that, joys-that, desires-that, embarrassments-that, disappointments-that, bitterness-that, etc. They all have propositional objects (by which I meant that their content is reported in indirect discourse). And credal feelings, like emotional ones, may be manifested or revealed, not only in speech but also by incidental grimaces, pallors, blushes, vocal ejaculations, intakes of breath, hand-gestures, body movements, and attitudes, etc. Indeed they may also be revealed by a person's actions, in the light of his known desires, aversions, etc. But again we should remember that there are other people, with just as many beliefs, who are more disposed to conceal those beliefs—whether in speech or in action or in both—than to reveal them.

Gloss no. 4. Acceptance here is not the same as supposition or assumption, in the standard senses of those terms. Thus the verb 'to suppose' commonly denotes an inherently temporary act of imagination, whereas acceptance implies commitment to a pattern, system, or policy—whether long term or short term—of premissing that *p*. Again, we can act on the assumption that *p* in order to test whether it is true that *p*. A mathematician may investigate in this way whether there is a *reductio ad absurdum* proof for not-*p*, for example, and if he is successful (and derives an obvious contradiction from *p*) it is not-p rather than *p* that will be accepted. Or a counter-espionage operative may feed information to a suspect on the assumption that he is an enemy agent in order to test whether he is indeed one, and only when the assumption is confirmed (by onward passage of the information) will it be accepted as a premiss

---

[2] As suggested by R. B. de Sousa, 'How to Give a Piece of Your Mind: or, the Logic of Belief and Assent', *Review of Metaphysics*, 75 (1971), 52–79.

for future strategy. Often too we are restricted to assuming that *p* for the moment, just because we don't at the moment have enough evidence to adopt the policy of premissing that *p*. Or maybe we say that we are only assuming that *p* in order to point out that it is arbitrary whether we take *p* or some other such proposition as our premiss in the given context.

Nor is acceptance that *p* the same as acting as if it is true that *p*. When the terrorists have thrown their first hand-grenade you may gladly accept, as you lie on the floor, that you can still move your limbs. But if you are wise you will act as if you are dead or paralysed, not as if you can still move your limbs. And, if George accepts that it is desirable for him to deceive Mary, he should—normally—act as if it is not desirable for him to deceive her. Also acceptance that *p* commits you to going along with the premiss that *p*, whereas acting as if it is true that *p* makes no such commitment.

Gloss no. 5. Acceptance and belief, in the relevant senses, have some well-known ancestors, or near-ancestors, in the history of philosophy. One can acknowledge these affiliations without necessarily sharing the same metaphysical presuppositions. Cartesian doubt about the truth of a proposition, for example, is very close to suspending acceptance of that proposition, just as to have an ordinary natural doubt about its truth is to experience a reluctance to believe it.[3] And Hume wrote that 'belief is more properly an act of the sensitive, than of the cogitative part of our natures'.[4] Omitting to notice its dispositional structure he said that 'belief is nothing but a peculiar feeling', and remarked on its being a feeling or sentiment that is 'different from what attends the mere *reveries* of the imagination'.[5] Similarly Peirce described the feeling of belief as 'a calm and satisfactory' state of mind, as compared with the 'uneasy and dissatisfied' state of doubt 'from which we struggle to free ourselves'.[6] And until about fifty years ago philosophers often used the word 'judgement' to cover what I am now calling 'acceptance'.

Such, then, is the basic distinction that needs to be drawn between belief and acceptance. Various consequences follow from

[3] R. Descartes, *The Philosophical Works*, i (trans. E. S. Haldane and G. R. T. Ross), Cambridge: Cambridge University Press, 1931: 145.

[4] D. Hume, *A Treatise of Human Nature* (ed. L. A. Selby-Bigge, revised P. H. Nidditch), Oxford: Clarendon Press, 1978: 183.

[5] Ibid., appendix, 624.

[6] C. S. Peirce, *Collected Papers*, v. (ed. C. Hartshorne and P. Weiss), Cambridge, Mass.: Harvard University Press, 1934: 230.

this distinction, as I have pointed out elsewhere,[7] such as that belief is involuntary while acceptance is voluntary and that (within subjective limits) acceptance is deductively closed while belief is not. But, so far as we grant belief and acceptance to exist at all, we can certainly note a tendency for them to be associated with one another in everyday experience. Having a belief that p can normally be taken to be some at least prima-facie reason for accepting that p, even though it may well not be the only, or the best, or even a sufficient reason. At the same time acceptance that p tends to cause or promote belief that p, as Pascal recognized in relation to religious doctrine. And, so far as acceptance and belief do in fact thus tend to associate together, this would explain the widespread tendency to confound the two concepts in philosophical reflection.

But there are also a number of contexts in which belief and acceptance do not in fact coincide, or in which strength of belief that p and degree of inclination to accept that p may vary independently. Some of these contexts are quite humdrum, as when for professional purposes a lawyer might accept that his client is not guilty even though he believes the opposite. But some have considerable philosophical importance. Thus in clarifying the nature of scientific knowledge epistemologists need to determine whether such knowledge culminates in a scientist's accepting a hypothesis or in his believing it or both. Again philosophical doctrines about the explanation of human actions are affected, because in addition to explanations in terms of belief and desire, which are both involuntary states, it is clear that folk psychology also offers explanations in terms of acceptance and goal-adoption, which are both voluntary states. And there are even certain hybrid patterns of explanation also. Self-deception, too, may be elucidated in terms of a clash between what a person unconsciously believes and what he decides to accept. And the treatment of Moore's paradox has to be adjusted appropriately if we acknowledge that, while a statement, testimony, or report that p gives it to be understood that the speaker believes that p, an assertion, concession, or admission that p gives it to be understood instead that the speaker accepts that p. However, while belief is prior to

---

[7] L. J. Cohen, 'Belief and Acceptance', *Mind*, 98 (1989), 367–89. See also L. Jonathan Cohen, *An Essay on Belief and Acceptance*, Clarendon Press, Oxford, 1992.

language, in the sense that beliefs, like other feelings, may be expressed in many non-linguistic ways, acceptance is not prior to language, in so far as taking it as a premiss that *p* presupposes the ability somehow to articulate the proposition that *p* into elements from which other propositions are derivable. Finally, there is an obvious parallelism to be investigated between the belief/acceptance duality in regard to folk-psychological concepts of cognitive states and the connectionist/digital duality in regard to scientific models of cognitive processes.

2. According to Stich[8] there are promising arguments against the everyday view that belief is a state or property of a person's mind. Most of Stich's arguments, however, are concerned with much-discussed general problems about the role of indirect discourse as an instrument in the characterization of mental reality. And such problems affect memory, hope, fear, desire, grief, joy, acceptance, and a wide range of other concepts just as much as they affect belief. So the resolution of those problems is neither eased nor hardened by the distinction between belief and acceptance. Their resolution therefore falls outside the scope of the present paper. It is merely assumed to be possible. For we should be rejecting too much—within the field of psychology—of what we normally take as data that require explanation if our arguments lead us to suppose that the idioms of indirect discourse have no role whatever to perform in the characterization of mental reality. It may well be the case that those idioms have no role to perform in the construction of explanatory theories that have scientific value. It might even be the case that different cultures divide up the mental spectrum differently, with some exotic conceptual systems recognizing mental states or attitudes that we do not, or not recognizing some that we do.[9] Perhaps some languages lack any idioms for indirect discourse. But it would remain an *ignoratio elenchi* to suppose that no mental states have articulable content, since the make-up of human memories, hopes, fears, desires, etc., constitutes an important part of what needs to be explained by any scientific psychology. If, for example, Freud's explanation of why we forget much of our infant experience is unsatisfactory, we need a better explanation.

[8] S. Stich, *From Folk Psychology to Cognitive Science: The Case against Belief*, Cambridge, Mass.: MIT Press, 1983.
[9] See R. Needham, *Belief, Language, and Experience*, Oxford: Blackwell, 1972.

Stich has another argument which is based on what he calls 'the sorry history of folk theories in general'.[10] But the fact that Newton engaged in many superstitious speculations about the prophecies of Daniel, the apocalypse of St John, etc., does not count against the validity of his theory of motion. So by parity of reasoning the falsity of folk astronomy (if there is such a thing) should not count seriously against the validity of folk psychology.

It is pertinent to concentrate instead on the one argument of Stich's that is concerned specifically and exclusively with the concept of belief in our own culture, i.e. in the folk psychology of twentieth-century civilization and is based on the existence of certain psychological findings. Consider, for example, an experiment of Storms and Nisbett.[11] The subjects in this experiment, whose getting-to-sleep times were all being monitored, were divided into two groups. The members of one group (the so-called 'arousal' group) were given a placebo to take fifteen minutes before going to bed and told that the pills would cause rapid heartbeat, irregular breathing, bodily warmth, and alertness, which are the typical symptoms of insomnia. The members of the other group (the 'relaxation' group) were told that the pills would have the opposite effect. The outcome was that arousal group subjects got to sleep 28 per cent faster on the nights they took the pill, while relaxation subjects took 42 per cent longer to get to sleep on the nights they took the pill. The arousal group subjects' results are explained by the experimenters as having been due to the fact that, in accordance with what attribution-theory would predict, these subjects tacitly or unconsciously 'attributed' their symptoms to the pills rather than to their own emotions and, being therefore less disturbed by the latter, got to sleep faster. Correspondingly the relaxation group subjects' results are explained as being due to the fact that, since these subjects' symptoms persist despite the pills, the subjects found their state of mind to be more disturbing than usual and consequently found it harder to get to sleep. But in a follow-up experiment, reported by Nisbett and Wilson,[12] the subjects speak out and tell a different story. Arousal group subjects were now told

[10] Stich, *From Folk Psychology to Cognitive Science*, 229.

[11] M. D. Storms and R. E. Nisbett, 'Insomnia and the Attribution Process', *Journal of Personality and Social Psychology*, 16/2 (1970), 319–28.

[12] R. E. Nisbett and T. D. Wilson, 'Telling More than we can Know: Verbal Reports on Mental Processes', *Psychological Review* 84 (1977), 231–59.

that—in the earlier experiments—they fell asleep faster after taking the pill, and relaxation group subjects were told that they fell asleep more slowly. And each subject was asked to report why the change in his or her sleeping-pattern took place. Arousal group subjects typically replied that they usually found it easier to get to sleep later in the week, or that they could now relax after doing well on an examination that had worried them beforehand, or that some personal problem seemed on the way to being resolved. Relaxation group subjects found similar sorts of reasons to explain their increased sleeplessness. But all denied that thinking about the pills was in any way responsible for what had happened to them. So the experimenters claim that in formulating their verbal reports subjects do not consult any memories of the actual processes by which the changes in their sleeping-patterns came about, but tend to apply some conventional theory about what is likely to cause such changes.

Stich infers that data of this kind lend support to the view that people have two 'more or less independent cognitive systems'.[13] One of the two is largely unconscious and affects non-verbal behaviour. That is the system at work in the subjects' minds as they actually grapple with their insomnia. The other cognitive system is largely conscious and is expressed in verbal behaviour. It is the system that produces the subjects' reports about their insomnia. And Stich contrasts this dualistic thesis with the monistic assumption that he imputes to folk psychology. According to that supposed assumption each person whose mind is made up on an issue has, at any one time, at most one cognitive attitude towards a particular resolution of the issue. Specifically, either he believes it or he disbelieves it, or he has no cognitive attitude towards it. The very same belief that underlies a sincere utterance that p may also generate a variety of non-verbal behaviour. But, according to the supposed folk-psychological assumption, there cannot be any inconsistency at any one time between the cognitive attitude that underlies a sincere utterance and the cognitive attitude underlying non-verbal behaviour that is related to the same issue. So if such an inconsistency is indeed demonstrated to exist in certain circumstances, the imputed assumption must be false. In other words, experimental findings like those of Storms, and Nisbett and Wilson,

[13] Stich, *From Folk Psychology to Cognitive Science*, 237.

show that folk psychology is wrong to assume a unitary cognitive system. Instead of a single system of belief it would be better to suppose 'two subsystems of vaguely belief-like states'.[14] One of the subsystems would interact with those parts of the mind that are responsible for verbal reporting, while the other would interact with those parts that are responsible for non-verbal behaviour. And though the two systems might often agree with one another, they might also often disagree, so that the verbal behaviour need not align itself with the non-verbal.

This argument of Stich's has been attacked by Horgan and Woodward[15] on the ground that the facts under consideration do not in fact require the existence of two separate cognitive systems. They can instead be explained, we are told, on the hypothesis of a single belief-system which sometimes operates consciously and sometimes unconsciously. Thus the subjects in the experiments described may be supposed to have believed one thing unconsciously (which they kept silent about) and something else consciously (which they reported to the experimenters). So, if one is prepared to allow the folk-psychological admissibility of unconscious belief, Stich has not made out a good case for holding that the everyday, folk-psychological concept of belief is empty.

Now there is nothing wrong with the view that unconscious belief is fully conceivable in folk psychology. As we have seen, because a belief is essentially a disposition, it may often remain unactualized and there are many reasons why this can happen. Nor is there anything wrong with the view that folk psychology may suppose an unactualized disposition to be the cause of some state of affairs. The fragility of a precious vase may cause its owner to tremble with fear when it is lifted. Instead, what is wrong with Horgan and Woodward's treatment of Stich's argument is that they assume the possibility of a person's both believing and disbelieving the same proposition at the same time. The proposition in question is something like: 'The cause of my worsened insomnia this week was that my emotions were more disturbing than usual, as I inferred from the fact that despite taking the relaxation pill I still had trouble getting to sleep', or 'The cause of my getting to sleep more easily this week was that my emotions were less disturbing

---

[14] Ibid. 231.
[15] T. Horgan and J. Woodward, 'Folk Psychology is Here to Stay', *Philosophical Review*, 94 (1985).

than usual, as I inferred from the fact that despite taking the arousal pill I still had little trouble getting to sleep.' There is no reason to suppose that subjects have ceased to believe one or other of these propositions unconsciously at the date at which they are asked to report why they think that their sleeping patterns have changed. So, if at that date a subject's report includes the statement that he disbelieves the proposition in question, he would indeed be ascribing to himself the belief that p at the same time as he has the belief that not-p. And the coexistence of these two beliefs is impossible. Whether or not a disposition is actualized, it cannot belong to something that also has the opposite disposition. A rod cannot be both flexible and resistant to bending, a plant cannot be both hardy and tender, and a person cannot both believe and disbelieve the same proposition at the same time. It follows that Horgan and Woodward's reply to Stich is not successful.

The right line to take against Stich is to argue, not that such a subject has flatly inconsistent beliefs, but that he *accepts* the negative of what he *believes*. We have already noticed several other types of situation in which what a person accepts runs counter to what he believes, and this happens particularly easily in the present type of situation because the belief is an unconscious one. Moreover, there are two specific reasons why the subject here should be regarded as reporting what he accepts rather than what he believes. The first is that that he says is tied in with the adoption of some conventional theory or hypothesis as the premiss for his explanation. What the psychologists suppose thus is that he voluntarily chooses the type of explanation that he gives. And the second reason is that, as we have seen in the preceding section, belief is prior to language in a sense in which acceptance is not. Acceptance is at bottom just an interiorization of the corresponding speech-act. So it is hardly surprising if in the experiments in question belief operates without any apparent linguistic mediation, while what the subjects accept is manifest in what they report.

Finally, we must recognize that, since the difference between the concept of belief and the concept of acceptance was revealed by philosophical analysis of everyday discourse, its folk-psychological credentials are as strong as that type of analysis produces. So the source of Stich's error is his failure to do justice to the richness of the resources with which folk psychology operates. He does not bear in mind that it employs a concept of acceptance as well as a concept of belief. There is thus no need here to construct two new artificial or 'scientific' concepts of 'vaguely belief-like' cognitive systems, as he suggests should be done, since the existing folk-psychological concepts of belief and acceptance are quite adequate to the task of describing what the psychologists claim to be going on. Indeed, the conceptual apparatus of folk psychology is strikingly vindicated by its ability to accommodate experimental data of the kind that we have been considering.

Of course, it may turn out that in some cases the subjects actually believe, and do not merely accept, that their reported explanations are true. But, if this could be established, it would have to count as evidence against the explanations derived from attribution theory. It is certainly impossible for the same person at the same time to believe both that p and that not-p.

INDEX